Child Welfare Services

Developments in Law, Policy, Practice and Research

Edited by Malcolm Hill and Jane Aldgate

Jessica Kingley Publishers
London and Bristol, Pennsylvania

Acknowledgements

The editors very much value the commitment to this publication shown by Jessica Kingsley. Much credit is due to all the contributors for meeting tight time schedules for drafting and revising chapters. We would like to thank Laura Lochhead, Elaine Hodge and Christina Cazalet for their secretarial assistance. Helpful advice has been given by Robbie Gilligan, Pauline Hardiker, Rupert Hughes and Jane Tunstill. Stewart Asquith is grateful to Nikki Loughran, Mike Montgomery, Maureen Buist and Cathlin McCauley for their research with him, which was drawn on for his chapter.

First published in the United Kingdom in 1996 by
Jessica Kingsley Publishers Ltd
116 Pentonville Road
London N1 9JB, England
and
1900 Frost Road, Suite 101
Bristol, PA 19007, U S A

Copyright © 1996 the contributors and the publisher

Library of Congress Cataloging in Publication Data
Child Welfare Services: Developments in Law, Policy, Practice and Research/edited by
Malcolm Hill and Jane Aldgate
p. cm.
Includes bibliographical references and index.
ISBN 1-85302-316-7
1. Child care services--Law and legislation--Great Britain.
2. Child care services--Government Policy--Great Britain
I. Hill, Malcolm. II. Aldgate, Jane. 1945–
KD3305, A75C48 1996
344.41' 0327--dc20
[344,104327]   95-36216 CIP

British Library Cataloguing in Publication Data
Child Welfare Services: Developments in Law, Policy, Practice and Research
I. Hill, Malcolm II. Aldgate, Jane
362.70941

ISBN 1-85302-316-7

Printed and Bound in Great Britain by
Athenaeum Press, Gateshead, Tyne and Wear

Contents

Part 3: The Continuum of Out-of-Home Care

Part 4: Evaluation and Outcomes

Figures

Tables

Preface

Putting together an anthology is both exciting and frustrating. It is an opportunity to gather together new, original material within a given theme, but always length sets boundaries around what may be included. Our intention has been to produce a volume commenting on recent changes in law, policy and practice which have affected the social responses to the upbringing of children, especially those living away from home. The legislation covered is primarily that which underpins professional social work services for the support, protection and welfare of children and their families. We also wished to share recent research findings which illuminate and inform those developments. Yet we are conscious of significant omissions and can only hope that readers who find their own interests and perspectives neglected may be fired to fill these gaps elsewhere.

What we believe is unique about this volume is that it draws on sources from the three jurisdictions of the United Kingdom and that of the Republic of Ireland, in order to reflect significant parallel changes in legislation which have taken place within the last five years. These developments reflect shared views: that children are generally best cared for within their families; that where they cannot live at home the State has a duty to ensure their welfare is promoted; and that whenever possible children and parents should be effectively included in all key decisions. Further, there is a good deal of common ground between the different countries in relation to good social work practice and its base of knowledge and theory. Nevertheless important differences remain in the systems and contexts, not only between the two states of the UK and Ireland, but also within the UK in response to the differing social, cultural and political heritages of Scotland and Northern Ireland.

The book is divided into four parts corresponding with four major themes. Part 1 reviews major developments in law, policy and related research. Part 2 looks at recent developments in the important practice area of child protection. Part 3 examines critical practice within a wide spectrum of services for children in out of home placements. These range from short-term respite accommodation, foster and residential care to adoption and services for care graduates. Part 4 ends the volume by illustrating from research aspects of the evaluation and outcome of child welfare practice.

Throughout the volume are threaded several overarching themes:

- the need for a long-term perspective on children's needs

- the participation of users in major decisions which affect them and in shaping services

- the desirability of maximising support to families in difficulties before or instead of removing children, whilst acknowledging the value of brief or even extended separations for children's welfare in some circumstances

- the value of users' views in the evaluation of services and guidance on their refinement

- the paramountcy of children's welfare

- the continuing significance to children of their families even when living apart

- the need for knowledge of and continuity with genealogical roots

- the importance of research in identifying good practice and influencing its further development.

Part 1 – legal and social policy developments

In Chapter 1, Malcolm Hill and Jane Aldgate give an overview of the main features of the Children Act 1989, most of which applied only in England and Wales. They show the connections between this comprehensive legislation for the upbringing of children and developments in research which have both influenced and monitored the law.

In Chapter 2, Kay Tisdall reviews the extent to which changing emphases in Scotland's legislation governing social work over the last two decades have responded to changed realities. She locates the Children (Scotland) Act 1995 within the context of social changes, recent reports and local government reform.

Chapter 3 brings the Northern Irish perspective. Here Greg Kelly and John Pinkerton analyse the evolution of policy leading up to the Children (Northern Ireland) Order 1995. This is almost identical to the Children Act 1989, apparently showing little regard for local circumstances or recent reports, but thanks to effective lobbying it seems that the implementation process will be much more inclusive and sensitive to Northern Ireland's particular needs.

Chapter 4 examines the legal changes underpinning Irish child welfare services in the 1990s. The Irish legislation is rooted in the constitutional belief in the paramountcy of the family but has increasingly recognised the need for children to be protected from adult abuse. Robbie Gilligan provides us with a fascinating glimpse of the tensions and significant changes in recent Irish child welfare law, as well as describing a number of practice initiatives.

Chapter 5 widens the child welfare arena into the social problem of juvenile crime. Stewart Asquith continues the theme of promoting children's welfare in exploring the relationship between explanations of juvenile crime and public policies, noting the undue influence of extreme cases, as in child protection. He summarises the conclusions of recent research, which indicate that intervention can be effective and that preventive action is likely to be most worthwhile when directed at social causes.

Chapter 6 remembers that both home and school are fundamentally influential on children's daily lives. Ruth Sinclair shows that there have been genuine efforts to advance the participatory rights of children in relation to social services, but that these have been deliberately marginalised in education legislation.

Part 2 – child protection

Part two moves on to examine a major aspect of child welfare services – child protection. In Chapter 7 Pauline Hardiker unravels the complexities of the English and Welsh definition of 'significant harm', illustrating the implementation of the law with some complex case studies drawn from recent social work practice.

In Chapter 8, Lorraine Waterhouse and Janice McGhee take us through recent developments in policy and practice developments in child abuse investigations, especially in Scotland. Drawing on recent research they consider children's, parents', social workers' and police views of the child protection system. They note how anxieties and fears on all sides can foster misunderstanding.

In Chapter 9, June Thoburn, Ann Lewis and David Shemmings highlight the important theme of participation. Their recent research shows how parental participation in the child protection process can promote children's welfare, especially when combined with continuity of positive social work support.

Part 3 – the care continuum

Jane Aldgate, Marie Bradley and David Hawley open this section in Chapter 10 with an example of one type of family support service – respite accommodation. The chapter draws on the authors' research to suggest that the development and outcomes of family support services benefit from the participation of parents and children. The process of user involvement can be an important act of empowerment.

In Chapter 11 Clive Sellick shows how short-term foster care is a crucial service for families under stress. Drawing on his own research, Sellick analyses the complexity of foster carers' roles. They need to be valued and supported, personally and financially.

Chapter 12 turns to longer-term foster care arrangements. Here, Colette McAuley highlights the meaning of foster care from the point of view of the children. She reveals many concerns and unresolved issues from the past. The importance of continuity of relationships and of listening to children about their evolving experiences is amply demonstrated.

Chapter 13 turns to residential care. David Berridge and Isabelle Brodie discuss the implications of recent inquiries, showing how concerted action has been taken which seeks to correct some of the long-standing problems of low status, poor pay and inadequate training. New research provides both positive and salutary messages for the development of residential services.

In Chapter 14, Murray Ryburn discusses recent issues and trends in adoption in England and Wales. As in earlier chapters, the link is drawn between poverty and parenting difficulties. Ryburn notes that policy has eschewed long-term family support measures in favour of transferring children to another family. He also argues that the reluctance to use other forms of long-term care or to encourage adoption with contact are contrary to children's rights as set out in the United Nation Convention on the Rights of the Child.

In Chapter 15, Eoin O'Sullivan places services for children looked after away from home in the context of the issues they face on leaving care in Ireland and in England and Wales. Attention is drawn to the common problem of homelessness for these children and others who become estranged from their families, with challenging comparisons made between the rhetoric of recent child care policies and the inadequacies of services for all homeless young people.

Part 4 – evaluation and outcomes of services

The final section on evaluation and outcome of services begins with Chapter 16 from Isobel Freeman, Alex Morrison, Fiona Lockhart and Moira Swanson. This continues the theme of participation, showing the value of consulting young people. Innovative methods were used to involve young people in the evaluation of service delivery and enable them to contribute to the planning process.

Chapter 17 from Harriet Ward shows how the concepts of promoting children's welfare and applying research findings have been translated into assessment and action schedules to measure the processes and outcome of services for children looked after away from home in England and Wales. Workers and carers have found the schedules useful in stimulating discussions, identifying unmet needs and planning.

Finally, the book is completed by Chapter 18 from Malcolm Hill, John Triseliotis, Moira Borland and Lydia Lambert. Here, the authors demonstrate the importance of research in measuring outcomes of services for young people and argue that both services and measurements of success are multi-faceted. Assessments of progress, satisfaction and achievements should all be part of the evaluative repertoire.

PART 1

Developments in Law, Policy and Related Research

CHAPTER 1

The Children Act 1989 and Recent Developments in Research in England and Wales

Malcolm Hill and Jane Aldgate

Origins and implications of the Children Act 1989

In England and Wales, many services for children and their families have been affected radically by the implementation of the Children Act 1989. This is a significant unifying piece of legislation which brought together the law about caring for, bringing up and protecting children which was previously inconsistent and fragmented across the face of the statute book. According to the Department of Health (1990), the Act

> rests on the belief that children are generally best looked after within the family with both parents playing a full part and without resort to legal proceedings. That belief is reflected in:
>
> - the new concept of parental responsibility;
> - the ability of unmarried fathers to share that responsibility by agreement with the mother;
> - the local authorities' duty to give support for children and their families;
> - the local authorities' duty to return a child looked after by them to his family unless this is against his interests;
> - the local authorities' duty to ensure contact with the parents whenever possible for a child looked after by them away from home. (DH 1990 p.1)

New principles were also introduced in relation to court proceedings – notably that the child's welfare shall be the paramount consideration; that delay should be avoided; and that no order be made unless an order is considered preferable to no order at all. In this chapter, we shall outline the implications of the new legislation in practice and then examine key research findings which have been reported since the Act was implemented. First, the evolution of the Act will be briefly considered.

Influences on the Children Act

Any major piece of legislation develops in response to a variety of influences. During the 1980s from a range of sources there were growing signs of a need to redraw the boundaries as regards the state, children and parents, and to remove some of the anomalies and overlaps between public and private law (Packman and Jordan 1991; Aldgate and Hill 1995).

There had been increasing concern in the courts that children in divorce cases were victims of an adversarial approach which often deprived them of continuing contact with a non-custodial parent. Research studies such as that by Mitchell (1985) had drawn attention to the plight of these children and the deleterious affect that prolonged court cases could have on their welfare.

There was also a growing recognition that the loss of parents was not confined to divorce cases. Over a decade from the mid 1970s, research had shown how easy it was for children in residential and foster care to lose contact rapidly with their birth families (Aldgate 1976; Millham et al. 1986). Furthermore maintenance of contact was associated with early return home. Most parents of children in out-of-home placements were shown to be willing and able to exercise responsibility towards their children, provided they were given a chance to do so (Rowe et al. 1984; Fisher et al. 1986).

Many people were also worried that it had become harder for families under stress to receive help and support, yet a greater readiness had developed to take compulsory action in relation to children. The trend was reported in a significant research anthology which drew together the findings from nine studies commissioned by the Department of Health and Social Security (DHSS 1985b). These findings were further endorsed by those from child abuse inquiries. On the one hand social workers were criticised for failing to act quickly to investigate and protect children from abuse (Hill 1990). On the other hand, as shown in the Cleveland inquiry (Butler-Sloss 1988), the powers of social workers to remove children from their homes in the middle of the night when no abuse had been proven, seemed in itself to constitute a further act of violence against children, disregarding their feelings and attachments to significant adults.

Thus, pressures built up for legislation which tempered the powers of local authorities and gave more attention to children's and parents' rights, compared with the Children Act 1975 (Harding 1991). This Act had sought to counteract the insidious damage to children subject to 'drift' in unplanned long-term placements (Rowe and Lambert 1973). The associated permanency planning movement achieved a great deal in enabling some children to return home and others to achieve a sense of full belonging in an alternative family when they had lost touch with their original families, but sometimes the policy of quickly seeking permanent substitute families was applied wholesale. Consequently parents who had turned to the State for help in times of stress and asked for their children to be in foster care for a while until they could resolve their problems found themselves facing adoption proceedings to deprive them of their children. The Family Rights Group built up a dossier of cases in the early 1980s of parents who had lost their parental rights unfairly and provided compelling evidence for the change in the law. In 1984, a High Court Judge expressed his concern that the law was being manipulated to the detriment of birth parents and in favour of adopters (Ormrod 1983; see also Ryburn this volume). Nevertheless there were also examples of successful partnership between social workers and parents, when workers were able 'to help parents retain their role as responsible, authority figures in relation to their children and active involvement in the processes, negotiations, and family dynamics of admission and discharge' (DHSS 1985b p.20).

It was seen as important that families should be able to seek help for everyday difficulties in parenting, without undue fears of a draconian response. As child care writers had argued for some time (Parker 1980), barriers between being in and out of care needed to be broken down and so lay to rest the ghost of the English Poor Laws which had separated recipients into the deserving and undeserving for four centuries. Short-term care could be seen not as an unfortunate failure, but as a positive means of 'preventing the permanent breakup of families by offering temporary relief' (DHSS 1985b, p.16).

Finally, the Act intended to de-stigmatise and unify services caring for all children in the community. It therefore extended its umbrella of family support to include children with disabilities, those with special educational needs and those living away from home long term either at boarding-schools or in hospital. Some of these children were known to be extremely vulnerable. The case for more suitable provision was fuelled in part by the scandals of child abuse and by the research of Robinson (1987) about the variable quality of services for children with disabilities.

Prompted by these developments, the government took the initiative to review the child welfare services. The Short Report (DHSS 1984) argued for more inclusive legislation which would embrace the needs of children with disabilities and those in hospitals and boarding-schools. The desirability of 'respite' and 'shared care' was stated in the Review of Child Care Law (DHSS 1985a), whilst the overarching concept of partnership between families and the State was spelt out in the White Paper (DHSS 1987) which preceded the Children Act 1989.

The new concept of parental responsibility

The concept of parental responsibility was central to the Act and marked a shift away from notions of parents' rights, except insofar as they derive from duties towards children:

> The Act uses the phrase parental responsibility to sum up the collection of duties, rights and authority which parents have in respect of their children. That choice of words emphasises the duty to care for the child and 'raise him or her to moral, physical and emotional health' is the fundamental task of parenthood and the only justification for the authority it confers. (DH 1989, p.2)

Parents are only given rights through the exercising of responsibility. The concept also accounts for a child's perception of who are significant adults, allowing inclusion of absent parents and other close relatives. Kinship and community are extolled as concepts fundamental to the well-being of children. 'There are unique advantages for children in experiencing family life in their own birth family and every effort should be made to preserve the child's home and family links' (DH 1990, p.2).

However, the way to promote the welfare of children is often found through helping their parents. Partnership with parents will not always be easy, but Marsh (1993) has indicated how potential conflicts can be avoided or ameliorated by open negotiation about options, resources and powers, with an emphasis on parental consent whenever possible.

Furthermore, the Act, for the first time in English law, recognised family diversity and the multi-cultural context of families in England and Wales. It required that these differences be taken account of and respected:

> Although some basic needs are universal, there can be a variety of ways of meeting them. Patterns of family life vary according to culture, class and community. There is no one perfect way to bring up children and care must be taken to avoid value judgements and stereotyping. (DH 1990, p.4)

The emphasis in the Act on working with parents on the basis of negotiation and voluntary agreement has been broadly welcomed, especially as 'the child remains centre stage' (Packman and Jordan 1991, p.323). The child's welfare is paramount and children's wishes must be ascertained and taken account of in all decisions. Moreover, it was hoped that services would become less defensive and controlling (Packman 1993). However, some believe that the stress on parental responsibility may have weakened the capacity of the state to act and plan effectively in children's interests in situations of potential harm (Eekelaar 1991). Similarly, in private law it has generally been seen as an advance that both parents are expected to exercise responsibility even when they separate, but women's aid organisations have pointed to the problems and pressures this new presumption can cause for women with violent partners.

Achieving a balance between child protection and family support

The Children Act was carefully constructed to provide a balance between child protection and family support. The Act calls on social workers to make enquiries as to whether children are at risk of significant harm (Hardiker this volume) and then to identify the services that may be necessary to avert or ameliorate that harm. Part III of the Act is devoted to family support services including the provision of family centres and voluntary out-of-home placements, which were renamed as accommodation (see Aldgate, Bradley and Hawley in this volume). The Act recognises that services for children in the community must be multi-faceted to reflect different aspects of children's development. It would be impossible for the current social services departments to provide all these services, so there is built into the legislation a mandate for social services to call upon other departments within local government such as leisure and recreation, and on local health and education services to assist them in their duties to provide services for children.

Such a response is particularly important in relation to children with disabilities, who are now designated 'children in need'. Bringing these children into the mainstream of services was a major achievement of the Act. Unfortunately, to date, with the exception of the work of Carol Robinson at Bristol University on respite care, there is little research to show how these children are faring under the Act.

Though the intention of the Children Act was to reach all children who are in need, it did not subscribe to a universal welfare system open to all. That would have been contrary to trends in other social policies during the 1980s. Rather it instructs social services to define 'children in need' according to local needs and to confine services to the most vulnerable. Although restricting services to children who are at risk of abuse is illegal, the tenor of this mandate has allowed some authorities to close their doors to all except those seriously at risk. Such an approach is in danger of undermining the family support emphasis in the Act.

Another potential danger is that of delegating the major provision of services to the voluntary sector. In line with the current UK governments belief in a mixed economy of welfare, encouragement is given to social services to work in collaboration with charitable and private social work agencies to widen the provision of services. Whilst voluntary agencies have a vital role to play in service provision, particularly of an innovative or specialist nature, consistency and continuity of provision of service is not always compatible with a market economy (Aldgate and Tunstill 1995).

Contrasts and tensions between the Children Act and other recent legislation

The thrust of parallel legislation affecting children and families has sometimes contradicted the ethos of the Children Act and threatens to undermine some of its positive effects.

First, English and Welsh legislation has taken a punitive attitude to juvenile offenders who come under the jurisdiction of the Criminal Justice Act 1991. This means that little therapeutic help is available to young offenders in the wider context of family support. Although the probation service offers some positive individual and group supervision, their terms of reference are increasingly being constrained by the Home Office to confine their duties to tight supervision relating only to the offence in question. This system is completely different from the Childrens Hearings system in Scotland (Asquith this volume) and sits uneasily beside the wider concept of family support for children in need in the Children Act.

The second piece of legislation which threatens the development of broad services for children in need is the 1988 Education Reform Act. This allows for schools to become self-governing and opt out of local government control of education provision. Governors have a far greater say over which children are admitted to their schools and over who is excluded. In some inner city areas particularly, this new arrangement has led to children being excluded from school for what might be interpreted as minor behaviour problems. It is difficult for these children to be found a new school since there is more opportunity to reject children who are undesirable pupils. Additionally, the introduction of national league tables based on grades achieved in national examinations discourages schools from admitting children with educational difficulties. Many children looked after by local authorities would come into this category (Aldgate 1990).

Third, the UK Health Service is now partly organised as self-governing trusts. General practitioners are budget holders and have to pay for places at specialist hospitals. This system has placed in serious jeopardy any reciprocity of services between social services and child psychiatry. All assessments and treatments at trust hospitals have to be paid for. As yet the impact of this change on children in need is not known, but some psychiatrists are concerned that it will disadvantage children in need of services who are in the care of poor local authorities.

One positive note in legislation parallel with the Children Act is the advent of the NHS and Community Care Act 1990, primarily designed to facilitate care in the community for disabled and chronically sick adults. This legislation should help to provide continuity of services for children with disabilities who are making the transition to adulthood.

Finally, as Ryburn notes in this volume, there is currently ongoing in England and Wales a review of adoption law. As yet it is uncertain in what direction there might be any changes but there are fears from preliminary documents that new adoption legislation may not place the same emphasis on continuity of race, religion and language demanded for children in the care system.

Research in the 1990s

Research and children's legislation

In the second half of this chapter we aim to provide an overview of patterns of research and findings published in the last five years. Given the time lag between fieldwork and publication, most of this material still relates to the period before the implementation of the Children Act in 1991 or else to the early stages of the impact of the new legislative context. This review does not purport to be comprehensive, but selects some of the key themes relevant to current and future practice.

As we have seen, research had an unusually important influence on the principles and details of the Children Act, although of course there were many other factors too. The interaction between research and legislation stretches back at least until the previous Children Act of 1975. Certainly research contributed to the strong emphasis in that Act on what became known as permanency planning, especially the work of Rowe and Lambert (1973), though the Maria Colwell Inquiry and Houghton Report were probably the most significant. However, the legislators had a strong commitment to evaluation, so that it was required that certain sections be monitored and investigated. This was true for adoption allowances and freeing for adoption, for instance (Hill, Lambert and Triseliotis 1989; Lowe et al. 1993).

We observed earlier that the 1980s witnessed path-breaking achievements by central government in sponsoring a number of co-ordinated studies and facilitating their dissemination (DHSS 1985b). A further compilation was published by the Department of Health in 1991. There have been many advantages in having co-ordinated research with government sponsors committed to incorporating findings in policy and practice, but there are also drawbacks, such as the sometimes restricted agenda and methodological concentration on interview or case record surveys (Bullock 1993).

Research and the spectrum of services and support

To provide a framework for making sense of the foci and messages of research, it is helpful to examine more recent investigations in relation to the spectrum or continuum of services (See Figure 1). This does not give an exhaustive picture of all elements of social services for children but indicates the principal ones under three main headings:

- services for children at home in the community

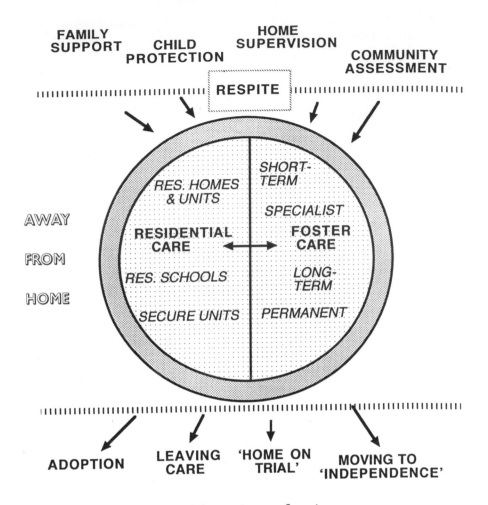

Figure 1.1 Research focus and the continuum of services

- services for children looked after away from home
- services for children after they have left 'accommodation' or care.

If we examine the continuum shown in Figure 1, it is apparent that empirical work has been very uneven in its coverage and changed its main emphases over time. During the 1980s most major studies were concerned with children then referred to as 'in care', i.e. mainly in foster care or residential care, although some did examine the admission processes or even have a comparison community sample (notably Packman, Randall and Jacques 1986). Many provided overviews of children in care and there were only a few which examined specific types of placement (e.g. Berridge 1985; Shaw and Hipgrave 1983, 1989).

There was a major interest in decision-making, planning and reviews (DHSS 1985b) and subsequently in outcomes (Triseliotis 1989; DH 1991).

This decade saw a number of studies on adoption, which accompanied its increased use for older or disabled children placed from care. The pioneering study by Stein and Carey (1986) put the issue of 'after-care' on the research and political agenda, leading to significant changes in practice.

There was very little research concerned with support to families and children at home, with preventive work or with restoration (rehabilitation). Perhaps even more surprisingly, in view of the huge attention given to child abuse and child protection following a series of scandals and inquiries (Parton 1991), this area of work received very limited systematic description, let alone evaluation within the social work field. A notable exception was the work of Corby (1987).

The picture has changed considerably during the 1990s, partly because of the Children Act. Some formerly neglected topics have come to the fore, whereas in other areas empirical information has dried up or shifted in emphasis. We shall look at the three main fields of the care continuum, but it is important to bear in mind that there are important themes which cut across or integrate the divides. These include decision-making, participation, rights and outcomes which are all important issues in policy, practice and research.

Children at home

There has been an upsurge of work on child protection and family support. The Department of Health (1995) produced a compendium of the key messages, prepared by members of the Dartington Research Unit. This summary begins by illustrating the difficulties of defining abuse. It notes how the threshold for intervention has been gradually lowered over the last century (DH 1995), although the concept of significant harm and the legal thresholds for action in the Children Act to some extent aim to ensure that compulsory intervention only occurs when there is genuine justification (Hardiker this volume). Child Protection Registers are seen by most professionals as a vital tool in assessing risk and recording concern, but even so they are often not consulted during initial referrals (Gibbons and Bell 1994; DH 1995).

Case conferences devote most attention to details of abusive incidents, with comparatively little time spent on planning future action (DH 1995). Involvement of parents was rare in the 1980s, but began to happen in some agencies before the Children Act, which has reinforced the trend. This is often difficult for all concerned, but participation in decision-making does appear generally to have aided parental understanding and eased the professional task (Thoburn this volume). Honesty, reliability and open communication have been shown to be important ingredients in enabling families to co-operate, even in circumstances of high tension and conflict.

Hallett and Birchall (1992) reviewed the factors which facilitate or inhibit co-operation, including differences in role and expectations, group processes and the degree of external (mainly governmental) mandate. Their subsequent empirical work showed that most professionals seemed to have a reasonable understanding of each other's roles and perspectives. They generally reported satisfaction with the quality of collaboration (Birchall and Hallett 1995). However, co-operation was most evident in the early stages, after which frequency of communication often dropped off markedly with social services usually taking on the main responsibilities (see also Farmer 1993a).

The great majority of children dealt with under child protection procedures remain at home (DH 1995). Indeed, a high proportion of the families concerned receive no positive service and few gain access to specialised treatment. This may help to account for the fact that 'between a quarter and a third of children were known to have been re-abused' (DH 1995 p.42). Fortunately, rates for 'serious' re-abuse were found to be much lower. A general conclusion is that too much time is spent on investigating relatively minor cases, whilst the needs and indeed expressed wishes for help of children, non-abusing parents, non-resident parents and siblings are often not heeded.

Different types of suspected mistreatment have different patterns of response. The Department of Health summary report concluded that isolated incidents of physical abuse 'seldom warrant much concern' (p.19), whilst even relatively minor, one-off events of sexual abuse 'may require a strong response' (p.19) – a conclusion which needs careful interpretation if the lessons of Cleveland and Orkney are not to be forgotten. The report notes the importance of emotional abuse and in particular stresses the vulnerability of children in households with little warmth and high levels of criticism. The most problematic category is that of neglect. A high proportion of cases in this group do not reach the case conference stage and contact with social services tends to cease soon after referral. Yet the families often have major material and other needs, which social services themselves neglect to attend to (Denman and Thorpe 1993; Gibbons 1995).

Overall the research on child protection suggests a need for a shift in approach from investigation to family support. This reinforces the message that a number of commentators have been giving for some time: that law and practice have become too preoccupied with child rescue and social control, insufficiently attentive to providing supportive services (Holman 1988; Parton 1991; Audit Commission 1994).

A national review has taken place of how Section 17 of the Children Act concerning children in need has been implemented over the first 18 months (Aldgate et al. 1994). There was great variation amongst local authorities in their interpretation of which children could be classified as in need, but there was a tendency to offer services to as narrow a range of children as possible. On the other hand, some social services departments can offer a very wide range of services, often in collaboration with health services and education departments.

There are now a wide variety of family centres and projects, as well as home support and volunteer schemes (Gibbons 1994). An investigation of day care and family support services showed that more families gained relevant help when there were a range of neighbourhood oriented and broadly based services available rather than conventional local authority provision alone (Gibbons, Thorpe and Wilkinson 1990). Open-access centres served a wider variety of families and met the needs of families with major difficulties who tended to avoid specialist projects because of stigma. A combination of material aid, mobilising networks and personal support is valued by parents, but some of their concerns may not be appreciated by professionals, e.g. about health or the environment (Gardner 1992; Smith 1992). Also there is still a tendency to focus on both the needs and perceived shortcomings of women, with much less attention given to men.

Little is known from research about longer-term support or supervision to families, whether following enquiries related to suspected abuse or for other children in need. Similarly, if we turn our attention to children who offend or have behaviour difficulties, there is a dearth of recent information about the nature and role of supervision. It is clear that strategies to divert young people from care or custody have been effective, but they require structured alternative programmes (Bottoms et al. 1990; Dennington and Pitts 1991; see also Asquith this volume). A study which covered parts of the North of England found that parents and young people were often unsure about the purpose of supervision and some social workers appeared to lack clear plans. Group workers were well regarded and group activities enjoyed, but families often saw this as having little impact on the original problems (Triseliotis et al. 1995).

For many years, Observation and Assessment Units were a prominent part of residential care provision, but now most have closed or changed function (Berridge this volume). Instead a number of areas now have community assessment programmes. Often differing systems apply depending on whether a case is seen as 'child protection', 'children in need' or children 'looked after'. An investigation in one authority with respect to adolescents showed that there were few major differences in process or outcomes between formal specialist assessments and routine assessments carried out by workers in their everyday work, although the former were more systematic (Sinclair, Garnett and Berridge 1995). It was concluded that assessment needs to be cumulative or cyclical rather than once and for all.

Children away from home

The 1980s witnessed a number of surveys which charted the careers of children across a range of placements in several authorities (e.g. Millham et al. 1986; Rowe, Hundleby and Garnett 1989). The current decade has built on those overviews mainly by focusing on specific types of placement, child or locality. However, evaluations of accommodation arrangements under the new Act are about to emerge. A national study by Packman and Hall (forthcoming) concluded that there has been a shift away from compulsory care placements in favour of 'voluntary' accommodation, reversing the trends of the 1980s. This has been especially noticeable for children who are first looked after in their teens. Likewise, Dickens (1993) found a reluctance to use the new provision for Child Assessment Orders, partly as a result of uncertainty about their nature and purpose, but also because of a wish not to antagonise parents.

An influential and innovative development in the relationship between research, policy and practice has been the evolution of the Looking After Children Project (Ward this volume). Here research expertise was used to devise dimensions and measures of children's progress; these were tested in practice; then revised versions were produced taking account of the evaluation. The implementation of this system in many areas across the country and elsewhere will not only assist in planning, review and taking action for individual children, but offers the opportunity for monitoring the progress of populations covering a wide range of circumstances and agencies.

There has been a cluster of studies looking at young people's views, mainly in relation to residential care (e.g. Buchanan, Wheal and Coker 1993). These studies demonstrate that some adolescents feel strongly that they wish to be fostered, whereas others are equally committed to residential care, but many in both groups cannot exercise their preferences. Most research has shown that there has been little choice of placement for children or parents, reflecting resource levels which are limited in scale and range (Cliffe with Berridge 1991, Triseliotis et al. 1995). Young people want to be actively involved in significant decisions and often voice resentment at reviews and other meetings they attend which are adult-dominated.

With a few exceptions, the circumstances and experiences of black children away from home has received little attention. Barn (1993) found that black children were over-represented in admissions to care. There were problems in assessment and engagement with families, but many children were placed in culturally appropriate settings.

RESIDENTIAL CARE

Research on residential care has continued to concentrate on the special provision rather than 'ordinary' establishments. Scant attention has been given to short-term placements (Bullock, Little and Millham 1993a).

Residential schools for children with emotional and behavioural difficulties ('EBD') vary considerably and perhaps excessively in the emphases of their regimes. For example they may encourage educational achievement, personal development, group management or behaviour modification principles (Grimshaw with Berridge 1994). Over a year, a sample of 67 children became more compliant at home and at school, whilst family relationships were for the most part sustained, but rates of offending and sexual exploitation increased. This picture of generally positive progress in residential schools fits with other findings (Hill, Triseliotis, Borland and Lambert this volume).

Harris and Timms (1993) examined policies about secure accommodation and analysed the characteristics of 399 children admitted to secure units. They concluded that, apart from an extreme minority, the residents hardly differed from those placed elsewhere, except in their absconding behaviour. Many led very unhappy and unstable lives, so were often relieved to gain psychological security in the physically secure setting. A study of young people attending Youth Treatment Centres identified that little attention was given to family and social relationships outside the institution, yet those with poorest outcomes were not necessarily grave offenders but those who lacked roots and support (Little 1993).

Feedback from young people about residential care indicates that they usually get on well with staff, though commonly regret the lack of continuity. Amongst their wishes are:

- more individualised care, smaller units, privacy, attention and support with school work
- respect from adults
- control of bullying
- wider peer contacts.

They also dislike staff favouritism (Fletcher 1993).

Baldwin (1990) offered a staff perspective from one local authority. She identified powerlessness amongst carers due to their lack of influence on the wider organisation of which they were part and their exclusion from influencing the circumstances from which children came. A programme of team-building within establishments appeared to fortify staff both in their work with residents and in their confidence in tackling wider issues.

FOSTER CARE

The large survey by Rowe et al. (1989) showed that most children in foster care experience short-term placements, whereas the bulk of previous research had concentrated on long-term or permanent placements. This discrepancy has begun to be rectified (Sellick this volume), although still not much is known from children's perspectives. Sellick (1992) found continuing dissatisfactions amongst short-term foster carers with the level and promptness of payments. Foster carers want social workers to be competent, reliable, supportive and respectful of foster carers' own knowledge and skills. Stone (1991) found that brief placements in foster care were valuable in supplementing family support, whilst respite care has been developed to help families undergoing stress (Aldgate this volume).

Research on specialist foster care for adolescents has usually shown the popularity of behavioural parenting based on the Kent model, and provided further support for its relative success with difficult adolescents (Shaw and Hipgrave 1989; Hazel 1990). In contrast, Downes (1992) in her intensive analysis of 23 placements emphasised the importance of past and present relationships. She identified the main issues in the families as centring on attachment and distance regulation. For instance, young people who were 'anxiously attached' seemed to need frequent accompanying and nurturance, whereas those who were more ambivalent oscillated between a desire for closeness and episodes of hostility or going missing. Foster carers evidently required careful preparation and training so they could adapt to the particular orientation of the young person and the often volatile demands.

Colton, Heath and Aldgate (1995) examined the role of foster carers in relation to education. It appeared that the foster families could not compensate for the deficits which children brought with them, although at least there was no further falling behind. Specialist input was needed as well as the commitment of foster carers. Foster children's educational progress appeared to be influenced by the stability of the placement. Those who expected to stay with their foster carers did better than those who were uncertain about their future (Aldgate, Heath and Colton 1992).

A major review of foster care research has just been completed by Berridge (forthcoming). He observed that there has been hardly any recent research specifically focusing on foster care by contrast with ten major studies of residential care currently in progress. He also noted that much attention has been given to specialist schemes, but the evidence is that these remain a relatively small and patchy part of the service.

Children who have moved back home or 'moved on'

Studies of young people leaving care (ceasing to be looked after) as a result of reaching an upper legal or administrative age limit have continued to document the major difficulties most face, in spite of the development of 'preparation', 'after-care' and 'through care' programmes. They still tend to face difficulties of finding and keeping accommodation, managing on often insufficient income, finding work, establishing close relationships and handling identity issues. Frequent changes of address are common. However, they are more likely nowadays to feel prepared for domestic chores (Pinkerton and Stein 1995). Risks of ending up homeless or in custody are high (Biehal *et al.* 1992). Young women seem to be especially vulnerable and lacking in support (Garnett 1992). Continued support from social workers or former carers provides a vital lifeline for some individuals, but is often absent. Despite the attention that this issue has received, reinforced by the Children Act, questions have to be asked about the viability and fairness of expecting some of the country's most disadvantaged youth to cope 'independently' at an age when most of their peers remain mainly or wholly at home.

Recent work has reminded us forcibly that the majority of children leave care much earlier than 16, usually to return home. Little attention had been given before to the nature and success of such departures compared to examinations of admission processes. Farmer and Parker (1991) looked at the circumstances of children who returned home on Care Orders or under Parental Rights resolutions, so these cases with legal orders were likely to encompass more difficult home situations in the first instance than children placed on a voluntary basis. Nevertheless, a worrying picture was revealed in which significant minorities of children encountered poor care or rejection again. Special education seems to have been particularly helpful at both the preparation and restoration stages in achieving positive results.

Bullock et al. (1993b) examined cases of children returning home through a wider variety of routes. They highlighted how return to family is sooner or later the destination of the great majority of children looked after away from home (86% in their estimate). However this was seen to be often an extended process of adjustment and readjustment. Sometimes family situations had stabilised or attitudes become more accepting, but in other instances family crises undermined the rehabilitation process (Little, Leitch and Bullock 1995). When provided, support from social workers or past carers usually helped facilitate successful reintegration, but often attention was minimal.

Adoption has increasingly become a destination for children leaving care over the last 20 years, although the proportion remains quite small in relation to the total number of children looked after away from home. Part of the same trend has been that a significant minority of freeing and adoption orders have been made despite the active opposition of one or both parents.. There are major problems of duplication and delay in the legal processes (Murch et al. 1993). Surprisingly perhaps, in a considerable percentage of such cases some form of contact with the birth family was maintained after adoption and this was not seen as threatening the placement (Ryburn 1994).

New information is appearing about placements for adoption or permanent new families made in the 1980s. For instance, placements of children of mixed parentage appear to have been more problematic both in matching of background and outcomes than for white or black children (Charles, Parvez and Thoburn 1992). The long-term study by Rushton, Quinton and Treseder (1993) indicates that the continued availability of social work support over years can be decisive in sustaining placements. Howe (1996) has completed a study of over 200 adopted persons, now in early adulthood. This highlights the lasting effects of pre-placement experiences and moves.

The linked issues of transracial and intercountry adoption remain contentious, as are the research methods and questions which have been used to shed light on outcomes for individual children concerned. There have been

further studies which suggest that children can do well on a range of measures
when placed transracially and often appear to develop a positive intercultural
identity (Bagley, Young and Scully 1993).

There is a growing body of work about seeking information or contact in
adulthood, the complexity and changeability of feelings on all sides and the
importance of counselling (Howe, Sawbridge and Hinings 1992; Feast 1992).

Conclusion

In this chapter we identified some of the factors and thinking which influenced
the Children Act 1989. The Act heralded a definite shift by local authorities
towards greater participation by young people and partnership with parents,
whilst retaining measures to safeguard children's interests. It also embraced a
philosophy of family support, particularly in relation to children in need. Recent
research suggests that some of the aims are being fulfilled, but as ever there are
shortcomings and new messages to learn.

It is important to keep in mind that the different aspects of the service
continuum are all connected. Many children move between them. Long-term
planning at the case and population levels should take account of typical
sequences, with particular attention to the risks, changes and supports
associated with each stage. There is evidence that one of the aims of the
Children Act – to make the boundary between support at home and away from
home more permeable – has been successful through more positive use of respite
and short-term placements.

Research indicates that family support work is valued, but ought to be
multi-faceted and openly available. Access to services has become more
confined to those families where a child is thought to be at risk. This is a crude
method of targeting, given the inherent difficulties of discriminating between
those who are at risk and those who are not. It excludes many other needy
children and their families. Narrow interpretations of the category 'in need' and
resource constraints have evidently contributed to this more restricted access to
family support than was hoped for by many who influenced the formulation
of the Children Act.

More account is being taken of children's own perspectives and views than
formerly, both individually and collectively (Sinclair this volume) but there is
a need to improve the mechanisms for doing so. This requires giving
information regularly, preparation for key meetings, care about attendance and
skilful chairing of meetings to ensure children are listened to. It is also important
to ensure that consultations are as wide as possible.

There is strong need for more information about the experiences of children
of different ethnic and religious backgrounds. It will be important to know
about the implementation and consequences of Section 22 of the Children Act

which established a duty to consider children's religion, racial, ethnic and linguistic background.

There are common findings about what people want from social workers, including honesty, respect, reliability, support and ready availability. Often though not invariably these personal qualities are present, but workers commonly do not have the time to be as available to so many parties as is wanted.

Both encouragement and warning signs can be derived from the first five years of developments in practice under the Children Act 1989. Securing children's welfare in a complex modern society is not straightforward and constant reassessment is required.

References

Aldgate, J., (1976) The child in care and his parents. *Adoption and Fostering 84*, 2, 29–40.

Aldgate, J., (1990) Foster children at school: success or failure. *Adoption and Fostering 14*, 4, 38–48.

Aldgate, J., Heath, A. and Colton, M. (1992) Placement stability and the education of children in long-term foster care. *Children and Society 6*, 2, 91 103.

Aldgate, J. and Hill, M. (1995) Child welfare in the United Kingdom: recent changes in policy and legislation. *Children and Youth Services Review 17*, 5/6, 575–596.

Aldgate, J., Tunstill, J., Ozolins, R. and McBeath, G. (1994) *Family Support and the Children Act – The First 18 Months, a Report to the Department of Health.* Leicester: University of Leicester School of Social Work.

Aldgate, J. and Tunstill, J. (1995) *Section 17 – The First 18 Months of Implementation.* London: HMSO.

Audit Commission (1994) *Seen but not Heard.* London: HMSO.

Bagley, C., Young, L. and Scully, A. (1993) *International and Transracial Adoptions.* Aldershot: Avebury.

Baldwin, N. (1990) *The Power to Care in Children's Homes.* Aldershot: Gower.

Barn, R. (1993) Black and white care careers: a different reality. In P. Marsh and J. Triseliotis (eds.) *Prevention and Reunification in Child Care.* London: Batsford.

Berridge, D. (1985) *Children's Homes.* Oxford: Basil Blackwell.

Berridge, D. (forthcoming) *Foster Care: A Research Review.* London: HMSO.

Biehal, N., Clayden, J., Stein, M. and Wade, J. (1992) *Prepared for Living?* (Leaving Care Research Project, Leeds University). London: National Children's Bureau.

Birchall, E. and Hallett, C. (1995) *Working Together in Child Protection.* London: HMSO.

Bottoms, A., Brown, P., McWilliams, B., McWilliams, W. and Nellis, M. (1990) *Intermediate Treatment and Juvenile Justice.* London: HMSO.

Buchanan, A., Wheal, A. and Coker, R. (1993) *Answering Back*, (Dolphin Project). Department of Social Work Studies, University of Southampton.

Bullock, R. (1993) The United Kingdom. In M. Colton and W. Hellinckx (eds) (1993) *Child Care in the EC*. Aldershot: Ashgate.

Bullock, R., Little, M. and Millham, S. (1993a) *Residential Care: A Review of the Research*. London: HMSO.

Bullock, R., Little, M. and Millham, S. (1993b) *Going Home*. Aldershot: Dartmouth.

Butler-Sloss, Mrs. Justice (Chair)(1988) *Report of the Inquiry into Child Abuse in Cleveland*. HMSO: London.

Charles, M., Parvez, S. and Thoburn, J. (1992) The placement of black children with permanent new families. *Adoption and Fostering 16*, 3, 13–19.

Cliffe, D. with Berridge, D. (1991) *Closing Children's Homes: An End to Residential Childcare?* London: National Children's Bureau.

Colton, M., Heath, A. and Aldgate, J. (1995) Factors which influence the educational attainment of children in foster family care. *Community Alternatives 7* 1, 15–36.

Corby, B. (1987) *Working with Child Abuse*. Milton Keynes: Open University Press.

Denman, G., and Thorpe, D., (1993) *Family Participation and Patterns of Intervention in Child Protection in Gwent*. Lancaster University: Department of Applied Social Science.

Dennington, J. and Pitts, J. (1991) *Developing Services for Young People in Crisis*. London: Longman.

Department of Health and Social Security (1984) *Report of The House of Commons Social Services Committee (The Short Report)*. London: HMSO.

Department of Health and Social Security (1985a). *Review of Child Care Law*. London: HMSO.

Department of Health and Social Security (1985b) *Social Work Decisions in Child Care*. London: HMSO.

Department of Health and Social Security (1987) *The Law on Child Care and Family Services*. London: HMSO.

Department of Health (1989) *An Introduction to the Children Act (1989)*. London: HMSO.

Department of Health (1991) *Patterns and Outcomes in Child Placement*. London: HMSO.

Department of Health (1995) *Looking After Children*. London: HMSO.

Dickens, J. (1993) Assessment and the control of social work: an analysis of the reasons for the non-use of the Child Assessment Order. *Journal of Social Welfare and Family Law*, 88–100.

Downes, C. (1992) *Separation Revisited*. Ashgate: Aldershot.

Eekelaar, J. (1991) Parental responsibility: state of nature or nature of the state. *Journal of Social Welfare and Family Law*, 37–50.

Farmer, E. (1993a) Going Home – what makes reunification work? In P. Marsh and J. Treseliotis *Prevention and Reunification in Child Care*. London: Batsford.

Farmer, E. (1993b) The impact of child protection interventions. In L. Waterhouse (ed) *Child Abuse and Child Abusers*. London: Jessica Kingsley.

Farmer, E. and Parker, R. (1991) *Trials and Tribulations*. London: HMSO.

Feast, J. (1992) Working in the adoption circle – outcomes of Section 51 counselling. *Adoption and Fostering 16*, 4, 46–52.

Fisher, D., Marsh, P., Phillips, D. and Sainsbury, E. (1986) *Children In And Out Of Care*. London: Batsford.

Fletcher, B. (1993) *Not Just a Name: The Views of Young People in Foster and Residential Care*. London: National Consumer Council/Who Cares? Trust.

Gardner, R. (1992) *Supporting Families: Preventive Work in Social Work Practice*. London: HMSO.

Garnett, L. (1992) *Leaving Care and After*. London: National Children's Bureau.

Gibbons, J. (ed.) (1994) *Family Support and the Children Act 1989*. London: HMSO.

Gibbons, J. (1995) Family support in child protection. In M. Hill, R. H. Kirk and D. Part (eds.) *Supporting Families*. Edinburgh: HMSO.

Gibbons, J. and Bell, C. (1994) Variations in the operation of English child protection registers. *British Journal of Social Work 14*, 701–714.

Gibbons, J., Thorpe, S. and Wilkinson, P. (1990) *Family Support and Prevention: Studies in Local Areas*. London: NISW/HMSO.

Grimshaw, R. with Berridge, D. (1994) *Educating Disruptive Children*. London: National Children's Bureau.

Hallett, C. and Birchall, E. (1992) *Coordination and Child Protection*. Edinburgh: HMSO.

Harding, L. F. (1991) *Perspectives in Child Care Policy*. London: Longman.

Harris, R. and Timms, N. (1993) *Secure Accommodation in Child Care*. London: Routledge.

Hazel, N. (1990) The development of specialist foster care for adolescents: Policy and Practice. In B. Galaway, D. Maglajlic, J. Hudson, P. Harmon and J. McLagan (eds.) *International Perspectives on Specialist Foster Family Care*. St Paul: Human Services Associates.

Hill, M. (1990) The manifest and latent functions of child abuse inquiries. *British Journal of Social Work 20*, 197–213.

Hill, M., Lambert, L. and Triseliotis, J (1989) *Achieving Adoption with Love and Money*. London: National Children's Bureau.

Holman, R. (1988) *Putting Families First*. London: Macmillan.

Houghton Committee (1972) *Report of the Departmental Committee on the Adoption of Children*. Cmnd. 5107. London: HMSO.

Howe, D. (1996) Adoption and attachment. *Adoption and Fostering 19*, 4, 7–15.

Howe, D., Sawbridge, P. and Hinings, D. (1992) *Half a Million Women.* Harmondsworth: Penguin.

Little, M. (1993) Specialised residential services for difficult adolescents: some recent research findings. In R. Bullock (ed) *Problem Adolescents.* London: Whiting and Birch.

Little, M., Leitch, H. and Bullock, R. (1995) The care careers of long-stay children: the contribution of new theoretical approaches. *Children and Youth Services Review.*

Lowe, N., Borkowski, M., Copner, R., Griew, K. and Murch, M., (1993) *Freeing for Adoption Provisions.* London: HMSO.

Marsh, P. (1993) Family reunification and preservation – the need for partnership between users and professionals. In P. Marsh and J. Triseliotis (eds) *Prevention and Reunification in Child Care.* London: Batsford.

Millham, S., Bullock, R., Hosie, K. and Haak, M. (1986) *Lost in Care.* Aldershot: Gower.

Mitchell, A. (1985) *Children in the Middle.* London: Tavistock.

Murch, M., Lowe, N., Borkowski, M., Copner, R. and Griew, K. (1993) *Pathways to Adoption.* London: HMSO.

Ormrod, R. (1983) Child care law: a personal perspective. *Adoption And Fostering 7,* 4, 10–16.

Packman, J. (1993) From prevention to partnership: child welfare services across three decades. In G. Pugh (ed) *Thirty Years of Change for Children.* London: National Children's Bureau.

Packman, J. and Hall, C. (forthcoming). Totnes: Dartington Social Research Unit.

Packman, J. and Jordan, B. (1991) The Children Act: looking forward, looking back. *British Journal of Social Work, 21,* 315–327.

Packman, J., Randall, J. and Jacques, N. (1986) *Who Needs Care?.* Oxford: Blackwell.

Parker, R. A. (ed) (1980) *Caring for Separated Children.* Basingstoke: Macmillan.

Parton, N. (1991) *Governing the Family.* London: Macmillan.

Pinkerton, J. and Stein, M. (1995) Responding to the needs of young people leaving state care: law, practice and policy in England and Northern Ireland. *Children and Youth Services Review.*

Robinson, C., (1987) Key issues for social workers placing children for family based respite care. *British Journal of Social Work 17,* 257–284.

Rowe, J. and Lambert, L. (1973) *Children Who Wait.* London: Abafa.

Rowe, J. Cain, H., Hundleby, M. and Keane, A., (1984) *Long-Term Foster Care.* London: Batsford.

Rowe, J., Hundleby, M. and Garnett, L. (1989) *Child Care Now: A Survey of Placement Patterns.* London: BAAF.

Rushton, A., Quinton, D amd Treseder, J. (1993) New parents for older children: support services during eight years of placement. *Adoption and Fostering 4*, 39–45.

Ryburn, M. (1994) Contact after contested adoptions. *Adoption and Fostering 18*, 4, 30–38.

Sellick, C. (1992) *Supporting Short-term Foster Carers.* Aldershot: Avebury.

Shaw, M. and Hipgrave, T. (1983) *Specialist Fostering.* Batsford: London.

Shaw, M. and Hipgrave, T. (1989) Specialist fostering 1988 – a research study. *Adoption and Fostering, 13*, 3, 17–21.

Sinclair, R., Garnett, L. and Berridge, D. (1995) *Social Work Assessment.* London: National Children's Bureau.

Smith, T. (1992) Family centres, children in need and the Children Act. In J. Gibbons (ed) *The Children Act 1989 and Family Support.* London: HMSO.

Stein, M. and Carey, K. (1986) *Leaving Care.* Oxford: Blackwell.

Stone, J. (1991) The tangled web of short-term foster care: unravelling the strands. *Adoption and Fostering 15*, 3, 4–9.

Triseliotis, J. (1989) Foster care outcomes. *Adoption and Fostering 13*, 3, 5–17.

Triseliotis, J., Borland, M., Hill, M. and Lambert, L. (1995) *Teenagers and the Social Work Services.* London: HMSO.

CHAPTER 2

From the Social Work (Scotland) Act 1968 to the Children (Scotland) Act 1995
Pressures for Change[1]

Kay Tisdall

The Bill that is now before the Committee is the result of a great deal of preparation and consultation. Its origins lie in the Child Care Law Review which reported in October 1990. Since then there has been a number of important reviews and reports which have contributed to our proposals – notably the reports of the Orkney and Fife child care inquiries. But the Bill is not just a series of responses to a multitude of recommendations – there were 400 in the various reports which have [been] issued since 1990. It is a coherent framework of legislation for the care of children and their families. (Hansard 5 December 1994)

So said the then Secretary of State for Scotland, the Rt. Hon. Ian Lang, at the first substantial debate on the Children (Scotland) Bill. Following amendments, this became the Children (Scotland) Act 1995. As Ian Lang suggested, the path to the new legislation was lengthy. Until 1995, the Social Work (Scotland) Act 1968 remained the foundation of child care legislation although a range of changes and additions had been made by the Children Act 1975, particularly in relation to adoption. The Scottish Office set up a Child Care Law Review in 1988. After the Review reported in 1990, the smooth path of policy revision was rocked by numerous scandals and reports – such as the removal of children under emergency child protection procedures in Orkney, and Sheriff Kearney's

---

1   The author would like to acknowledge the assistance provided by Professor Lorraine Waterhouse in commenting on an earlier draft of this chapter.

inquiry into Fife Region's child care policies.[2] Five years after the review process began, Scotland received its White Paper, *Scotland's Children* (August 1993), and the Children (Scotland) Bill was introduced into Parliament in November 1994.

This chapter focuses on the development of the Children (Scotland) Act 1995 and particularly on child protection, the children's hearings and child care provision. It begins with the 1968 Act and then discusses some of the following challenges to child care services due to changing realities and concepts, which have led to the eventual development of new Scottish children's legislation. It will be suggested that the new children's legislation addresses some of the realities and incorporates some of the concepts, but it does not do so comprehensively nor adequately in all areas. The chapter ends by exploring whether the new Act does indeed provide a 'coherent framework' for children and their families, as declared by Ian Lang (in the quote above).

The Social Work (Scotland) Act 1968: origins and major provisions

In 1961, a Committee under the chairmanship of Lord Kilbrandon was appointed by the Secretary of State for Scotland, with the mandate to review the arrangements for dealing with juveniles in need of care or protection, and juvenile delinquents. When the Committee reported in 1964, it began with the assumption that all children appearing before juvenile courts, whether because they were in need of care or protection or because they had committed offences, were all exhibiting symptoms of the same difficulties: 'the true distinguishing factor, common to all children concerned, is their need for special measures of education and training, the normal up-bringing process having, for whatever reason, fallen short' (p.13). The Committee proposed that decisions on guilt and innocence would remain with the judiciary but a separate system of children's hearings would make decisions on care. This separate system would be supported by a social education service department set up within the education authority.

The White Paper *Social Work and the Community* (1966) brought forward Kilbrandon's recommendations with a notable difference. Rather than a social education service, a separate and comprehensive social work department would be created. The new social work department would not only service the children's hearings, but bring together social services for people of all ages. The White Paper thus went far beyond Kilbrandon's mandate to consider children: it incorporated the growing belief that professional social work had common principles, objectives, and methods for working with individuals and families (Martin 1983; Murray and Hill 1991).

---

2 For further description of these situations/reports, see later in chapter.

The resultant Social Work (Scotland) Act 1968 provided the legislative foundation for social work departments, with the requirement for local authorities to have a Social Work Committee and a Director of Social Work. The new Departments were made responsible for 'fieldwork' and a range of services: residential, day care and domiciliary (Martin 1983 p.109). In Part III of the Act, the new system of children's hearings was indeed enacted, largely as suggested by the Kilbrandon Committee.

As legislated in the 1968 Act, the children's hearing system has three key actors: the Reporter to the Children's Panel; the social work department; and the Children's Panel. The Reporter is a senior local authority officer, with experience in both legal and child care issues. The Reporter is responsible for examining cases brought to her/his attention (referrals), and assessing whether a child is in need of compulsory measures of care and should therefore be brought before a children's hearing tribunal. The social work department of the local authority is responsible for investigating cases on behalf of the Reporter and for implementing any measures of care imposed on a child by the hearing. Lay people volunteer to become part of their local community's Children's Panel and, if selected, receive training.

A children's hearing is an informal tribunal where three panel members (one of whom acts as chairperson) discuss the background and circumstances of the child referred by the Reporter, with the child and his or her family. Then the hearing makes a decision on any compulsory measures of care they consider necessary. Appeals against the grounds of referral or the children's hearings' decisions are heard by the Sheriff (Murray 1983; Kearney 1987; Murray and Hill 1991).

An important feature of the 1968 Act is the duty in Section 12 (1): 'It shall be the duty of every local authority to promote social welfare by making available advice, guidance and assistance...' The duty is further specified for children, to diminish the need for taking in or keeping a child in care, or for referring a child to a children's hearing (subsection 2). Local authorities have the power to provide not only assistance 'in kind' but also in cash. To many early observers, this positive promotion of welfare in the 1968 Act was revolutionary, and notably absent from parallel legislation in England and Wales (Younghusband 1978 p.252; Cooper 1983 p.50; Martin 1983 p.109).

Changing realities and changing concepts

Since the 1968 Act was created over two decades ago, families have changed radically.[3] Rates of divorce have increased, a higher proportion of children are

---

3　The following statistical information has been obtained from Children in Scotland (1995).

being born to single mothers, and the population has diversified with the growth of black and minority ethnic populations. People are marrying at older ages, and young people are increasingly reliant financially and practically on their parents long past their teens. More and more mothers with young children are going outside their homes to work and thus causing a rising demand for child care.

The range of crises facing families has multiplied. Homelessness and poor housing are growing problems: in 1992–93, Shelter (Scotland) estimated that over 33,000 children were in homeless households and 5 per cent of Scottish housing stock was 'below tolerable standard'. At least 5,000 young people sleep rough every year in Scotland. Official unemployment rose to 9.4 per cent in 1994, and young people aged 16–24 made up one-quarter of unemployed people in Scotland. The divide between incomes has widened until the top 1 per cent earned 13 times more than the bottom 50 per cent of earners (1992), and the number of children living in poverty has increased to over one-third of all children.

Children and young people are increasingly coming to public attention either as offenders or as victims of child abuse. The number of child protection referrals to social work departments has grown dramatically (from 95 in 1972 to 7228 in 1993) – whether abuse is more prevalent or more is reported is unknown. The number of referrals to the Reporter has similarly increased. In 1990, one-fifth of the Scottish prison population was under 21.

These changing realities, along with rising expectations of services, has led to growing demand and resulting stresses on social work services. Perhaps inevitably, a rash of inquiries and reports in the early 1990s outlined the deficiencies in the organisation and practice of social work and the children's hearings. Two such examples were the Fife and Orkney inquiries.

Sheriff Kearney led the Inquiry into Fife Social Work Department's child care policies, reporting to Parliament on 27 October 1992. The Inquiry investigated policies pursued by the Department under the Social Work (Scotland) Act 1968 and related legislation: '...in the use of voluntary and compulsory measures of care for children, and in particular, in the advice given to children's hearings before they decide on or review compulsory measures of care for children referred to them' (p.v). The Social Work Department's policy document, which promoted avoiding out of home and compulsory measures of care at all costs, was a particular focus of attention. The Inquiry found '...difficulties which can be caused when the delicate balance of the system is disturbed by the precipitate introduction of the simplistic and mechanical approach to child care work which we discovered' (p.616).

Recommendations were made specifically to the Fife Social Work Department, such as advocating a more flexible approach to child care and revising policy documents to emphasise general principles of good child care practice. The Inquiry also took a wider view and commented on various aspects of child care: for example, the need to acknowledge the importance of all three parties (social work departments, Children's Hearings and Reporters) in the child care system; the limited resources available to Departments, which constrained children's hearings decisions; the isolation and potential vulnerability of Reporters, who should have some structure for appropriate support; the need for specialised training in child care; and the need to study the child care system, throughout Scotland, in greater depth.

On the same date as the Fife Report, Lord Clyde's *Report of the Inquiry into the Removal of Children from Orkney in February 1991* was also submitted to Parliament. The Report considered the action of the agencies involved in the removal of nine children in Orkney by social workers, as a result of suspected sexual abuse.

The situation had a lengthy history. In 1987, a father was convicted of physically and sexually abusing his children. Three years later, seven children from this family were taken into care because of alleged abuse of children by their sibling. Social workers came to believe that organised sexual abuse was occurring on the island, due to the disclosures of these children. Following an investigation by the Orkney Social Work Department, the Royal Scottish Society for the Prevention of Cruelty to Children and the police, 'place of safety' orders were obtained from a Sheriff and nine children removed from their homes and admitted into public care on the mainland. Following child protection procedures, the children were then referred to the Reporter. The parents of these nine children denied the grounds of referral and their cases went to the Sheriff Court. The Sheriff held that the proceedings had been flawed by procedural irregularities. Evidence in relation to the alleged abuse was never heard and the nine children were returned to the families.

Lord Clyde's Report made 194 recommendations, suggesting considerable reform in the procedures of child protection, children's hearings, and social work training. For example, strengthened inter-agency co-operation was advocated in identification and investigation of sexual abuse. Greater consideration should be given to the Sheriff's being able to exclude a suspected abuser from contact with the child, and to having a child advocate or 'safeguarder' (an independent person concerned with the best interests of the child) involved in emergency child protection procedures.

Lord Clyde recommended that the European Convention on Human Rights and the United Nations (UN) Convention on the Rights of the Child should be taken account of in child care law reform and most particularly in child protection. (For further discussion of the Orkney Inquiry, see Asquith 1993.)

Children's rights and parental responsibilities

The two Conventions referred to by Lord Clyde were gaining increasing attention in Scottish child care policy and practice. Alleged contraventions of the European Convention on Human Rights can be taken to the European

Court. The references to the Court within debates on the Children (Scotland) Bill (Hansard 7 and 9 March and 5 July 1995) suggest the considerable impact the Convention – and the threat of court cases – has on Scottish Office thinking in the areas of child protection and the children's hearings.

The UK government signed the UN Convention on the Rights of the Child in 1991, and thus committed itself to operationalising the articles contained within the Convention. The Convention itself identifies three key principles (p.1):

- all rights guaranteed by the Convention must be available to all children without discrimination of any kind (Article 2)

- the best interests of the child must be a primary consideration in all actions concerning children (Article 3)

- children's views must be considered and taken into account in all matters affecting them (Article 12).

Other articles can then be divided into three areas: participation, protection and provision (p.2).

The UN Convention furthers the recognition of children as individuals, with needs and rights of their own, rather than as chattels of their parents. Correspondingly, there has been a shift in the discourse on parenting in Scotland. Rather than beginning with parents' rights over children, the Scottish Law Commission's *Report on Family Law* (No. 135) recommended beginning with the parents' obligations towards their children – parental *responsibilities.* Article 18 of the UN Convention states that children have the right to have both parents involved in their upbringing and development, as long as such involvement is not against their best interests. In turn, Report No. 135 encouraged *joint parenting*: a child's right to both parents should not be erased because of problems between the parents. The concepts of 'parental responsibilities' and 'joint parenting' both demonstrate the focus on children as individuals, whose rights must be considered in parental decisions.

Limited resources and targeting need

In the early days of implementing the 1968 Act, social work departments faced a constantly expanding demand for personal social services. The almost inevitable consequence, according to Martin (1983), was the prioritisation on crisis situations instead of the 'carefully planned long-term preventive work' (p.110) promoted in the 1966 White Paper. This prioritisation had changed little two decades later.

Increased numbers of child protection referrals, children in poverty and homeless children and young people, have placed growing demands on Scottish social work departments and their local authorities. Yet funding to social work departments has been constrained. Local authorities complain of the lack of resources provided by the Scottish Office (*The Scotsman* 17 January 1995). Immediate crises have to be dealt with, and as child protection referrals increase, so have complaints that preventive work – actually to prevent the need for such referrals in the first place – is being ignored (Hill 1990). Statutory duties understandably are prioritised and non-statutory provision (such as day care services) become increasingly precarious. As demands have increased and resources have decreased, conceptually there has been a shift from advocating universal provision of services and benefits to targeting those most in need (Secretary of State for Social Services 1985).

Local Government reform

Local authorities are not only being faced with a crisis in revenue and services, but considerable upheaval with the new Local Government etc. (Scotland) Act 1994. The two-tier system of local government will revert to a unitary system in 1996. Housing services will no longer be separated from social work and education; all three will be the responsibilities of the new authorities. Twenty-nine new councils will be created on mainland Scotland, with the three existing Island councils continuing to serve Orkney, Shetland and the Western Isles. Social work and education, previously delivered by nine Regional Authorities, will be the responsibility of considerably smaller units. To provide services, powers are given in the Act for local authorities to work together in either Joint Boards or Joint Committees.

A number of concepts are driving local government reform, which are likely to have considerable impact on children's services. By going from the bigger Regional Councils to the new smaller unitary authorities, decision-making and services are *decentralised*. The 1994 Act requires the new authorities to develop proposals for further decentralisation and the Act firmly supports the continuation of Community Councils. (One notable reversal to the decentralisation trend is the creation of a national Reporter's service, under the aegis of a Principal Reporter for Scotland.)

Decentralisation is promoted as a way to ensure local authority services meet the needs of the local population. However, new local authorities may not be able to sustain certain services with their smaller populations and correspondingly smaller budgets. Specialised services, such as those for children with complex disabilities, and non-statutory services, such as Strathclyde Region's early years provision, appear particularly at risk. While provision is made in the Act for local authorities to work together, it is feared that these services will be lost in the turmoil of transition or the difficulties of cross-authority collaboration.

Decentralisation is also promoted because it is expected to bring local government 'closer to the people', heightening both political accountability and local involvement. Indeed, the Scottish Office constantly refused to put strengthened requirements on local authorities during debate on the Bill, because it advocated 'non-prescription': local authorities would be able to decide for themselves what structures they would have and how their services would be delivered. No longer will local authorities be required to have Social Work or Education Committees, nor Social Work or Education Directors, although, after much lobbying, local authorities will retain a requirement for a chief social work officer. The structure of local authorities may radically change in the future. For example, rather than separate social work and education departments, a children's department could be created, or someone with a housing background may manage a department including social work and education. Indeed, some new local authorities are already planning joint housing and social work departments. Such changes provide both opportunities and fears: will inter-agency collaboration within a local authority finally become a reality? will certain social services be de-prioritised and all but statutory duties disappear?

The move to smaller units of government enhances the need for individual local authorities to look outside themselves for service provision. Local authorities are increasingly likely to become 'enabling authorities,' purchasing services rather than providing them directly. Children's services are therefore likely to be provided increasingly by voluntary and private organisations. This matches a corresponding promotion of the 'mixed economy of welfare' by the Conservative government, where not only public services but voluntary organisations and private agencies should provide welfare services (Scottish Office 1994). Such changes raise both opportunities and fears for voluntary agencies: will they have increasing opportunities to provide services or be forgotten in the upheavals? will they become welded to a contract culture that guides and constrains their services, so that they lose their capability to innovate and to advocate for children and their families?

Children (Scotland) Act 1995

Throughout the passage of the Local Government etc. (Scotland) Act 1994, the Government promised that Scottish children's legislation would be introduced 'as soon as parliamentary time was available'. After much lobbying by agencies working with children and their families and by Parliamentarians, the Children (Scotland) Bill was introduced in 1994 using special Parliamentary procedures. On 19 July 1995, the Bill was given Royal Assent.

The Act brings together aspects of family, child care and adoption law that affect children. This in itself is a departure from the Child Care Law Review (1991) and the White Paper (1993), which identified the need to resolve the interface problems between the systems but themselves made few recommendations or attempts to co-ordinate the systems.

The influence of changing realities and concepts, described earlier in this chapter, can be seen in the Act. To meet the depressing realities faced by many young people leaving local authority care, the Government has slightly extended the duties for after-care support. New duties and powers are placed on local authorities to provide accommodation for children who need it. Child protection procedures are radically overhauled, with new Child Protection Orders for emergency situations, short-term Child Assessment Orders and a new Exclusion Order for alleged abusers.

Children's hearings are to be updated by including an extra tier of appeal and the possibility for a children's hearing to exclude a parent and the press. To meet European Convention requirements, the Act provides a new power to the Sheriff, who will be able to vary the decision of a children's hearing on appeal. The Ayrshire case (concerning allegations of satanic or ritual child abuse and subsequent handling of the allegations by social workers, police and the children's hearings) erupted as the Bill was going through Parliament, and amendments were made to ensure that children's hearings could be directed to hear new evidence. Various changes are made in adoption law, including consideration of a child's welfare into adulthood (thus recognising the older age at which many children are now being adopted and the long-term needs of adoptees) and continuation of the birth parent's status in step-parent adoptions (thus recognising the increasing number of re-constituted families).

In his introduction to the Bill, Ian Lang emphasised, 'The Bill is founded on principles derived from the United Nations Convention on the Rights of the Child...' and calls the first three clauses of the Bill, which set out the main responsibilities and rights of parents, 'a clear and important statement' (Hansard 5 December 1994). Joint parenting is promoted – '...a new climate where the emphasis will be on both parents playing an active part in raising their children' (Hansard 5 December 1994) – particularly by the change from 'custody' and 'access' to 'residence' and 'contact' orders as suggested by the Scottish Law Commission.

Rights for children are scattered through the Act, with the right of children to have their views considered located in at least eight sections. Courts and children's hearings will now have to consider the appointment of a safeguarder (an independent person to report on the child's best interests) in a wider range of situations. In a new Parliamentary procedure, young people who had experience of local authority care spoke to MPs of their views on the Bill, raising issues concerning after-care support, children's hearings and the proposed exclusion orders (Hansard 6 February 1995).

Those perceived as most 'in need' are targeted in the Act. Local authorities will have a new duty to 'safeguard and promote the welfare' of 'children in need' (including children with disabilities). For the first time in mainstream child care legislation in Scotland, children with and affected by disabilities are specifically mentioned – thus paralleling the UN Convention's requirement not to discriminate against children with disabilities (Article 2) but also to provide services that particularly meet their needs (Article 23).

Non-discrimination is further promoted by the requirement to have regard to children's 'religious persuasion, racial origin and cultural and linguistic background' in three places in the Act: for young people looked after by local authorities; in providing services for 'children in need'; and in adoption decisions.

Local authorities will have to prepare, publish and review children's service plans. These plans will set out how a local authority will provide child care services. Plans will have to be prepared in consultation with such agencies as Health Boards and trusts, voluntary organisations, the Principal Reporter and the Children's Panels in the area. For many of those concerned with children's services, it is hoped that these plans will ensure that the new local authorities do address and plan for children's services (Hansard 6 February 1995).

Compared to the new children's legislation elsewhere in the UK (the Children Act 1989 in England and Wales, and the Children (Northern Ireland) Order 1995), the Act has several innovations. The after-care duties and powers, while limited to children who have been in and left care at various ages, do require local authorities to provide 'advice, assistance and guidance'. Other UK legislation has the weaker duty to 'advise and befriend' and only a power to 'assist', although although an older age limit is set for young people who have left care. Scottish legislation is the first to introduce the new concept of 'parental responsibilities', an exclusion order for an alleged abuser (although England and Wales are likely to have theirs soon in a new Act), a statutory duty to have children's service plans, and specific recognition of children affected by disability. The unique children's hearings system is retained. However, the influence of other UK legislation has been greater than anticipated by the Child Care Law Review and the White Paper. A range of agencies across Scotland are deeply disappointed to have certain measures imported from other UK legislation: children will be 'looked after' by the local authority rather than being 'in care' (Hansard 6 June 1995), the category of 'children in need' is included and children's rights can be ignored when the public is 'at risk of serious harm' (the latter two are discussed below).

Changing realities and concepts: does new Scottish children's legislation address them?

Earlier in the chapter, changing realities and concepts have been described that have had considerable impact on services for children and their families. How well does the new Act address the impact of such realities and recognise the conceptual changes?

The remit of the Act does not allow for attention to be paid directly to unemployment and poverty. However, even within its scope, the Act is accused of failing to meet the needs of young people leaving local authority care: for example, by only raising the local authorities' duty to provide after-care support by one year to the age of 19 and only providing such help for young people who were in local authority care at the age of 16. The Government has not extended the after-care duty further because of the feared cost, and sees the new age limits as focusing on 'those in the greatest need' (Hansard 13 and 28 February and the 7 June 1995).

The category of 'children in need' similarly limits costs by targeting a specific group of children (Hansard 6 June 1995). Just as the Government was recognising the constricted interpretation of 'children in need' as 'children at risk of abuse' in England and Wales (Stone 1995), Scotland was introducing the same category. The category is profoundly disagreed with by a significant proportion of those working with and representing children and their families, for being stigmatising and static, crisis-driven and negative (Hansard 6 February 1995). It represents a significant retreat from the preventive vision presented by the Kilbrandon Committee, the promotion of welfare legislation in Section 12 of the Social Work (Scotland) Act 1968 and the positive welfare duty promised by the 1993 White Paper (in paragraph 3.3). At its latest stages, Lord Fraser provided certain assurances that 'children in need' services could include preventive and community services but these will only be addressed in guidance and not in the legislation (Hansard 5 July 1995).

The new Act will be implemented within the new structure of local authorities. It follows the Government's previous insistence on non-prescription, by not substantially expanding the duties on local authorities. New additions – such as after-care support past the age of 19, provision of day care to all children, provision of accommodation – are typically powers (and thus discretionary) rather than duties (which are legal requirements). As a result, new local authorities faced by resource constraints, and with their own political priorities, could have vastly different and perhaps diminished services for children and their families. Scotland's children and their families may face a patchwork of services, where their needs might be well met if living in one local authority but ignored in another.

The present duties for children's service plans do not specify that plans be based on an assessment of local need, which should then be used to prioritise services. The provisions thus run the risk of copying failures of children's service plans in England and Wales: 'Services tend to be provided reactively on the basis of past and present referrals, rather than proactively on current information about the extent of need' (Secretaries of State for Health and for Wales 1994 para. 2.40). Thus, while targeting is recognised in the category of 'children in need', clear identification of those in need and targeting of services towards them in planning is not required by the new Act.[4]

---

4   Following pressure from Opposition MPs, there is hope that the Government will address this in guidance (see Hansard 28 February 1995).

While the Government's promotion of children's rights is welcomed, a section by section analysis of the Act indicates numerous gaps. One of the most striking is the new power of local authorities, courts and children's hearings to abrogate the rights of children, 'for the purpose of protecting members of the public from serious harm'. While the Government sees this as necessary to balance the increased obligation on local authorities, courts and children's hearings to place the welfare of a child in care as the paramount concern (rather than a primary concern), agencies ranging from the Association of Directors of Social Work to the Association of Children's Reporters regard this as an extreme response to the perceived problem (Hansard 6 February 1995). Despite repeated Opposition amendments, the Government refused to delete the clause or even accept an amendment for a reduced regard to a child's welfare as a *primary* concern in such circumstances. Assurances, however, have now been given that the clause is not intended to allow a permanent disregard for a particular child's rights (Hansard 5 July 1995).

Despite criticism from the UN Committee on the Rights of the Child (January 1995) that corporal punishment by parents is still legal in the UK, the Government refused to accept amendments to limit parental punishment of children (Hansard 1 May, 6 June and 5 July 1995) – saying such amendments were unnecessary.

The new Exclusion Order for an alleged abuser does demonstrate attention to children's rights. When determined to be necessary to protect a child from a suspected abuser, a local authority can make an application to a Sheriff to exclude the abuser rather than to remove the child from home. Such a provision respects the child's right to remain with (the rest of) his or her family, rather than feeling doubly victimised – by the abuse itself and also from being separated from familiar and supportive surroundings.

When the Bill was first introduced, adults' civil liberties were still favoured over the rights of children, as the exclusion order was not to be available on an emergency basis. The very purpose of such an Order was undermined, since to protect a child in the short term the only option may be to remove the child. As one young person said in the Oral Evidence to the Special Standing Committee: 'It does not matter if it is two days or two years... We get put into care for being abused – it is us who are taken away so we are still the victims. It seems as if you are a victim your whole life' (Hansard 6 February 1995). After intense debate in the House of Commons Committee Stage, the Government did agree that an emergency order should be made available and introduced amendments in the House of Lords. This was a considerable victory for children's rights – not only in the new provision itself, but also because the words of the young person above greatly influenced the views of MPs.

Scotland's Children Legislation – a coherent framework for the next century?

Is the Children (Scotland) Act 1995 a coherent framework that will meet the needs and rights of children and their families, into the next century? While many of the provisions in the Act are welcomed by organisations, young people and parents themselves, serious doubts remain.

The children's hearing's system may be seriously undermined by the power of a Sheriff to change a children's hearing decision on appeal. While the Government sought to reassure that this provision should be little used (Hansard 7 March, 7 June and the 5 July 1995), this new power undermines a fundamental tenet of Kilbrandon: the separation of welfare and justice decisions into two different systems.

Children's rights are included in many parts of the Act, but there is no overarching set of principles at the beginning of the Act (as in the Children Act 1989 and the Children (Northern Ireland) Order 1995), and there are significant gaps in relation to children's rights, as raised above.

Doubts have been raised about whether the Act adequately recognises the impact of local government reform on the new legislation's implementation: in such areas as children's service plans; the reliance on local authority powers rather than duties; and the lack of national monitoring required (Hansard 28 February 1995).

Whether the Act meets the needs of children and their families into the next century is likely to be less dependent on the new children's legislation by itself and more dependent on its combination with the Local Government etc. (Scotland) Act 1994. How the new local authorities structure themselves and deliver the services for children and their families, in combination with the changes required by the new children's legislation, could produce a considerably different picture in just a few years.

After a long wait and heated debates, Scotland has only just received its own Children Act. The results of the Act's implementation on policy and practice will not be known for several years after that. Its resulting effects on the lives of children will only be ascertainable at an even later date. At this point, one can hope that the Act and its implementation will meet the promises of Ian Lang:

> In scope, the Bill goes rather beyond the provisions of the Children Act 1989 for England and Wales. It will provide Scotland with its own Children Act based on Scots law and Scottish needs. At its heart is the child, and running through the Bill are the themes of the child's welfare as the paramount consideration and the need to listen to the child's view. (Hansard 5 December 1994)

References

Asquith, S. (ed) (1993) *Protecting Children – Cleveland to Orkney: What Lessons to Learn?* Proceedings of a one day conference organised by Children in Scotland and the National Children's Bureau. Edinburgh: HMSO.

Committee on the Rights of the Child (1995) Concluding observations of the Committee on the Rights of the Child: United Kingdom of Great Britain and Northern Ireland. In *Consideration of Reports Submitted by States Parties Under Article 44 of the Convention.* Eighth Session.

Cooper, J. (1983) Scotland – the management of change. In *The Creation of the British Social Services 1962-1974.* London: Heinemann Educational Books.

Fife Inquiry (1992) The Report of the Inquiry in Child Care Policies in Fife. Return to an Address of the Honourable the House of Commons, 27 October 1992, chaired by Sheriff Kearney. Edinburgh: HMSO.

General Assembly of the United Nations (1989) *The Convention on the Rights of the Child.* Adopted by the General Assembly of the United Nations on 20 November 1989.

Hansard House of Commons Official Report (1994) *Scottish Grand Committee,* Monday 5 December, Edinburgh. London: HMSO.

Hansard House of Commons Official Report (1995) *Special Standing Committee. Children (Scotland) Bill,* Second Sitting, Monday 6 February, Morning, Glasgow. London: HMSO.

Hansard House of Commons Official Report (1995) *Special Standing Committee. Children (Scotland) Bill,* Fourth Sitting, Monday 13 February, Afternoon, Edinburgh. London: HMSO.

Hansard House of Commons Official Report (1995) *Special Standing Committee. Children (Scotland) Bill,* Eighth Sitting, Tuesday 28 February, Afternoon Part II, Westminster. London: HMSO.

Hansard House of Commons Official Report (1995) *Special Standing Committee. Children (Scotland) Bill,* Tenth Sitting, Tuesday 7 March, Morning, Westminster. London: HMSO.

Hansard House of Commons Official Report (1995) *Special Standing Committee. Children (Scotland) Bill,* Ninth Sitting, Thursday 9 March, Morning, Westminster. London: HMSO.

Hansard House of Commons Official Report (1995) *Parliamentary Debates,* Monday 1 May 1995, Westminster. London: HMSO.

Hansard House of Lords Official Report (1995) *Committee of the Whole House off the Floor of the House. Children (Scotland) Bill,* First Sitting, Tuesday 6 June, Westminster. London: HMSO.

Hansard House of Lords Official Report (1995) *Committee of the Whole House off the Floor of the House. Children (Scotland) Bill,* Second Sitting, Wednesday 7 June, Westminster. London: HMSO.

Hansard House of Lords Official Report (1995) *Parliamentary Debates*, Wednesday 5 July, Westminster. London: HMSO.

Hill, M. (1990) The manifest and latent lessons of child abuse inquiries. *British Journal of Social Work* 20, 197–213.

Kearney, B. (1987) *Children's Hearings and the Sheriff Court.* London/Edinburgh: Butterworths.

Kilbrandon Report, Scottish Home and Health Department and the Scottish Education Department (1964) *Children and Young Persons Scotland.* Report by the Committee Appointed by the Secretary of State for Scotland. Presented to Parliament April 1964, Cmnd. 2306. Edinburgh: HMSO.

Martin, F. M. (1983) Personal social services. In J. English and F.M. Martin. (eds) *Social Services in Scotland*, Second Edition. Edinburgh: Scottish Academic Press.

Murray, K. (1983) Children's hearings. In J. English and F.M. Martin (eds) *Social Services in Scotland*, Second Edition. Edinburgh: Scottish Academic Press.

Murray, K. and Hill, M. (1991) The recent history of Scottish child welfare. *Children and Society* 5, 3, 266–281.

Orkney Inquiry (1993) *The Report of the Inquiry into the Removal of Children from Orkney in February 1991.* Return to an Address of the Honourable the House of Commons, 27 October 1992, chaired by Lord Clyde. Edinburgh: HMSO.

The Scotsman (1995) Councils ready for big cuts in spending. *The Scotsman*, 17th January.

Scottish Education Department and the Scottish Home and Health Department (1966) *Social Work and the Community: Proposals for Reorganising Local Authority Services in Scotland.* Presented to Parliament by the Secretary of State for Scotland by Command of Her Majesty, October 1966, Cmnd. 3065. Edinburgh: HMSO.

Scottish Law Commission (1992) *Report on Family Law*, No. 135. Edinburgh: HMSO.

The Scottish Office (1991) *Review of Child Care Law in Scotland.* Report of a Review Group appointed by the Secretary of State, chaired by J.W. Sinclair. Edinburgh: HMSO.

The Scottish Office (1994) *Working Together: The Scottish Office, Volunteers and Voluntary Organisations.* Edinburgh: The Scottish Office.

Secretary of State for Social Services (1985) *Reform of Social Security: Programme for Action.* Presented to Parliament December 1985. London: HMSO.

Secretaries of State for Health and for Wales (1994) *Children Act Report 1993.* Presented to Parliament by command of Her Majesty, Cmnd. 2584. London: HMSO.

Social Work Services Group (1993) *Scotland's Children: Proposals for Child Care Policy and Law*, Cmnd. 2286. Edinburgh: HMSO.

Stone, K. (1995) Which way now? *Community Care* 1–7 June, 20–22.

Tisdall, E.K.M. with Donnaghie, E. (1995) Children in Scotland. In *Scotland's Family Factsheet.* Edinburgh: HMSO.

Younghusband, E. (1978) Developments in Scotland leading up to and following the Social Work (Scotland) Act, 1968. In *Social Work in Britain: 1950–1975.* London: George Allen and Unwin.

CHAPTER 3

The Children (Northern Ireland) Order 1995
Prospects for Progress?

Greg Kelly and John Pinkerton

Introduction

The Children (Northern Ireland) Order became law on 15 March 1995. Echoing the language that launched the Children Act 1989 in England and Wales, the Northern Ireland Department of Health and Social Services described the Order as 'the most comprehensive piece of legislation ever enacted in Northern Ireland in relation to children'. It predicted that the Order 'will have a profound effect not only on children and families but also on a wide range of organisations and disciplines in the social services, voluntary organisations, the courts, the education system, the health service and on individuals providing childminding, day-care and other services for children' (DHSS:NI 1995).

Based on the twin principles of the paramountcy of the welfare of the child and the promotion of parental responsibility, the Order can be seen to express a United Kingdom, and indeed international, consensus on how best to meet the needs of children and their carers. However as Michael Freeman (1992) has warned: 'It is easy to take the words for the act and think that because the words have been enacted the condition of children's lives have changed.' Taking up that caution, this chapter aims to explore the prospects of realising in practice the sound principles within the Order. That exploration requires recognition of those features of the child care system that have developed in Northern Ireland which are particular to the region and those which reflect developments elsewhere, in particular within England and Wales. The chapter overviews the historical background to the Order in a way that gives attention to the 'parity principle' which dominates social policy in Northern Ireland. It highlights both shifts in professional culture and organisational change. A brief summary of the Order is then provided along with comments on the consultation process that immediately preceded it and on the plans for implementation that are at present being pursued. Finally three areas are identified where key challenges will have to be met if the fundamental principles of the Order are to become a reality in practice. These are professional practice, organisational context and resources.

'Parity' and child welfare

Northern Ireland shares a state with three other nations – England, Scotland and Wales. It also shares an island, and some would say its nationhood, with another state – the Republic of Ireland. One result of this complex set of relations has been the persistent and often violent contest over national identity and the legitimacy of political structures. The glare of that struggle – euphemistically known locally as the 'Troubles' – can blind people to the more mundane but equally important implications that Northern Ireland's peculiar situation has on every area of life. Child care is no exception. In many ways civil society in Northern Ireland provides children and young people with a context to grow up in that is clearly Irish – in the high proportion of children within its demographic structure (of a population of around a million and a half people over a quarter are under 18 years old), extensive poverty and traditional cultural values (Kilmurray and Richardson 1994). Yet it is also the case that there are no formal relationships between the two child welfare systems on the island Child welfare in Northern Ireland is part of a UK state system

In matters of child welfare, as in most areas of social policy, the principle of maintaining 'parity' with England and Wales is seen by politicians, policy makers and commentators as the driving force behind developments in Northern Ireland. Evason has usefully summarised 'parity':

> The people of Northern Ireland pay the same taxes as the rest of the United Kingdom for the same cash benefits and, with regard to the other services, the aim is that provision should be of a similar standard to that attained elsewhere, but they need not be identical. (Evason 1976)

From this parity perspective the Children Order could be seen as simply an extension of the English and Welsh Children Act of 1989 to Northern Ireland. To take that view however is to take a superficially neat but over-simplified and very short-term view of the origins of the Order. Such a view both misunderstands parity and rules out serious consideration of the local forces affecting child welfare developments. Even a cursory glance at the period since the second world war suggests that keeping in step has not been quite as straightforward as seems to be suggested by the idea of parity Until the Children (NI) Order is implemented in the autumn of 1996, the primary child care legislation in Northern Ireland will continue to be the 1968 Children and Young Persons Act; which is essentially the English and Welsh Children and Young Persons Act of 1963. Thus Northern Ireland law has not been affected by the major reforms of the 1969 Children and Young Persons Act in England and Wales nor by any of the subsequent legislation prior to the 1989 Children Act.

This apparent failure to apply the parity principle in the period between the Children and Young Persons Act of 1968 and the Children Order of 1995 coincides with the most recent and prolonged period of the 'Troubles'. The mass civil disobedience and armed confrontations of the late 1960s and early 1970s led to the suspension of the Northern Ireland parliament and the imposition of 'Direct Rule' from Westminster in March 1972. Despite a number of attempts to revive some form of regional assembly, Direct Rule still continues, with legislation being enacted by Order in Privy Council at Westminster and executive powers being exercised by a team of Northern Ireland Ministers under the Secretary of State. Whilst such political turmoil could have been expected to disrupt and delay legislative developments, particularly during the early 1970s, there is no constitutional reason for their not having taken place at all. In fact it has been observed that during this period 'the process of assimilation between the law in Northern Ireland and the law in England has, if anything been fortified' (Dickson 1989 p.4). Thus it seems reasonable to see this disruption in parity as something more than just a rather long delay in implementing English and Welsh legislation, only now rectified by the enacting of the 1989 Children Act in the form of the Children (NI) Order 1995.

Attempting to read what lies behind the lack of parity in children's legislation for almost 30 years requires an understanding of parity as something more than simply delayed implementation of English and Welsh law. Rather parity has meant in practice the creation of local legislation through delay and quasi-imitation, which allows for reflection of much of the letter of the Westminster law but at the same time expresses the balance of social forces within Northern Ireland itself. 'The impetus normally came from Britain and the extent to which British examples were followed depended on the relative strengths of the various lobbies, both within and outside the government' (Buckland 1979 p.150).

A kind of parity – the 1950s and 1960s

If parity is recognised as denoting this rather more complex relationship between Northern Ireland and Westminster rather than simply as following suit, a history of post-war developments emerges which allows for a better understanding of the social forces and dynamics that will give effect in practice to the Children Order. The first piece of children's legislation in Northern Ireland after the war was the 1950 Children and Young Persons Act. This can be read as simply the application to Northern Ireland of the English and Welsh legislation of two years earlier. But against such a reading it can be pointed out that at the time the English and Welsh legislation was passing through Parliament a Northern Ireland Government White Paper on services for children and young people was stressing that 'the answer to the problem as it exists in Northern Ireland does not lie in slavish adoption of the system either existing or proposed in Great Britain' (Government of NI 1948 pp.12/13). The 1948 Act was the basis for Northern Ireland's 1950 legislation but this acceptance was on the terms of the Unionist Party which controlled the local Stormont Parliament.

What this meant in the immediate post-war period was the development of a greatly weakened version of the interventionist welfare state being established in the other parts of the UK. Elsewhere there was a political will to replace the large regimented institutions of the Poor Law with compensatory, primarily home based, child welfare services for deprived children (Bolger et al. 1981). That service was delivered by Children's Departments staffed by trained children's officers (Packman 1981). In Northern Ireland the general lack of political commitment to interventionist welfare state institutions ensured a less ambitious system of local government welfare departments with responsibility for deprived children as just one of a number of client groups (Caul and Herron 1992). This lack of political commitment to statutory services was reinforced by the cultural importance attached to family responsibility and by the extensive provision of substitute care by religious institutions.

By the time of Northern Ireland's second piece of post-war children's legislation a decade and a half later the enthusiasm of the Unionist government for social reform was no greater. The Children and Young Persons Act (NI) 1968 appeared to be the result of the parity principle, as it was almost word for word the 1963 English and Welsh legislation, but it is better seen as a way of pre-empting the more fundamental changes being debated at the time in England and Wales in preparation for the 1969 Children and Young Persons Act. Having accurately read the more interventionist and preventative intentions of the Labour Government (Bolger et al. 1981), the Unionists pre-empted any parity pressure for similar local reform by passing the earlier 1963 Act in 1968 (Kelly 1979). Whilst prevention has its place within the 1968 Northern Ireland legislation it is restricted by the general spirit of the Act. State intervention was in the main reserved for exceptional situations of delinquency or inadequate parenting and was dependent on the decision of the juvenile court.

Any possibility of parity later forcing the reforming 1969 legislation on to the Northern Ireland statute book was lost in the early 1970s through a combination of UK and Northern Ireland factors. A new political climate was developing in England and Wales as the economic and social problems of the 1960s undermined the post-war consensus on the leading role of state service provision. Alternative views were emerging which argued for a reduction in public spending and increased individual responsibility. At the same time the political tensions and the linked social and economic problems that had always given Northern Ireland a distinct identity within the UK boiled over into communal, paramilitary and state violence in a way that made the differences between Northern Ireland and other parts of the UK all too clear.

The period from 1969 to 1972 not only saw the end of Stormont and the start of Direct Rule from Westminster but also the discrediting and dislocation of local government services. Local government had been the site of many of the grievances over religious and political discrimination. With a significant section of the Northern Ireland community having no faith in the institutions of the local state, that power had to be relocated. As the central UK state had no intention of directly empowering the local communities which were engaged in both inter-communal and anti-state violence, the option taken was technocratic management from above (O'Dowd *et al.* 1981). As part of this attempt to manage the crisis, a number of democratically unaccountable, but well-resourced, public service agencies were established. Included in this initiative was the establishment of what in UK terms was a unique structure of combined Health and Social Services Boards (Caul and Herron 1992). The Health and Personal Social Services (Northern Ireland) Order 1972 took social services from local government control into the National Health Service. Personal social services, including child care, became the responsibility of these nominated Boards. This removed them from party politics but also effectively reduced democratic accountability and increased professional and managerial power.

The dominance of child protection – the 1970s and 1980s

Located within the Health and Social Services Boards and led by the social work profession, child care in Northern Ireland during the 1970s began to take on the increasing preoccupation with child abuse and child protection that was to become so characteristic of child welfare services in the English-speaking world. This development within England and Wales has been well charted, emphasising how public inquiries and media campaigns were instrumental in changing the focus of child care social work from attempting to support and resource families to an almost exclusive concern with policing families for child abuse and neglect (Parton 1985, 1991; Frost and Stein 1989). From the mid 1970s onwards Northern Ireland developed substantially the same defensive policing practice as England and Wales, with similar procedural mechanisms – the case conference, the child abuse register and the widespread use of the Place of Safety Order. Within Northern Ireland, however, this happened without there being a local child abuse inquiry with the associated media interest and professional trauma.

What pushed Northern Ireland child care services and practice towards the authoritative assessment and intervention required by child protection work was the ease with which this style of work fitted well with the strategy of technocratic management from above. This gave rise to a rapid development of the service both in numbers of staff and organisational systems. Northern Ireland social workers were able both to articulate and to develop a seemingly appropriate and relatively high status service by drawing on a professional culture and training that represented experiences and preoccupations in Great Britain and internationally. One effect of this was to create distance between them as professionals and the troubled and troublesome communities in which they worked.

As social services consolidated and expanded throughout the 1970s, it was recognised that there was a need to review arrangements for children and young people in the light of both the new situation of the services in Northern Ireland and developments in law, policy and practice in other parts of the UK and internationally. In 1976 a Children and Young Persons Review Group was set up with Sir Harold Black as Chair. When the Review Group reported in 1979 it emphasised that 'the primary determinant of children's behaviour…is the social, moral and economic climate' (DHSS:NI 1979). In the context of Northern Ireland this meant recognising that a significant proportion of the child population experienced multiple socio-economic deprivation (Evason 1976) and that all children were having to cope with the rapidly changing nature of modern society and the continuing problem of political violence and social instability (Cairns 1987).

At the same time the Black committee noted the continuing strength of relationships within the family, extended family, church and community and suggested that these were acting as a partial counterbalance to the difficulties children and young people were having to face. From that starting-point, the Report argued that the best way to promote child welfare was for the state to bolster these strengths. The Report proposed a 'Strategy for Help' which emphasised prevention and the meeting of children and young people's needs through resourcing the family and other formal and informal child care institutions and networks.

Despite having emphasised the broader context in which child care services needed to be considered, the Black Report appeared oblivious to the implications of actual developments within both local communities and statutory services during the 1970s (Pinkerton 1983). Material deprivation and the 'Troubles' had sapped much of the energy that the Black Committee held to be available within communities. There had been some community development initiatives but these tended to draw on a highly exclusive, territorial sectarianism often in association with a degree of paramilitary organisation. The closed technocratic management of child protection that had increasingly become the defining characteristic of public child care services did not lend itself to the risky, open and creative resourcing of families and communities in partnership that the proposed 'Strategy for Help' required.

Not surprisingly the Black Report failed to have any significant impact on the direction of child care within the Health and Social Services Boards during the 1980s. Not only was there no constituency able or willing to take forward the Committee's proposals effectively at the time, but also the possibility of a full debate was cut short by Kincora – Northern Ireland's major child care scandal (Pinkerton and Kelly 1986). In 1980 newspaper allegations were made in the South of Ireland about long-standing sexual abuse of young men by staff in a Belfast hostel. There were suggestions of involvement and cover-up by Unionist politicians and paramilitaries and by police and British military intelligence. It took five years and several inquiries before the Hughes Report (DHSS:NI 1986a) drew the matter to a close by providing a detailed account of the affair and a long list of recommendations emphasising administrative systems and methods of staff selection. Thus both the political dimensions of the case and what it had to say about power relations between young people and adults within residential care were neatly side-stepped. The Kincora affair had directly linked child care with the Troubles, with the result that closed defensive practice amongst professionals was further encouraged.

Thus through an interweaving of international, British and local Northern Ireland concerns and social forces, by the mid 1980s the dominant form of statutory child care in Northern Ireland was that of monitoring situations of risk in a way that offered little if anything to help families find ways of improving their situations. A DHSS advisory committee on child care reporting at that time noted that services were 'concerned solely with the symptom of family failure, child abuse or neglect and not with actually trying to prevent or overcome the problems that are contributing to the situation' with the result that 'services will tend to be given a wide berth by families with problems.' (DHSS:NI 1986b p.42). This view was endorsed by a number of local studies conducted in the late 1980s.

A study of decision making in Northern Ireland leading to admissions to care (Kelly 1990) indicated that social workers used compulsory means to admit children to care with even greater frequency than their colleagues in other parts of the UK. In an aggregate of three studies carried out between 1987 and 1989, 30 per cent of the children were taken into care using a Place of Safety Order compared to 17 per cent in Rowe's study of six English authorities (Rowe et al. 1989). It was concluded that normal practice was to use compulsory means of admission to care where the reasons for admission were abuse or neglect, despite the fact that there was confirmed abuse in only a quarter of the cases and in one study 70 per cent of those admitted by Place of Safety Order were back with their families within twelve months. A side effect of this practice was the high proportion of children and young people at home on care orders. A study of these placements noted the absence of therapeutic work and described the social work involved as 'a sustained "watching brief" allowing for monitoring and reactive management' (Pinkerton 1994 p.103).

Into the 1990s with the new Children (NI) Order

Statutory child care in Northern Ireland at the start of the 1990s could be characterised as a relatively closed professional world of child protection. Child sexual abuse was a major preoccupation (Kennedy 1990) and whilst there was an acute awareness, in the aftermath of the Cleveland Inquiry, of the widespread criticism of overly intrusive intervention, the response was concern to develop expertise in disclosure work and improve legal and administrative systems rather than to question the fundamental direction of the service. Social work staff in statutory child care at all levels had trained and developed their careers in a child protection culture and, effective as they may have become in that area, they tended to cast most family problems and failures in parenting using the mould of abuse. Parents in trouble and the working class communities from which they mainly came saw social workers not as supports but as threats, their role not to help but more to police their families. They represented another expression of a state which had never been trusted by the nationalist section of the working class and from which the unionist working class communities had become increasingly alienated.

It was into this context that the Children (NI) Order was introduced. There had been signs on a number of occasions in the late 1980s that new legislation was likely and in 1989 a fairly brief consultation paper from the Office of Law Reform and the DHSS (Office of Law Reform/DHSS 1989) promised early publication of draft legislation. It was made clear that this would follow the 1989 Children Act in consolidating and harmonising public and private law relating to children in a single coherent statutory framework. In the event the Order repeats almost word for word the Children Act. Where there are changes, this generally reflects the differences between administrative structures in Northern Ireland and those of England and Wales (Warner 1993). The main provisions are:

- the introduction of the principle of parental responsibility that continues even when the children are not living with parents
- the restructuring of private law, in relation to divorce and matrimonial provisions, and linking it to the public law which relates to the responsibilities of the Health and Social Services Boards
- the introduction of a unified family court system
- the introduction of a flexible range of new orders in private law to be used only when in the child's best interests
- the duty on Health and Social Services Boards to safeguard and promote the welfare of children who are 'in need' and to support parents in bringing up children 'in need' in their own home

- the promotion of partnership with parents if children are in care and specifically to consult parents and children about any decisions made in relation to them; parents will also have extended rights to question decisions in court

- the replacing of existing orders in care proceedings with a single care order

- the creation of three new orders in child protection – the emergency protection order, the child assessment order and the recovery order. (DHSS:NI 1993)

When the draft Order was published in 1993 the explanatory document that accompanied it reiterated a commitment to reflect the general thrust of the recommendations of the Black Report but it was hard to see any evidence of that in legislation – except in so far as aspects of Black coincided with the English and Welsh Act.

The three year delay between the 1989 consultation paper and the publication of the Draft Order in 1993 allowed for the development of a broadly based professional consensus that was favourable towards the Children Act, impatient for new local legislation but adamant that it must be fitted to Northern Ireland's particular circumstances. Reflecting this view the DHSS's own Advisory Committee welcomed the central aims of the draft Order but regretted that 'the major differences between NI and GB have not been taken sufficiently into account thereby giving the impression that the Order is English and Welsh legislation imposed on NI culture' (CPSSAC 1993 p.2/3). Much of the work around developing and articulating this consensus was carried out by the Children Order Group. It had been formed in 1992 to stimulate discussion and debate across the broad range of interests, statutory and voluntary, which would be affected by the Order, such as social work, law, health and education.

Despite the work of the Children Order Group, which received fulsome praise from all sides during the debate on the Order (Hansard 1995), only minor changes were made to the Order as originally drafted. The more significant effect of the lobbying was to build up commitment to the Order within the professional community which raised the political profile of the legislation within Government. Faced with this pressure, and the experience of the implementation of the Children Act, the DHSS developed a strategy based on the twin and possibly conflicting goals of speedy yet participatory implementation. To that end once the Order was passed a Project Board was established comprising a small group of senior staff from the DHSS and from the Department of Education and the Court Service. This Board was given the task of directing the implementation of the Order in a co-ordinated fashion and established an intermeshing structure of consultative and working groups to deal with training, dissemination, information systems and the development of regulations and guidance.

Finding a constituency for effective implementation

Effective implementation of the Children (NI) Order depends on its finding a constituency capable of taking it forward. The legislation has not emerged directly from any democratic political process in Northern Ireland. As with the 1950 and 1968 Acts, parity has yet again meant legislation from England and Wales which requires shaping not so much in the letter of the law but more in its practical application. What is different from the earlier legislation is that, following the Health and Social Service developments of the 1970s and 1980s, professional groups, and particularly social work, have the opportunity to play a leading role. The activity of the Children Order Group, prior to the legislation and the focused but inclusive strategy being adopted for the preparation for implementation by the DHSS, suggests there is the professional capacity to meet this challenge. However there are crucial issues of resources, organisational context and professional practice that place a question mark over that capacity.

Resources

No one disputes the fact that the Children (NI) Order will require both the redirection of existing resources and considerable new resources. However the amount of funding required and its use is in contention. In commenting on this issue, a senior member of the Social Services Inspectorate commented: 'I have pointed up the possibility of some transfer of resources away from child protection, in favour of prevention, but I would be very cautious indeed about pushing the boat out too far in that direction' (Chambers 1994).

The estimates of projected costs produced by the four Health and Social Services Boards add up to £45 million (CCNI News 1995). This includes an estimate of over £20 million to meet obligations towards children 'in need', child minding and day care. The Boards' estimated £6 million would be needed for developing services for children with disabilities which to date have been patchy and uncoordinated. Child protection services will also have to be developed, at an estimated cost of £3 million, to ensure a partnership approach with parents, a more proactive approach in the courts and higher standards of assessment to demonstrate significant harm. Additional responsibilities towards care leavers have been estimated to cost £2 million. On top of those figures there will be considerable costs for changes to court services, development of the new Guardian *Ad Litem* service, plus developments in associated services such as education. Finding the necessary scale and direction of resources is clearly not going to be easy in the existing climate of UK central government politics.

Organisational context

It is also UK Government policy that has created the rapid and radical change in the organisations that will carry responsibility for implementing the Order

– the Health and Social Services Boards. Social services have been subject to the fundamental changes in National Health Service philosophy, management and accountability designed to reform the Health Service. The Chief Social Services Inspector expressed the frustration felt by many at the rate of organisational change:

> 'The ink was hardly dry on the Boards' proposals for reorganisation when the Department issued yet another consultation letter.' (McCoy 1993 p.13)

> 'The discussion the Department proposed to have with the Boards was overtaken by yet another NHS reform package.' (McCoy 1993 p.15)

In the rest of the UK the personal social services have remained a part of local government and so the Health Service changes were planned without social services being part of the equation, but they have been implemented in full in Northern Ireland and applied to social services in the same measure as to the Health Service. Apart from occasional references to the significance of the 'integrated service' there has been little in the way of government-led research, inquiry or debate on the appropriateness of imposing a structure – including hospital Trusts and the internal market – on community based social service with statutory functions. The Children Act, drafted and designed to be implemented within a democratic local government structure, is being imported into the quango-led competitive culture of the health Trusts. Considerable lobbying on the part of the Children Order Group and others eventually led to the clarification of the legal issues with the passing of the Health and Personal Social Services (NI) Order 1993 which gave the Department of Health and Social Services the power to devolve responsibility for statutory functions to the newly forming community Trusts.

The development of community Trusts has created a situation of pseudo-competition in which crude indicators of need and service such as per centages of children in foster care are used in league tables of performance. This can encourage a competitiveness that distorts service planning and takes insufficient account of the assessed needs of individual children and families. The much vaunted independence of Trusts carries with it the risk of losing co-operation between Trusts. This may cause the loss of economies of scale that make the provision of specialist units possible. In addition the financial pressures on the Trusts are likely to discourage the provision of adequate services to children 'in need' and their families. The temptation will be to develop criteria that allow services to stay within the tried and tested, but constraining, confines of child protection. At the same time the organisation of services around the purchaser/provider split has promoted concern for quality, efficiency and value for money which is producing a greater commitment to innovation, training, research and evaluation of practice. The purchaser/provider split provides the opportunity to write into the Trust or provider specifications standards explicitly based on the principles of the Children (NI) Order, and thereby produce clearer organisational commitment to the new directions required by the legislation.

Professional practice

When the 1989 Children Act was introduced it was acknowledged that the new directions it required called for a radical shift in professional attitudes and style of work – even though there had been a stream of reforming legislation over the previous twenty-five years. In Northern Ireland, where there has been no new legislation since 1968, the degree of change required to put the Children (NI) Order into practice is proportionately greater. An example of this is the testing of professional decisions by second opinions through the development of the Guardian *Ad Litem* (GAL) service. Prior to the Children Order there has been no provision to appoint GALs in care cases. Following implementation of the new legislation the expectation is the appointment of GALs 'in nearly all public law cases under the Order' (DHSS:NI 1993).

A second example of the extent of change called for in professional practice is use of Wardship. One of the ways the Northern Ireland system adjusted to the growing influence of professionals within an increasingly complex child protection field was to avoid the crude adversarial forum of the magistrates' court by making extensive use of the Wardship jurisdiction (O'Halloran 1988). There is even some evidence that it was being used as a replacement for the Place of Safety Order (Southern Area Child Protection Committee 1994). This will have to cease under the new Order which seeks to ensure that the inherent jurisdiction of the High Court will not be used to circumvent the statutory applications prescribed under the Order. Both child care professionals and their legal colleagues will have to find ways to blend due process with the complexities and risk-taking in child welfare assessment and planning.

The extent of change required in the professional culture to match the spirit of the new Children Order is most sharply brought into focus by the issue of parental involvement. Much recent UK and international research indicates that most child abuse referrals are the result of poor parenting by under-resourced, isolated parents, whereas the child protection response is dominated by practice based on the experience of the small percentage of parents who seriously abuse or neglect their children (Thorpe 1994). Having been part of that trend, can professionals in Northern Ireland now move from the relative security of the technocratic management of child protection and develop the political skills of risky and challenging partnership work? One recent local study showed that almost half the parents did not attend the case conferences they were invited to. Of those who did attend, most thought the idea of partnership with social services was unrealistic. 'Parents' reservations on the notion of partnership appear to stem from their consciousness of agency and statutory power.'

(Southern Area Child Protection Committee and Queens University Belfast 1994 p.59).

The same study did, however, reveal real development in professional opinion, away from a position of some hostility prior to the introduction of the policy. Ninety-four per cent of the professionals who attended conferences with parents present felt that their presence was helpful. The study also looked at parental participation during the emergency protection phase and described the conflict and emotion that was inherent in these situations and which set the agenda for much parent–social worker contact. None the less, while most parents were 'overwhelmingly negative' about their experience of social services, a majority thought in hindsight that the investigation and/or removal was in their child's best interests.

That view is gaining wider currency within the local communities which, whilst still wary of social services, recognise the reality of child abuse, in particular child sexual abuse following a number of well-publicised cases (SSI 1993; Moore 1995). These communities are also more willing and able to work in partnership with the statutory services as they have become increasingly well organised and resourced through job creation and community development initiatives. As with the development of child welfare users' groups, such as the Voice of Young People in Care and Parents Aid, it is important not to exaggerate the strength of these developments. But the Children (NI) Order clearly has a resonance with a more combative attitude amongst users and communities, that they have rights not only to services, complaints procedures and legal redress, but also to resources that will empower them to take on the responsibilities that the Government's community-oriented policies invoke.

Another important ally in the shift away from narrow child protection to the open partnerships required by the spirit of the Children (NI) Order is the voluntary sector. It has always been strong in Northern Ireland and has taken the opportunities of the last two decades to modernise and recast its relationship with both statutory bodies and communities. Voluntary organisations have developed a strong voice through their umbrella organisation, Child Care Northern Ireland, and have both all-Ireland and European links which are likely to become increasingly significant. Again it is important not to exaggerate these developments and to recognise the destabilising effect that Government policies and funding have had on the voluntary sector. But in a mixed economy of social care and with the advantage of being able to engage families and neighbourhoods with less of the stigma attached to social services, the voluntary sector is likely to be a crucial ingredient in any constituency capable of taking forward the Children (NI) Order.

Conclusion

The application of the parity principle to child care during the post-war period has provided Northern Ireland with legislation which mirrored that enacted for England and Wales but which has been shaped by local forces. Child care throughout the UK in the last 20 years has not been a job for the faint hearted. Whenever it seemed impossible for the situation to get worse in terms of the complexity of the task, the pressure to get it right and the lack of public support – it did. In Northern Ireland there have been the added pressures of working in a society racked by violent political conflict and in organisations that have undergone fundamental and recurring change. It is not surprising that at times either simply coping with the pressures within the child care programmes or flight to other programmes of care have seemed the dominant response. It is surprising that this dark period in the service's development has led to the introduction of the most challenging and visionary child care legislation in the history of Northern Ireland.

The fact that the Children (NI) Order 1995 is being introduced as the peace process gathers momentum is coincidental but fortuitous. It adds to the sense that perhaps this is the opportunity for fundamental change. The Order sets an agenda for realigning child care away from being a monitoring and policing service and towards empowerment through partnership. In this respect it embodies the values most workers came into child care to give expression to and the service wanted by most users, whether children, young people or carers. Implementing the Order represents an opportunity to explore the limits of relationships between the state, the voluntary sector and service users. Returning to Freeman's caution at the start of this chapter, it is clear from the Northern Ireland experience that no piece of legislation can banish the uncertainties that go with putting into practice the word of the law. There is no alternative to the risky and demanding business of acting and becoming engaged in the interplay of individuals and social forces. Only by doing so is there any chance of constructing a constituency capable of ensuring that real progress is made in the condition of children and young people's lives through the Children (NI) Order.

References

Bolger, S., Corrigan, P., Docking, J. and Frost, N. (1981) *Towards Socialist Welfare Work*. London: Macmillan.

Buckland, P. (1979) *The Factory of Grievances*. Dublin: Gill and Macmillan.

Cairns, E. (1987) *Caught in the Crossfire*. Belfast: Appletree.

Caul, B., and Herron, S. (1992) *A Service for People*. Belfast: December Publications.

Central Personal Social Services Advisory Committee (1993) *Response to the Draft Children Order*. Belfast. DHSS.

Child Care NI News (1995) February, Belfast CCNI.

Chambers, N. (1994) The Children (NI) Order: strategic options open to boards and key providers in Northern Ireland. In McAuley, C. and McColgan, M. (eds) *The Children (NI) Order: Challenges Ahead.* Belfast: QUB.

Department of Health and Social Security (Northern Ireland) (1979) *Report of the Children and Young Persons Review Group.* Belfast: HMSO.

Department of Health and Social Security (Northern Ireland) (1986a) *Report of the Committee of Inquiry into Children's Homes and Hostels.* Belfast: HMSO.

Department of Health and Social Security (Northern Ireland) (1986b) *Supporting Families Under Stress.* Belfast: DHSS.

Department of Health and Social Security (Northern Ireland) (1993) *Draft Children Order – Notes of Guidance.* Belfast: DHSS.

Department of Health and Social Security (Northern Ireland) (1995) *Taking Forward the Children (NI) Order 1995.* Belfast: DHSS.

Dickson, B. (1989) *The Legal System of Northern Ireland.* Belfast: SLS.

Evason, E. (1976) *Poverty: the facts in Northern Ireland.* London: CPAG.

Freeman M (1992) Taking children's rights more seriously. *International Journal of Law and the Family 6,* 1, 52–71.

Frost, N. and Stein, M. (1989) *The Politics of Child Welfare.* Hemel Hempstead: Harvester Wheatsheaf.

Government of Northern Ireland (1948) *The Protection and Welfare of the Young and the Treatment of Young Offenders.* Belfast: HMSO.

Hansard (1995) 254, 47, 8 February 404–432.

Kelly, G. (1979) Social work in the courts in Northern Ireland. In H. Parker (ed) *Social Work and the Courts.* London: Arnold.

Kelly, G. (1990) *Patterns of Care.* Belfast: Dept of Social Work, Queens University.

Kennedy, M. – The Research Team (1990) *Child Sexual Abuse in Northern Ireland.* Antrim: Greystone Books.

Kilmurray, A. and Richardson, V. (1994) *Focus on Children – Blueprint for Action.* Northern Ireland: Focus on Children.

McCoy, K. (1993) Integration – a changing scene. In Social Services Inspectorate *Perspectives on Integration.* Belfast: DHSS.

Moore, C. (1995) *Betrayal of Trust - The Father Brendan Smyth Affair and the Catholic Church.* Dublin: Marino.

Office of Law Reform/Department of Health and Social Security (1989) *Consultation Paper on Proposed Changes to Some Aspects of the Law Relating to Children in Northern Ireland.* Belfast: Office of Law Reform/DHSS.

O'Dowd, L., Rolston, B., and Tomlinson, M. (1981) *Northern Ireland – Between Civil Rights and Civil War.* London: CSE Books.

O'Halloran, K. (1988) *Wardship In Northern Ireland.* Belfast: SLS.

Packman, J. (1981) *The Child's Generation*, Second Edition. London: Blackwell and Robertson.

Parton, N. (1985) *The Politics of Child Abuse*. London: Macmillan.

Parton, N. (1991) *Governing the Family*. London: Macmillan.

Pinkerton, J. (1983) The politics of Black. In B. Caul, J. Pinkerton and F. Powell *The Juvenile Justice System in Northrn Ireland*. Belfast: Ulster Polytechnic.

Pinkerton , J. (1994) *At Home In Care*. Aldershot: Avebury.

Pinkerton, J. and Kelly, G. (1986) Kincora affair – the aftermath. *Youth and Policy* Summer, 17-25.

Rowe, J., Hundleby, M. and Garnett, L. (1989) *Child Care Now*. London: BAAF.

Social Services Inspectorate (1993) *An Abuse of Trust – The Report of the Social Services Inspectorate into the Case of Martin Huston*. Belfast: DHSS.

Southern Area Child Protection Committee and Queens University Belfast (1994) *Evaluation of Policy on Parental Participation in Child Protection*. Southern Area Child Protection Committee.

Thorpe D (1994) *Evaluating Child Protection*. Buckingham: Open University Press.

Warner, N. (1993) United Kingdom. In B. Munday (ed) *European Social Services*. Canterbury: University of Kent.

CHAPTER 4

Irish Child Care Services in the 1990s
The Child Care Act 1991
and Other Developments

Robbie Gilligan

Introduction

This chapter examines the prospects for the Irish child care system following upon the enactment of the Child Care Act 1991, which is the most significant legislative initiative in this field since the Children's Act 1908. Wider developments in relation to the primary strands of the Act – child protection, alternative care and family support are also reviewed.

While the Child Care Act 1991 is a major watershed in child care policy, it emerges in a time of unprecedented interest and activity in the child care field generally. Several other pieces of legislation relevant to child care have been enacted in recent years (e.g. Status of Children Act 1987; Judicial Separation and Family Law Reform Act 1989; Adoption Acts 1988 and 1991; Criminal Law (Rape) (Amendment) Act 1990; Child Abduction and Enforcement of Custody Act 1991; Criminal Evidence Act 1992; Adoptive Leave Act 1995). The courts have also had increasing opportunities to issues judgements in child care cases and Ireland[1] has ratified the United Nations Convention on the Rights of the Child. A number of high profile child abuse cases have triggered public and media interest in the area. These cases have run the gamut from chronic abuse within families to abuse by priests and allegations of abuse by staff members in homes run by religious orders. The cases have also had a considerable impact on the political system and in some instances on the Catholic Church, whose leader in Ireland has described child abuse by clergy as bringing 'pain, shame, humiliation and suffering' to the whole Church (Daly

---

1   This chapter does not cover the law and services in Northern Ireland, which have
     been discussed in Chapter 3

1995). Responding to the public shock at the details of the first of these high profile cases, known as the 'Kilkenny Incest Case' (Wood and Cooper 1993) the Minister for Health established an Inquiry Team to investigate failures in responses by different services to a case which had involved gross physical, emotional and sexual abuse. The Inquiry Team's prompt report (McGuinness 1993) has proved very influential and led to the government immediately committing £35 million of new money to implementing the recommendations of the report and the terms of the Child Care Act 1991. This response is all the more remarkable to those familiar with the earlier history of state involvement in Irish child care policy. In addition to the effects of other legal changes and the impact of high profile cases, current child care reform is being lent momentum by impending legal and social reform in areas of relevance to child care: education, health and juvenile justice.

The emergence of a state-led child care system

The full history of Irish child care policy since the foundation of the Irish State in 1922 remains to be written. A major task of that history will be to explain the marginality of the State, over many decades, in terms of child care policy and services (see Gilligan 1989 for a discussion of possible factors influencing the state's passivity). Two examples can illustrate this trend of relative inactivity by the state. Firstly, it was only in the early to mid 1970s as an Irish version of the welfare state emerged that the statutory health services began in the most tentative way to employ numbers of social workers in child care or other roles. In the same period the government began to plan for the reform of child care services (Task Force on Child Care Services 1975, 1981; Committee on Reformatories and Industrial Schools (Kennedy Committee) 1970). Secondly, the Irish state seemed reluctant until recently to use coercive authority in the child care arena. As late as 1983 the proportion of children in public care on a court ordered basis was only 28.4 per cent, a proportion which had risen to 49.3 per cent in 1991 (the latest year for which data are available: Department of Health 1986, 1994c). A further example of a hesitancy to use powers is in the legal processing of cases of infanticide where the Irish rate of prosecution is estimated, on the basis of official statistics in the period 1972 to 1991, to be four to five times less than the English rate (Dooley 1995, p.28).

Major social changes since the 1960s, in particular the impact of mass unemployment averaging between 15 and 20 per cent since the late 1970s, may have given the same momentum to a wider state role in child care, which perhaps the Second World War had earlier given the British state. Greater urbanisation and industrialisation from the 1960s onwards, a growth in crime rates especially in some of the larger urban centres, and the emergence of a serious drug problem in parts of the capital city, Dublin, have all stemmed from and contributed to conditions which have begun to prompt the emergence of a state-led child care system.

The organisation of Child Care Services

Public child care services are provided through the eight regional health boards
as part of an integrated system of health and personal social services. All the
health board regions are further divided into community care areas with
populations of 120,000 approximately. Each area is served by a community
care team. The use of the term 'community care' in the Irish context predates
its appearance as a tenet of recent British health policy and has a different sense.
It refers to all non-institutional multi-disciplinary field work services provided
by health boards for children and adults. Community care teams comprise
members of a range of disciplines including public health nursing, social work,
public health medicine, psychology, speech therapy and dentistry. (General
practitioners have a somewhat semi-detached relationship to this system,
because of their private contractor relationship to the health boards).

Clearly it takes more than the stroke of an administrative pen to accomplish
integrated teamwork within and across such a range of disciplines. Problems
of trust and communication can be exacerbated by various factors including the
lack of sufficiently clear protocols for inter-professional sharing of
responsibility (Kelly 1995). Experience varies greatly but local factors such as
shared accommodation and committed leadership can improve
inter-professional co-operation.

While the voluntary sector is an important provider in the health system,
operating many hospitals and residential and community services for the
disabled, this reflects a historical pattern rather than some ideologically driven
policy à la Thatcherite Britain. Indeed the current trend is strongly in the
direction of tighter integration and accountability of voluntary sector providers
within the wider system (Department of Health 1994a, p.33; Duffy 1993).
Within child care, the voluntary sector is active in residential services, adoption
services and in community-based preventive services. It has no role however in
the investigative phase of child protection work or in foster care, these being
solely the preserve of health board social work services. New draft regulations
on foster care, however, propose opening up the possibility of health boards
contracting out the assessment of foster carers to voluntary agencies.

The Child Care Act 1991 and Health Boards

The Child Care Act 1991 gives powers and duties to health boards and courts
in relation to the welfare of children at risk. The Act strives for a fine balance
between the rights of children and of parents and for a new emphasis on
accountability, planning and evaluation in child care services. The Act is being
implemented on a gradual basis, but it has been announced that the majority
of the Act will be in force by the end of 1995.

The Act requires each health board to 'promote the welfare of children in
its area who are not receiving adequate care and protection' (Section 3.1).

Section 8 requires health boards to undertake initial baseline and subsequent annual reviews, of the adequacy of their 'child care and family support services' and gives some hint as to the specific categories of children the legislators envisaged the Act serving. Health boards, in undertaking such reviews, are to have regard to particular broad categories of children who 'are not receiving adequate care and protection and in particular:

- children whose parents are dead or missing
- children whose parents have deserted or abandoned them
- children who are in the care of the board
- children who are homeless
- children who are at risk of being neglected or ill treated
- children whose parents are unable to care for them due to ill health or for any other reason'. (Section 8.2)

The Act defines as a 'child' all those up to 18 years who are not married. Broadly the Act has three focal areas of concern: child protection, children in care and family support. In performing its functions under the Act a health board is required to give 'due consideration to the wishes of the child' in decisions affecting the child. The Act also requires Boards to 'co-ordinate information from all relevant sources on children not receiving adequate care and protection', thus implying that a board must have good working links with all relevant bodies. The Act also gives health boards new powers to monitor and enforce new national standards in relation to foster care, residential child care, placement with relatives and pre-school day care.

Section 5 of the Act places a duty on health boards to receive into voluntary care those children who need it. There is also, in a controversial alternative to the care option, a duty on boards to provide 'accommodation' for young people, where the board is satisfied that the youngster has no access to accommodation which they can 'reasonably occupy' (O'Sullivan this volume). In the case of compulsory care the Act requires Boards to seek care orders where they deem this necessary.

A care order under the Act will give a health board 'like control over the child as if it were his parent' and will remain effective until age 18, or for such shorter period as the court determines. Children who are the subject of care orders may be placed in a foster family, children's home, or with relatives. To make an order a court must be *satisfied* that a child has been or is being 'assaulted, ill treated, neglected, or sexually abused', or that the 'child's health, development or welfare', has been, is being, or is likely to be, avoidably impaired or neglected. The Act also provides for supervision orders where the Court decides there are '*reasonable grounds to believe*' that the grounds for a care order apply (a lesser test). In addition to those cases where a court makes a supervision order instead of a care order, supervision orders may be made where health boards specifically seek them.

Supervision orders can be made on application by a health board or where a court decides not to grant a care order application. Health boards may apply for a supervision order in order to secure access to the child in its home or to secure compliance with 'medical or psychiatric examination, treatment or assessment'. A supervision order is effective for one year (renewable on application) and 'authorises a health board to have a child visited' as often as considered necessary, in order to allow a health board 'to satisfy itself as to the welfare of the child' and 'to give to parents…any necessary advice as to the care of the child'. A court may, on the application of a health board, at any time during the currency of an order, 'give directions as to the care of the child, which may require the parents of the child to cause him to attend for medical or psychiatric examination, treatment or assessment at a hospital, clinic, or the place specified by the court'. Parents may appeal to court in relation to the manner in which a supervision order is being carried out.

Relevant to the health boards' functions under the Child Care Act is Section 6 of the Domestic Violence Bill 1995 which empowers health boards to apply for a legal remedy (safety order or barring order) on behalf of a victim (or their dependant) of incidents threatening their safety or welfare.

Child protection

According to Department of Health national statistics, there has been a ninefold increase, from 182 to 1609, in confirmed reports of child abuse of all types in the ten years 1984–93. In 1993, confirmed cases represented 40 per cent of all reports received. The rate of confirmed cases in the same year was 1.4 per 1000 persons under 18 years (based on 1991 Census data). Responsibility for the management of child abuse cases has been vested in the Director of Community Care, the (medical) head of multi-disciplinary field services at community care area level (Department of Health 1987), but this formal responsibility for local management of child abuse cases is expected to be reassigned later in 1995 as part of a wider reorganisation of health service management.

In practice, the operational management of cases is generally devolved to social work teams, although in the case of pre-school children it is possible that a public health nurse (who combines many of the functions of the British district nurse and health visitor) may act as key worker. Area medical officers may also be involved in the assessment and monitoring of a child's developmental progress. These disciplines, and others including teachers, general practitioners and gardaí (police) may attend case conferences. Individual health boards are beginning to develop their own guidelines for staff on the management of these cases.

An Garda Síochána [guardians of the peace] – the national police force – have given high priority to the prevention of violence against women and children. They have called it 'probably our most under-reported crime' and ranked it as second only to the threat posed by terrorism and organised crime in a list of five priorities which the force has set itself for the period 1993–97 (Garda Síochána 1993, p.1).

A supplement to the 1987 national Child Abuse Guidelines (Department of Health 1987) has recently been published (Garda Síochána and Department of Health 1995). These offer guidance on health board – garda co-operation in child protection and offer new definitions of different forms of child abuse: physical abuse, sexual abuse, neglect and, interestingly, emotional abuse. The Department of Education has also issued guidelines to teachers on how to respond to suspected cases of child abuse affecting school students (Department of Education 1991).

Health board social work services are generally not available out of hours, which has prompted calls for a 24 hour field social work service (ISPCC 1995, p.21). The largest of the health boards, the Eastern Health Board which serves a third of the population nationally including Dublin, has begun recruiting for an out of hours intervention service for children in crisis in May 1995 (*Irish Times* 12 May 1995).

Investigation and assessment of child sexual abuse referrals
In the management of cases of suspected child sexual abuse, the task of assessment of suspected sexual abuse may be undertaken in some regions by *hospital* based teams in dedicated specialist units, whereas in other regions it may be undertaken by *community* based multi-disciplinary teams whether operating on a specialist full- or part-time basis or an *ad hoc* basis as circumstances or demand may require. The former approach emerged from a Working Party drafting new Child Abuse Guidelines at the time (Department of Health 1987). This also recommended the establishment of multi-disciplinary child sexual abuse assessment centres (Hensey 1988), the first two of which were established in Dublin in 1987 (Ryan and Fitzpatrick 1991). In three of the eight health boards including the largest Eastern Health Board, there are now such hospital based units with multi-disciplinary teams (typically headed by a child psychiatrist who is assisted by social workers and psychologists). These teams take referrals of suspected cases from community care social workers, general practitioners or directly from parents/caregivers. The assessment process generally involves interviews with the child, caregivers and those professionals involved.

In explaining this use of specialist centres or teams, it seems plausible to speculate that senior management in the health services had begun to appreciate (through a number of cases involving health boards in the superior courts) that sexual abuse cases risked embroiling boards in litigation which other types of child care cases typically did not. They were attracted, presumably, by the value of an aura of clinical specialism and medical authority combined with multi-disciplinary expertise as some kind of buffer against legal and other challenges to professional judgement in what was seen to be such a fraught area. The appointment of such medically led teams also reflected the strong influence of the medical profession in child care services. While these units have made a contribution to provision, there are occasional reservations expressed by some fieldworkers about the danger that reliance on specialist units disempowers frontline workers in terms of their professional skills. Certain aspects of the therapeutic or diagnostic value of the current operation of one such unit (which is broadly representative of the other units) have been questioned, too (Keary and Fitzpatrick 1994). Frontline workers may also feel envious at the resources devoted to specialist provision when, at least in certain high social stress areas, there are difficulties in terms of staff shortages and a high volume of referrals (*Irish Times* 13 May 1995).

Treatment of victims

If the management of services in the acute phase in child protection is not without difficulties, the picture is even less satisfactory in respect of ongoing treatment for victims or their families. There are limited resources devoted to child therapy, and while family therapy may be more common it is still an exaggeration to suggest that it is something which 'child care professionals use widely in child abuse cases' (O'Hagan 1994). Attempts to incorporate family therapy approaches to child protection and the repair of relationships in cases of intra-familial sexual abuse have been written up by a number of Irish family therapists (Colgan McCarthy and O'Reilly Byrne 1988; Butler, Farrelly and O'Dalaigh 1993).

Treatment of offenders

In recent years, certain initiatives by practitioners have begun to reflect the growing appreciation of the need for a focus on treatment not only of victims but also of perpetrators in the areas of child sexual abuse and domestic violence. A small group of social workers and psychologists working in community and clinical settings on the Northside of Dublin took the initiative to establish a treatment group for adolescents with a history of perpetrating sexual abuse (and a parallel group for their parents) (McGrath 1991, 1992). That this programme relied on the initiative and commitment of these professionals is a sign of the weakness in planning and strategy in the Irish child care services. On the other hand it reflects a strength in terms of the autonomy, enthusiasm and competence of these workers who wanted – and were allowed – to fill a space left by a planning vacuum. In another example of a practitioner-led initiative a social worker in a family centre in a Dublin working class suburb helped establish, in

One or more of:

Physical Abuse

Physical Injury to a child, including poisoning, where it is known or suspected that the injury was deliberately inflicted.

Sexual Abuse

The use of children by others for sexual gratification. This can take many forms and includes rape and other sexual assults, allowing children to view acts or to be exposed to, or involved in, pornography, exhibitionism and other perverse activities.

Emotional Abuse

The adverse effect on the behavior of a child caused by persistent or severe emotional ill-treatment or rejection to ongoing domestic violence.

Neglect

The persistent or severe neglect of a child, *whether wilful or intentional* [emphasis in original], which results in serious impairment of the child's health, development or welfare.

Source: Garda Síochána and the Department of Health (1995)

Figure 4.1. Official Definitions of Abuse

1989, the first branch of MOVE – Men Overcoming Violent Experience, a self-help movement for men who are willing to take responsibility in trying to end violent behaviour in their relationships. There are now up to ten such groups or branches across the country linked to MOVE, which very strongly sees itself as contributing one strand of the necessary range of responses to the needs of victims of domestic violence (Ferguson and Synott 1995).

Child abuse prevention programme

The Child Abuse Prevention 'Stay Safe' Programme is a national primary school based prevention programme developed by a child psychiatrist and psychologist and written specifically for Irish conditions. Individual schools, which enjoy considerable autonomy in the Irish system, make their own decision (with parents) to opt in or out. To date 55 per cent of schools are teaching the programme (Bhreathnach 1995). In its development phase eight social workers (one from each health board) and eight teachers were seconded to serve the needs of primary schools nationally. The programme offers curriculum materials for use in class with seven- to eight-year-olds and at a later stage a further version with 10–11-year-olds. Its operation and development is not without controversy. There have been objections from groups with a right wing religious standpoint who oppose what they see as its moral message and its threat to parental authority and autonomy (Casey 1993). This is a debate which the proponents (McIntyre 1993) appear largely to have won at least in terms of national policy as reflected in a commitment in the recent White Paper on Education to 'the continuing development of the Stay Safe Programme and its extension to all schools' (Department of Education 1995, p.161) and in the recently published national Health Promotion Strategy (Department of Health 1995b, p.19).

Increasing significance given to domestic violence

Domestic violence figures increasingly as a policy issue in health and social care generally (Second Commission on the Status of Women 1993, p.334–5; Department of Health 1994a; Department of Health 1995a) and as a concern of service providers. Very significantly in terms of child protection, 'exposure to ongoing domestic violence' is now cited as one form of emotional abuse in the most recent national guidelines agreed between An Garda Síochána and the Department of Health (see Figure 4.1). Furthermore, the Domestic Violence Bill 1985 greatly extends the remedies available to victims, including provision for health boards to act on behalf of a fearful victim. Factors likely to have contributed to this trend include the impact on policy makers and professionals of the findings of the Kilkenny Incest Case Inquiry Team (McGuinness 1993), the keen interest of two successive female Ministers for Justice, and the skilful lobbying and research work of Women's Aid (Cronin and O'Connor n.d.; Women's Aid 1995).

Alternative care away from home

Children in public care are placed in foster care or residential care. It is rare for children legally in care to be placed at home. The Child Care Act 1991 offers a new option of placement with a relative – a measure which has already been operated informally on a limited basis by some health boards. There are approximately 3000 children (or 2.6 per 1000 under 18 years) in the care of the eight regional health boards responsible for public care (Department of Health 1993). This figure has been rising slowly but steadily over the past 15 years or so. The 1980s also saw a doubling, to half, in the proportion of children in health board care on the basis of a court order. The proportion of children who are fostered has also been growing (Gilligan 1993b), and the latest data indicate that 74 per cent of youngsters in care are placed in foster families, with the remainder in different forms of residential care (Department of Health 1995c). Children admitted to care at a younger age, and those whose present age is younger are more likely to be in foster care (O'Higgins 1993). The Child Care Act 1991 places a duty on health boards to 'facilitate' access to a child in care for a parent or other person with a 'bona fide interest'. This may reflect growing professional awareness of the importance of family contact for children in care. A recent study in one health board found that only 21 per cent of children in care had no access visits in the four week study period, while 60 per cent of children had two or more such visits (Gallagher 1995). While these findings are not necessarily representative of the national picture, they may still give some hint of the value placed on family contact by professionals and by parents or relatives.

Foster care

Fostering is not only the dominant form of care but also represents the most important source of long-term alternative family care for children in the Irish public care system. This is because of legal and cultural impediments to the widespread use of adoption as an option for the permanent placement of children in the care system against parental wishes (O'Halloran 1994). The Adoption Act 1988 has opened up this latter possibility, although its complex process for dispensing with parental consent probably restricts the number of children affected.

While foster care has enjoyed a clear resurgence in the past fifteen years or so, prospects for the future may not be so buoyant. Difficulties in recruitment and retention are reported. Perhaps the future lies less in the realm of traditional models of foster care, but more with the use of relatives on the one hand and specialist carer schemes on the other. The Eastern Health Board has been to the fore in pioneering new approaches for Ireland. It has launched a carer scheme (for time-limited placements for older youngsters with challenging needs) and a scheme seeking to recruit placements for traveller children within traveller families (indigenous gypsy minority). It is also about to launch in conjunction with a drugs agency a support scheme for the children of drug-using parents which will include resources for family placement where necessary (Eastern Health Board 1995, p.141–3). A further sign of the broadening of the traditional concept of fostering is the fact that 6 per cent of the children in care placed in families by the Eastern Health Board are now placed with a relative (ibid. p.81), a proportion that seems set to rise.

Residential care

The great majority of residential places have traditionally been provided by voluntary bodies – usually religious orders, although now many religious-run units are closing as the orders find the complexity of managing modern residential child care services beyond their capacity. Since 1983, virtually all these centres have been in receipt of 100 per cent agreed budget funding, although there has been criticism of inconsistencies in funding levels between comparable centres (Streetwise National Coalition 1991). While in receipt of state funding, the residential units have until recently been relatively free of any bureaucratic accountability. Three factors are forcing the pace of change in this, however. First, a number of alleged scandals in children's homes have come into the public domain. Second, funding health boards are experiencing increasing frustration at the unwillingness or inability of residential units to accept or retain children who manifest serious behaviour problems, of a kind increasingly characteristic of children needing residential placement (Commission on Health Funding 1989). Third, voluntary sector children's homes face the same pressures of accountability to which the voluntary sector in the whole health care system is to be exposed.

While the residential sector is in decline in overall terms, there is some growth – especially in short to medium places for adolescents – at what might be regarded as opposite ends of the spectrum. There has been a tendency for policy to favour a switch to new smaller units with about six beds, often in or close to the neighbourhood from which residents are drawn (Gilligan 1982) or serving a given catchment area. On the other hand there are now moves to open the first secure unit(s) in the child care system. Health boards have heretofore assumed that they lack the legal authority to detain a child in secure conditions. However in a series of recent court cases (e.g. F. a minor and the Minister for Education, the Minister for Health, Ireland and the Attorney-General), the Courts have found on a case by case basis that the state has a constitutional obligation to provide care for children with special behavioural problems even where this necessitated 'containment with treatment'.

New awareness of risk of abuse to children in public care
A number of allegations by former residents have sensitised the public and professionals to the vulnerability of children in care. In late 1994, the Department of Health circulated new directions to the managements of children's homes on the recruitment and selection of staff, including a requirement for a police check before a final appointment is made (Department of Health 1994b). A report is soon to be published on an inquiry into allegations of abuse by staff at Madonna House – a children's home in Dublin.

Family support

While prevention and family support is in volume terms by a long way the Cinderella of child care provision, there is still encouraging evidence of energy and innovation to be found in this field in most parts of the country. Initiatives tend to be localised and there are few programmes established on a national basis. In the early childhood field, the Community Mothers Programme in the Eastern Health Board has been an influential development which is now being adopted by some other of the health boards. This is a programme of low key domiciliary parent education and support to mothers with young children. It is delivered by local women who are experienced mothers and who are recruited, trained and supported by specially designated public health nurses. Adapted from a British model which relays its child care and health promotion messages through health visitors (Barker 1984), the Irish model has been subject to evaluation which found statistically significant gains for participating mothers and their children when compared with non-participating controls (Johnson, Howell and Molloy 1993; Johnson and Molloy 1995).

There is quite a range of parenting programmes on offer throughout the country under the varied auspices of schools, Churches, health boards, adult education, voluntary and community organisations (Ryland 1995). There has also been an explosion of daytime adult education programmes driven by women's grass root demands and interests (Inglis 1994), many of which address at least initially issues of personal development and parenting. There have also been initiatives to offer therapeutic support groups to parents, which in one reported instance has generated significant improvements for the parents and their children (Mullin, Proudfoot and Glanville 1990).

The Task Force on Child Care Services (1975) recommended the development of *neighbourhood youth projects* (NYPs) aimed at offering activities and supports to young people at risk and their peer group in their own locality. Three projects have survived from the mid to late 1970s, one in Cork City and two in inner city Dublin (Clarke, Lahert and McCabe 1994). Now the programme of service development under the Child Care Act 1991 has revived interest in the concept of the Neighbourhood Youth Project as health boards grapple with the provision of preventive services to adolescents. Two new projects have developed in Galway city, another in Blanchardstown, a Dublin suburb, and there appear to be more in the pipeline. Projects tend to have at least three to four staff, usually drawn from a variety of professional backgrounds, child care work, youth work, social work and community work. Each project develops its own approach to the target youngsters and their peers within a broad framework of individual and group work. The first Galway project has developed a special commitment to working closely with the parents of the young people who are involved (Dolan 1993).

There has also been a growth in neighbourhood based resource centres or family centres offering a range of facilities and supports to local families. These may be run directly by health boards or more likely by voluntary bodies. In order to meet the needs of specific high risk families, a number of new approaches have been developed including Claidhe Mór, an innovative multi-method therapeutic family centre in Dublin (Butler and McTeigue 1994). This centre has helped introduce to Ireland the Dutch method for enhancing parental child management skills – video home training (Weiner, Kuppermintz and Guttman 1994). Some other innovations in the wider system include the deployment of supervised lay family support workers or professional child care workers in the service of individual children and families, in order to lower stress and/or the risk of admission to care (Eastern Health Board 1995).

Important family support work occurs under the auspices of other agencies including the Combat Poverty Agency (Harvey 1994) and the Department of Education which has sponsored the new Early Start programme (compensatory pre-school provision in high social stress areas) (Fitzgerald 1994). The potentially very important Home–School–Community Liaison Scheme now involves 105 teachers released from classroom duties at primary level and others at second level (Irish National Teachers Organisation 1995, p.5). It has been argued that the full potential of family support under the Child Care Act 1991 can only be realised if health boards not only give it priority within their own sphere of operation but also cultivate and support such relevant initiatives by other services (Gilligan 1995).

Issues for the future

Legal reform

A number of matters relevant to child care and the law are likely to require policy attention in the reasonably near future. These include constitutional reform, mandatory reporting (that is the duty on certain categories of professionals to report suspicions of abuse), and training for the judiciary.

CONSTITUTIONAL EMPHASIS ON PARENTAL RIGHTS

The country's written Constitution is frequently criticised from a child care perspective for what is seen as a bias towards the interests of parents, although in the view of one authority 'the provisions of the Irish Constitution have on balance played a valuable role in curbing excessive state intervention in the name of child protection' (Duncan 1993). The Kilkenny Incest Case Inquiry Team (McGuinness 1993) lent their voice to calls for constitutional change to ensure a Constitutional presumption of priority for the rights and interests of the child. A forthcoming review of the Constitution may provide an opportunity for such reform.

MANDATORY REPORTING

While there is no provision for mandatory reporting of child abuse cases currently, the possibility of its introduction is under active review (Department of Health 1994a). Such a measure has been called for or supported by a wide range of opinion, including the Law Reform Commission (1990), the Irish Society for the Prevention of Cruelty to Children (ISPCC 1995), the Inquiry Team into the Kilkenny Incest Case (McGuinness 1993), and even a previous Minister for Health while in office (Howlin 1993).

TRAINING FOR THE JUDICIARY

While various members of the judiciary have let it be known that they do not favour the idea of obligatory formal training for work in areas such as child care, it seems likely that some formula will have to be found which satisfies the concerns of a wide spectrum of opinion on this matter (Women's Aid 1995; Law Reform Commission 1990, p.97). The considerable increase in the volume of child care cases before the Courts which is likely to flow from the Child Care Act 1991 will probably bring this about sooner rather than later.

A new emphasis on research and evaluation

There is a strong case for a strengthening of the research, evaluation and management information capacity of the Irish child care system. The paucity of research in an area such as foster care has been lamented on a number of occasions (Gilligan 1990; O'Sullivan and Pinkerton 1994). While there are examples of service or programme evaluation (Farrelly 1994; Johnson, Howell and Molloy 1993) these are still all too rare. So too unfortunately is practitioner led research such as that of Hynes and Jennings (1989). It is essential also to use research to assess the extent of an emerging problem as in the case of child sexual abuse (McKeown and Gilligan 1991) or bullying at school (O'Moore 1995). Research can also be a valuable mechanism for illuminating the views of service users as to the value or impact of that service (Boldt 1994; Hannan and Shortall 1991; Farrelly 1994; Smyth and Keenaghan 1993; Ruddle and O'Connor 1992). Work of this kind needs to be steadily and purposefully augmented. It is essential also that the quality and immediacy of official statistics be considerably enhanced.

Other developments required

Additional public money must continue to be invested in order to resource adequately the national system of services to international standards. Special support must be delivered to certain groups where evidence exists of a disproportionately high risk of admission to care or other disadvantageous conditions, e.g. children of travellers (O'Higgins 1993; Task Force on the Travelling Community 1995); of drug users (Woods 1994; Clarke 1994) and of inner city residents (McKeown 1991). There is a need to move faster in the direction of routine participation by clients in decision-making fora as recommended by the National Economic and Social Forum (1995, p.52–3), or in the process of service planning (Price 1993). It is important that the child care agenda is not dominated by a narrow preoccupation with child protection, but retains a balance which favours prevention and family support (Gilligan 1995). A clear strategy must be developed to cope with the implications of the gradual but inexorable diminution and change in the Catholic Church's role in the provision of child care services (Gilligan 1993a). A strong and vibrant voluntary sector in the child care system must be cultivated, both as an end in itself and as a replacement for the former role of the Church. Finally the necessary policy, planning and training work must also be undertaken in order to ensure that the rhetoric of inter-agency and inter-professional co-operation has some realistic prospect of becoming a reality.

References

Barker, W. (1984) *The Child Development Programme: A Collaborative Programme Linking Parents, Community and Health Visitors.* Bristol: Early Childhood Development Unit, University of Bristol.

Bhreathnach, N. [Minister for Education] (1995) *The Stay Safe Programme – Press Release.* 23 January.

Boldt, S. (1994) *Listening and Learning – A Study of the Experiences of Early School Leavers from the Inner City of Dublin.* Dublin: Marino Institute of Education.

Butler, G., Farrelly, M. and O'Dalaigh, L. (1993) Working with intra-familial child sexual abuse. In H. Ferguson, R. Gilligan and R. Torode (eds) *Surviving Childhood Adversity – Issues for Policy and Practice.* Dublin: Social Studies Press.

Butler, G. and McTeigue, D. (1994) *Claidhe Mór Family Centre.* Dublin: Claidhe Mor Family Centre.

Casey, G. (1993) Why I am opposed to "stay safe". *Intercom* June 10–11 Commission on Health Funding.

Clarke, B. (1994) Drug using parents – the child care issues. *Irish Social Worker 12,* 2, 9.

Clarke, B., Lahert, J. and McCabe, F. (1994) *The Neighbourhood Youth Projects – North Inner City Dublin 1979–1994.* Dublin: Eastern Health Board.

Colgan McCarthy, I. and O'Reilly Byrne, N. (1988) Mistaken love: conversations on the problem of incest in an Irish context. *Family Process 27*, 181–199.

Commission on Health Funding (1989) *Report of the Commission on Health Funding.* Dublin: Stationery Office.

Committee on Reformatories and Industrial Schools (Kennedy Committee) (1970) *Report.* Dublin: Stationery Office.

Cronin, J. and O'Connor, M. (n.d.) The Identification and Treatment of Women Admitted to an Accident and Emergency Department as a Result of Assault by Spouses/Partners – A Pilot Project between Women's Aid and St. James Hospital 1993. Dublin: authors (mimeo).

Daly, C. (Cardinal) (1995) Needing forgiveness. *Intercom 25*, 1, February, 6–8.

Department of Education (1991) *Procedures for Dealing with Allegations or Suspicions of Child Abuse.* Circular 16/91 Primary Branch Dublin Department of Education.

Department of Education (1995) *Charting our Education Future – White Paper on Education.* Dublin: Stationery Office.

Department of Health (1986) *Children in Care 1983.* Dublin: Department of Health.

Department of Health (1987) *Child Abuse Guidelines.* Dublin: Department of Health.

Department of Health (1994a) *Shaping a Healthier Future – A Strategy for Effective Health Care in the 1990s.* Dublin: Stationery Office.

Department of Health (1994b) *Recruitment and Selection of Staff to Children's Residential Centres.* [Letter to management of children's residential centres] 9 November.

Department of Health (1995a) Violence against women and children pp.52–53. In Department of Health *Developing a Policy for Women's Health – A Discussion Document,* pp.52–53 Dublin: Stationery Office.

Department of Health (1995b) *A Health Promotion Strategy: Making the Healthier Choice the Easier Choice.* Dublin: Department of Health.

Department of Health (1995c) *Survey of Children in the Care of Health Boards in 1992.* Dublin: Department of Health.

Dolan, P. (1993) *The Challenge of Family Life in the Westside A Six Week Course for Parents of Young People attending the Neighbourhood Youth Project. Dissertation in Partial Fulfilment of the Requirements for the Advanced Diploma in Child Protection and Welfare 1992–3.* Department of Social Studies, University of Dublin, Trinity College.

Dooley, E. (1995) *Homicide in Ireland.* Dublin: Stationery Office.

Duffy, M. (1993) The voluntary sector and the personal social services. *Administration 41*, 3, pp.323–344.

Duncan, W. (1993) The constitutional protection of parental rights – a discussion of the advantages and disadvantages of according fundamental status to parental rights and duties. In J. Eekelaar and P. Sarcevic (eds) (1993) *Parenthood in Modern Society*. Kluwer Academic Publishers, pp.431–445.

Eastern Health Board (1995) *Review of Adequacy of Child Care and Family Support Services 1994*. Dublin: Eastern Health Board.

Farrelly, J. (1994) *The Transition Unit – A Residential Programme to Prepare Families Who Have Been Homeless for Settlement in the Community*. Dublin: Focus Point Project Limited.

Ferguson, H. and Synott, P. (1995) *Intervention with Men who Batter – Issues for Social Work in the Republic of Ireland*. Paper presented at Irish Association of Social Workers Conference, Limerick, 11 May.

Fitzgerald, E. (1994) [Ministerial contribution in adjournment debate] Parliamentary Debates *Dail Eireann*. 21–22 June columns 285–288.

Gallagher, S. (1995) Parents, families and access to children in care: the implications of the Child Care Act 1991. In H. Ferguson and P. Kenny (eds) *On Behalf of the Child: Professional Perspectives on the Child Care Act 1991*. 121–141, Dublin: A and A Farmar.

An Garda Síochána (1993) *An Garda Síochána Strategic Plan 1993–97*. Dublin: An Garda Síochána.

An Garda Síochána and Department of Health (1995) *Notification of Suspected Cases of Child Abuse between Health Boards and Gardaí*. Dublin: An Garda Síochána and Department of Health.

Gilligan, R. (1982) *Children in Care in their Own Community*. Dublin: Society of St Vincent de Paul.

Gilligan, R. (1989) Policy in the Republic of Ireland: historical and current issues in child care. In P. Carter, T. Jeffs and M. Smith (eds) *Social Work and Social Welfare Yearbook 1*. Milton Keynes: Open University, 61–73.

Gilligan, R. (1990) *Foster Care for Children in Ireland – Issues and Challenges of the 1990s*. Dublin: University of Dublin, Trinity College, Department of Social Studies Occasional Paper No. 2.

Gilligan, R. (1993a) *Child Care and Family Support – Choices for the Church*. Dublin: Conference of Major Religious Superiors.

Gilligan, R. (1993b) Ireland. In M. Colton and W. Hellinckx (eds) *Child Care in the EC – A Country-specific Guide to Foster and Residential Care*. Aldershot: Arena.

Gilligan, R. (1995) Family support and child welfare. In H. Ferguson and P. Kenny (eds) *On Behalf of the Child: Professional Perspectives on the Child Care Act 1991*, 121–141. Dublin: A and A Farmar.

Hannan, D. and Shortall, S. (1991) *The Quality of their Education – School Leavers' Views of Educational Objectives and Outcomes*. General Research Series Paper No. 153 Dublin: Economic and Social Research Institute.

Harvey, B. (1994) *Combating Exclusion – Lessons from the Third EU Poverty Programme in Ireland*. Dublin: Combat Poverty Agency and associated organisations.

Hensey, O. (1988) Child sexual abuse: Cleveland – Irish implications. *Irish Medical Journal 81*, 1, 3–4.

Howlin, B. (1993) [contribution as Minister for Health] Parliamentary Debates – *Seanad Eireann*. 7 July columns 726–7.

Hynes, M., and Jennings, S. (1989) Community notification of child sexual abuse. *Irish Medical Journal 82*, 3, 115–117.

Inglis, T. (1994) Women and the struggle for daytime adult education in Ireland. *Studies in the Education of Adults 26*, 1, 50–66, April.

Irish National Teachers Organisation (1995) Allocation of posts for the school year 1995/6. *Tuarascáil 2*. March.

ISPCC (1995) *Preventing Child Abuse – Supporting Healthy Families: A submission to Government on the Continuing Child Care and Protection Crisis in Ireland*. Dublin: ISPCC.

Johnson, Z., Howell, F. and Molloy, B. (1993) Community mothers programme: randomised controlled trial of non-professional intervention in parenting. *British Medical Journal 306*, 1449–52.

Johnson, Z. and Molloy, B. (1995) The community mothers programme – empowerment of parents by parents. *Children and Society 9*, 2, 73–85

Keary, K. and Fitzpatrick, C. (1994) Children's disclosure of sexual abuse during formal investigation. *Child Abuse and Neglect 18*, 7, 543–548.

Kelly, A. (1995) A public health nursing perspective. In H. Ferguson and P. Kenny (eds) *On Behalf of the Child: Professional Perspectives on the Child Care Act 1991*, 60–83. Dublin: A and A Farmar.

Law Reform Commission (1990) *Report on Child Sexual Abuse*. Dublin: Law Reform Commission.

McGrath, K. (1991) Adolescent sex offenders group therapy project. *Irish Social Worker 10*, 2, 17–18.

McGrath, K. (1992) *Inter-agency Cooperation in the Provision of Group Therapy for Adolescent Sex Offenders and their Parents*. Paper presented at the Ninth International Conference on Child Abuse and Neglect, Chicago, 2 September.

McGuinness, C. (Chair) (1993) *Kilkenny Incest Investigation – Report presented to the Minister for Health by South Eastern Health Board*. Dublin: Stationery Office.

McIntyre, D. (1993) The stay safe programme. *Intercom*. June.

McKeown, K. (1991) *The North Inner City of Dublin – An Overview*. Dublin: Daughters of Charity.

McKeown, K. and Gilligan, R. (1991) Child sexual abuse in the Eastern health board area of Ireland in 1988: an analysis of 512 confirmed cases. *Economic and Social Review 22*, 2, 101–134.

Mullin, E., Proudfoot, R. and Glanville, B, (1990) Group parent training in the eastern health board: programme description and evaluation. *Irish Journal of Psychology 11*, 4, 342–353.

National Economic and Social Forum (1995) Consultation and participation pp.52–53. In *Quality Delivery of Social Services. Forum Report No. 6*. Dublin: National Economic and Social Forum.

O'Hagan, K. (1994) Ireland's response to child abuse. *Violence Update 4* 5, 3 and 10, January.

O'Halloran, K. (1994) *Adoption in the Two Jurisdictions of Ireland*. Aldershot: Avebury.

O'Higgins K. (1993) *Family Problems – Substitute Care*. Dublin: Economic and Social Research Institute.

O' Moore, A. M. (1995) Bullying behaviour in children and adolescents in Ireland. *Children and Society 9*, 2, 54–72.

Price, B. (1993) Client participation in the development of practice and policy within an agency. *Irish Social Worker 11*, 3, 12–13.

Ruddle, H. and O'Connor, J. (1992) *Breaking the Silence: Violence in the Home – The Women's Perspective*. Dublin: National College of Industrial Relations/Mid-Western Health Board.

Ryland, J. (1995) *A Study of Parenting Programmes in Ireland*. Dublin: National Children's Resource Centre, Barnardos.

Ryan, I. and Fitzpatrick, C. (1991) St. Clare's and St. Louise's child sexual abuse assessment units: an analysis of their origin, function and work practices. *Irish Journal of Psychological Medicine 8*, 68–71.

Second Commission on the Status of Women (1993) *Report to Government January 1993*. Dublin: Stationery Office.

Smyth, E. and Keenaghan, C. (1993) *The View 'Back There' – An Assessment of Needs from a Community Perspective Commissioned by the Western Health Board*. Dublin: National College of Industrial Relations.

Streetwise National Coalition (1991) *At What Cost – A Research Study on Residential Care for Children and Adolescents in Ireland*. Dublin: Focus Point.

Task Force on Child Care Services (1975) *Interim Report*. Dublin: Stationery Office.

Task Force on Child Care Services (1981) *Final Report*. Dublin: Stationery Office.

Task Force on the Travelling Community (1995) *Report of the Task Force on the Travelling Community*. Dublin: Stationery Office.

Weiner, A., Kuppermintz, H. and Guttman D. (1994) Video home training (the Orion Project) – a short-term preventive and treatment intervention for families with young children. *Family Process 33*, 4, 441–453.

Women's Aid (1995) *Discussion Paper on Violence against Women by 'Known' Men*. Presented to the Minister for Justice 20th January 1995. Dublin: Women's Aid.

Wood, K. and Cooper, A. (1993) *The Kilkenny Incest Case*. Dublin: Poolbeg.

Woods, M. (1994) Drug using parents and their children: the experience of a voluntary/non-statutory project. *Irish Social Worker 12*, 2, 10.

CHAPTER 5

Children, Crime and Society

Stewart Asquith

The main purpose of this chapter is to explore the relationship between explanations of crime and offending by children and young people on the one hand and the development of preventive policies and practices on the other. The focus will in particular be on the implications of increasing acceptance of what might be broadly termed 'social explanations' for the development of crime prevention strategies. In that respect there will be little discussion of actual systems of juvenile justice and administrative structures for dealing with young offenders in the United Kingdom. Rather, my purpose is to examine what changes crime prevention strategies, and indeed governments themselves, may have to embrace in order to realise a truly preventive philosophy. In doing so, the contribution of current research will be considered (Asquith *et al*. 1995).

Dealing with children and young people who offend: a crisis in philosophy?

Logically, policies and practices devised to deal with crime and offending by the young should be based on clear explanations for the behaviour. Farrington puts this well when he states: 'Methods of preventing delinquency should be grounded in knowledge about the causes of delinquency or at least in knowledge about risk and protective factors that predict delinquency' (Farrington 1994).

But in relation to crime and delinquency, the measures employed to deal with offenders may not necessarily bear much relationship to the explanations offered for their behaviours in the first place. Thus policies may be developed in the absence of any clear information on what the causes of the behaviour are and indeed may fly in the face of the contribution of research. Detention centres and the value of the 'short, sharp shock', for example, were advocated forcefully by the government in the early 1980s despite the conclusion of a number of research projects pointing to their ineffectiveness and opposition from a number of practitioners. There are striking similarities with current arguments for 'boot camps' and military style regimes for young offenders (see Montgomery 1995).

What is also clear is that the advocacy of measures for dealing with children and young people who offend, whatever form they may take, usually entail implicit assumptions about the nature of children, childhood and the stages of development and growth which children pass through. In that respect much can be learnt from the social and political reaction to particularly horrific cases such as the Bulger case. Explanations for what happened in that case varied from descriptions of the children who murdered James Bulger as 'evil' or 'wicked' who should be punished and even, some argued, hanged for what they did, to explanations based on a need to examine the familial and social environment to consider what changes need to be made in the way we afford social and life experiences to our children (King 1995; Asquith 1995).

Such 'difficult' cases clearly identify the complex interplay between public stereotypes of children and childhood, particularly where children 'do wrong', and the principles on which more formal responses are based. Qvortrup (1994) clearly states this relationship between notions of childhood and the social institutions with which children come into contact: 'Childhood is the life-space which our culture limits it to be, i.e. its definitions through the courts, the school, the family, the economy and also through psychology and philosophy' (p.3).

It is clear that policies and practices for dealing with young offenders have to be based on some view of human nature or at the very least on some explanation of just why it is that certain children and young people turn to crime. Conversely, it would seem pointless to direct our attention and divert scarce resources to policies and practices which in fact bore no relationship to the factors which propel individuals on to criminal or delinquent careers.

Most European countries, including the UK, are currently reviewing their juvenile justice systems and there is clear evidence of particular sets of explanations and accompanying views of the nature of children and childhood informing the development of policies and practices. In particular, there is a move away from explanations which focus only on the individual child and the development of policies and practices which favour explanations based on the need to understand the child in his or her total environment. This tension between individualistic and more social explanations, as we shall see, continues to inform current policy and practice (Asquith 1995).

But if the current debates on juvenile offending in British newspapers are anything to go by, there is considerable confusion both over what factors can legitimately be held to be the causes of offending and what measures are the more appropriate to be taken in the attempt to reduce offending by young people.

On 7 June 1995, the *Daily Telegraph* reported that a call for the reintroduction of flogging of young offenders who commit violent crimes was defeated in the House of Commons by a vote of 153 to 58 (Kirkbride 1995). The sponsor of the Corporal Punishment (Reintroduction) Bill had argued that the bill, which would have applied to youngsters between the ages of ten and

18, was necessary to curb the increasing numbers of violent crimes committed by young people. What the report also noted though was that the Bill would have been contrary to the European Convention on Human Rights which bans corporal punishment. It could also have argued that it would have contravened the United Nations Convention on the Rights of the Child which the UK ratified in 1991.

On 15 May 1995, the *Independent on Sunday* had also carried reports on what should be done about crime and delinquency (Mills 1995). In complete contrast, it was noted that a number of police chiefs supported a study by National Association for the Care and Resettlement of Offenders (NACRO) on *Crime and Social Policy* in which the growth in crime was attributed in large part to poverty, inequality and unemployment. A plea was made in the report to move away from a 'cops, courts and corrections' perspective and to make a massive investment in the family and society. The ability of the criminal justice system in itself to substantially reduce offending was seen to be inevitably limited: 'At present too many resources are devoted to punishing and controlling those who commit crime and too little to preventing its occurrence in the first place.' Instead of the traditional demand, which we have all become familiar with, for the need for more police and resources to combat crime through the criminal justice system, the report demanded that more support be given to families, including nursery provision, more services for young people and better training for those with a responsibility for children. The Report also argued that education, health, employment and penal reform all go hand in hand in order not simply to reduce crime but to enhance the life experiences of children and young people. From this perspective, the punitive approach will inevitably fail, because it touches only a limited section of the population and does nothing to lay the basis for a long-term reduction in crime and offending behaviour. By this view, socio-economic factors are key variables in the search for explanations of crime and only when they are taken into consideration can a truly *preventive* strategy be developed.

Nevertheless, much publicity was given to a recent research-based report which appeared to reject the idea that social and economic factors in and of themselves can explain the apparent trend in rising crime rates. The study by Rutter and Smith (1995) argued that anti-social behaviour by young people could not be blamed on unemployment, poor housing or broken homes. Rather, crime amongst the young could be attributed to the rise in post-war freedom and individualism which accounts for the increase in psychosocial disorders experienced by the young. For Rutter and Smith, there has been a separation of the young from positive influence of adults through the development of a distinct youth culture, the increase of separation and divorce and other such factors. This has contributed to a generation of young confused people growing up in a moral vacuum, which, they argue, has led to a growth in crime and suicide amongst young people. Where Rutter and Smith appear to differ most

markedly from others who argue that the apparent increase in crime is caused
by social and economic factors, is in their assertion that poverty, unemployment
and economic disadvantage cannot in themselves explain the situation that
young people find themselves as we head toward the end of the twenty-first
century (see also Cohen 1995). Though they do offer an account of criminal
and related behaviours based on social and economic explanations, they
postulate no direct causal link between crime and poverty as such.

What we also have to be aware of is that the confusion and ambiguity about
explanations of crime, particularly by the young, leaves room open for more
controversial *individualistic* theories. In particular, the inheritance of biological
positivism from the nineteenth century Italian criminologists regularly appears
in debate and discussion about predicting and controlling crime in the attempt
to realise what might be called the 'logic of difference' – that is, that offenders
are in some significant way different from the rest of society who do not commit
crime.

From this point of view, crime control has a rather simple logic. Single out
those factors which differentiate offenders from the rest of us and preventive
strategies can be based on the eradication of those factors. What those factors
are is, of course, a source of some controversy and various alternatives have been
offered in the history of criminology. What is more relevant for our purposes
though is that the 'logic of difference' not only tends to underpin commonly
held stereotypes about those who offend, how to identify them and how to
deal with them, but is also in evidence in current professional explanations. For
example, the CIBA Foundation held a Conference in London in February 1995
on The Genetics of Criminal Behaviour. Michael Rutter (one of the authors of
the Rutter and Smith report) argued that: 'Research into the genetics of
criminality could lead to a better understanding of how risk factors operate,
which is important for intervention and prevention' (Naysmith 1995).
Biological positivism is by no means without its current advocates.

Two clear trends can be detected. One is an increasing polarisation in the
types of explanations for offending behaviour by children and young people
into two groups: those who, on the one hand, attribute alleged increases in
crime to factors within individuals (whether in terms of individual responsibility
or individualistic causal factors) and those, on the other, who assert the
criminogenic influence of more social, economic and structural factors.

The other trend involves an increasing convergence in the explanations
offered for offending behaviour by the young, or for other childhood problems
such as child abuse, poor educational attainment, poor health and so on. That
is, the *factors* employed to account for delinquent and offending behaviour by
the young are increasingly strikingly similar to those employed to explain, for
example, child abuse or ill health. Similarly, there is convergence in acceptance
and understanding of the kinds of *preventive strategies* required if we are truly to

reduce offending, prevent child abuse and generally improve the life experiences of our children.

There is of course nothing new in the dichotomy of explanations for offending behaviour between the individual and social factors – that has been a characteristic feature of the history of criminology. But what is increasingly obvious is the clear polarisation of policies and practices (largely based on this individualistic–social dimension) suggested as to how we should deal with those young people who offend. In relation to the UK (or more accurately England and Wales), long criticised by European commentators for having a more punitive approach to crime, the polarisation of views is supported by a high degree of commitment to individualistic explanations and associated punitive policies for young offenders. For example, in relation to the Bulger case, the Prime Minister, John Major, himself stated that 'we should condemn more and understand less'. This was echoed later by his Home Secretary, Michael Howard, who asserted that: 'We should have no truck with trendy theories which try to explain away crime by blaming social-economic factors…criminals should be held to be accountable for their actions. Trying to pass the buck is counterproductive and dangerous' (see Cohen 1995).

Graham (1996) noted the influence of such thinking on the 1994 Criminal Justice and Public Order Act which 'represents a partial reversal of the diversionary trend which characterised the 1980s'. It introduced a range of new measures which essentially extend the courts' remand and sentencing powers to younger offenders by introducing secure training orders for 12- to 14-year-old persistent offenders; extending the provisions of section 53 of the Children and Young Persons Act on detention for grave offences to 10- to 13-year-olds; increasing the maximum length of detention in a Young Offenders' Institution from 12 to 24 months for 15- to 17-year-olds and allowing courts to remand 12- to 14-year-olds.

What also has to be recognised though is that criticisms of an individualistic approach also apply to measures and policies for dealing with offenders which are based on a commitment to a welfare philosophy and meeting the needs of offenders. Thus, the Scottish Children's Hearings system can be also be viewed as focusing attention on the offender and paying less attention to social considerations in explaining and developing of policies of crime prevention. Whereas the report of the Kilbrandon Committee (HMSO 1964), on which the Scottish system of juvenile justice is based (see Tisdall this volume), emphasised a preventive philosophy in which families were to be supported in caring for their children, measures have in practice been directed largely at individuals and the wider preventive thrust of the Kilbrandon philosophy never realised. The current trend towards an acceptance of explanations of offending behaviour in terms of social factors rejects policies and measures based on individualistic explanations whether they are punitive or welfare oriented.

In the general review of juvenile justice systems currently underway in the international arena, there are a number of common issues to be addressed, most of which are related in some way to the individualistic-social dichotomy. These would include:

- the extent to which punishment is an acceptable option for young offenders
- the age of criminal responsibility
- the relationship between community based services and custodial provision
- the relevance of the court or tribunal model of decision-making
- the relevance to children and young offenders of traditional notions of criminal justice and search for alternatives such as 'restorative' or 'reparative' justice (Walgrave 1996)
- the integration of young offenders into mainstream social life
- the degree of commitment to the rights of children caught up in formal justice processes (Cappelaere 1994)
- the nature of preventive philosophies.

In the UK context, it does appear that there is considerable resistance to preventive philosophies in the light of a high degree of commitment to punishment and retribution; a low age, by European standards, of criminal responsibility (ten in England and Wales and eight in Scotland); an acceptance of 'children's jails' in association with a questioning of the validity of alternative scenarios for dealing with offenders; and a general hardening of the language of delinquency control in its presentation of children and young people as threats to society. A comparison of the social and political reactions to the James Bulger case with the death of Silje Redergard in Norway is particularly instructive in this respect (Asquith 1996). In contrast to the fairly severe reaction shown by many members of the public to the Bulger case involving demands for life imprisonment or even hanging for these 'evil' children, the Norwegian public, including the mother of the dead child, generally expressed concern that the future lives of the children involved should not be destroyed by what they had done.

Responses to offending by children and young people: twin tracking

Much of the argument for the adoption of punitive approaches to dealing with juvenile offenders is based on an acceptance of the increase in juvenile crime. However, as argued above, the development of policies and practices for dealing with offenders do have to be based on a clear understanding of just what it is that is being dealt with. The data available do not support the over-generalised claim that juvenile crime is on the increase. That is too simplistic an interpretation and the evidence needs to be reviewed in more detail.

What has to be borne in mind is that when we speak of developing policies for responding to juvenile crime, or for that matter crime by adults, what is largely being spoken about is a male population. By and large juvenile and criminal justice systems deal mainly with male offenders and females are relatively invisible in the crime statistics. Moreover, the majority of offences are committed by the young offenders who tend to come from working class sections of the community. No argument is being made here that this implies that working class males therefore commit more offences than others – simply that the official crime statistics do present a profile of young working class males as being the main group of offenders. This of course may well reflect that the statistics and the legal categories employed relate largely to working class crime and ignore other types of criminal activity. The majority of recorded offences are property offences involving theft and burglary with a minority of offences involving violence against the person.

A review of crime statistics since the Second World War reveals that in most Western industrialised countries, including the UK, there was a steady and significant increase in the rates of crime until the 1980s and particularly with regard to juvenile crime (Kyvsgaard 1991; Junger-Tas 1994). As Utting, Bright and Henricson (1993) observe, official statistics almost certainly under-represent the level of offending by young people in the community. According to surveys such as the British Crime Survey and the work of Anderson, Kinsey and Smith (1990), involvement in criminal behaviour by young people is higher than the official statistics would lead us to believe.

However, what most countries noted in the 1980s was that there was a general decline in the rates of recorded offending behaviour by the young. In particular, the decline was greater in relation to the younger offenders, particularly those under 13. Nevertheless, there appear to be clear gender differences in that though the rates of offending by girls also declined, the decline was much less marked than for boys.

In terms of the types of offences committed and the changes over time it appears to be the case that the decline has been greatest in relation to the general category of property offences. There has however been a small increase in offences against the person. (For a fuller discussion see Junger-Tas 1994.)

What is also clear is that throughout the international arena there is great variation in the degree of seriousness of the types of behaviour displayed by young people. In Europe there is of course concern at the increase in violent offences committed by young people but it bears little comparison with the kinds of behaviours displayed in American inner cities (Garbarino and Kostelny 1995). Nevertheless, the more serious cases involving young offenders attract particular media and public attention and it is these cases which inform our stereotypes of offending by young people and may also influence developments in juvenile justice as a whole.

The implication of all this is that there are two broad categories of children and young people who commit offences. There is, firstly, a large group of young people who commit property offences, in which the damage or loss is of relatively low value. The other is a smaller group of children and young people who commit the more serious offences or who repeatedly offend.

What has characterised the search for new paradigms of juvenile justice over the past decade or so is what might be termed the 'twin track' approach. By this is meant the development of distinctive types of policies for the two categories of young offenders. In particular, for the majority of offenders traditional criminal justice approaches are increasingly seen to be inappropriate. Such offenders have steadily been diverted from the criminal justice system at different stages in the process, by means of a range of alternatives from prosecution (such as mediation and reparation strategies) and a variety of alternatives to custody.

More punitive and severe measures are seen as appropriate for that group of serious and persistent offenders. There is a danger that policies for crime prevention and delinquency control are influenced disproportionately by the more serious cases which tend to attract political and public awareness. The number of cases with the same degree of seriousness as the Bulger case, involving the murder of a young child by two children barely at the age of criminal responsibility, is very small. Nevertheless, the case has had a profound impact on debates about how juvenile offenders should be dealt with (King 1995; Levy 1994; Roberts 1993; Asquith 1996). A characteristic feature of responses to such as the Bulger case is that there is a knee jerk reaction both to seek both immediate and short-term responses to offending by children and full-scale reconsideration of the juvenile justice system and other child associated institutions, such as the education system. They also tend to rehearse arguments about the responsibility of young offenders and the need for and acceptability of punishment. As in so many other fields of social policy, the development of long-term preventive strategies is placed lower on the political and public agenda.

Nevertheless, all the indications from recent research do suggest that punishment of young offenders, whatever its political or moral acceptability, is ineffective and that long-term preventive strategies must inevitably address the social and familial context in which children find themselves.

Preventing offending by children and young people: some considerations

The development of preventive strategies is of course not new and a number of preventive models have been developed in relation to offending by children and young people (Graham 1993). For example, '*situational crime prevention*' seeks to reduce offending by 'target hardening'. This involves, extending the range of security and surveillance techniques available to reduce opportunities for offending to take place. It is on such an argument that a whole host of techniques have been employed such as neighbourhood watch schemes; better security devices for cars; increased surveillance of shops and property and the promotion of video surveillance in city centres. One effect of the Bulger case was to increase greatly the demand for the installation of video cameras in public places (McCalpine 1994). One consequence of such measures is, of course, that public places are increasingly being subjected to surveillance and scrutiny.

The criminal justice system itself has adopted a number of preventive strategies based on a variety of philosophies including punishment, deterrence, and rehabilitation. What concerns us most here though are those preventive strategies which direct attention at the social and familial context in which children find themselves and the implications they hold for the development by governments of appropriate policies and practices. No attempt will be made here to define in detail a particular preventive strategy – that is not my purpose. Rather, I intend to consider the kinds of issues which will necessarily have to be addressed for a realistic and effective preventive philosophy to be developed

A number of general themes can be identified:

Marginalisation and alienation of children and young people
The literature illustrates clearly that children and young people are increasingly marginalised and alienated from mainstream society. Such a claim is based not solely on surveys of young people themselves but also on evidence of policy and practice developments in the UK (Montgomery 1995) and elsewhere (Asquith 1995). The changing social, political and economic climate has exposed young people as vulnerable, disenfranchised, exhibiting low self esteem and expressing dissatisfaction with the social and physical environments in which they live. At the time of writing, the trouble in Bradford where there have been riots on the streets largely involving youth has also been attributed by the police and other authorities to the marginalisation and dissatisfaction of our children and young people.

The effects of disadvantage
Increasing numbers of children and their families experience the effects of poverty with all the associated correlates such as poor health, low educational achievement and behavioural problems (Bradshaw 1990). The increasing gap between rich and poor may well exacerbate the difficulties encountered by such families and attempts to control delinquent behaviour which ignore the established facts of disadvantage will inevitably fail.

Importance of parenting role

The importance of the parenting role in assisting children to healthy emotional and physical development cannot be understated. Throughout the literature, the parental contribution was emphasised in terms both of the positive and the negative contribution it can make to growth and development. No assertion is being made here that parents are to blame for behavioural problems such as delinquency. A more social explanation is prevalent in the literature in which the need is identified for help and support to be given to those who find themselves in the parenting role. Where parents are in a situation of disadvantage, the difficulties associated with the parenting role may well be compounded. Similarly, it is also clear that the break-up of families through divorce and separation is not in itself necessarily negative for children. The *quality* of the parenting offered to and experienced by children is the crucial factor.

The need for early intervention

What is clear from a review of the literature is that a strategy of prevention should target the early life experiences of children and in particular, pre-school children. There are undoubted long-term benefits which could derive from such an investment, not just in terms of the reduction of delinquency but in a number of other areas of children's lives (Farrington 1994). Persistent and serious offenders do seem to have experienced particularly problematic childhoods in terms of deprivation and parenting, with poor parenting a crucial factor. The effects of high risk factors however can also be mitigated by a variety of what Loughran (1995) calls 'insulatory factors'. Preventive strategies should focus on the social and environmental context in which offenders find themselves and resources should be diverted from more traditional criminal justice measures and practices.

Ineffectiveness of incarceration and effectiveness of alternatives

Research literature has repeatedly demonstrated the ineffectiveness of both punishment *and* incarceration. In terms of prevention, 'after the event' measures fail completely to tackle the very factors which may cause the behaviour in the first place. As a result, the Penal Affairs Group rejected the idea of American style boot camps for dealing with young offenders (BBC News 28 March 1995). By contrast it is clearly not the case that nothing works, despite the claims associated with what has become known as the Martinson thesis (see Montgomery 1995). A search of the literature and an audit of policies and practices identifies those factors which are associated with successful programmes. For example, successful programmes are associated with:

- cognitive behavioural projects such as social skills training
- aggression reduction techniques

- clarity of focus and objectives in projects
- the combination of a number of measures
- diversion strategies such as mediation and reparation programmes and community based programmes.

As Waller suggested in 1992, '…we know what works. But it usually costs money.'

In general there is increasing acceptance that programmes which divorce the young offender from his or her family, social and community environment with all the support networks he/she may have, will ultimately fail. Conversely, programmes which add resources to the general social environment in which young people find themselves have a greater chance of success, and of long-term success at that. Again, to repeat what has been emphasised above, the allocation of resources and political will can be even more effective at the *early* stages in the lives of children who may be at risk in a number of ways. The message from the literature is clear – the earlier the intervention is in alleviating high risk factors in the lives of children, the greater is the opportunity to influence positively children's growth and development and realisation of their potential.

Policies, programmes and information: fragmentation and deficit

From an audit of policies and practices it is clear that there are a wide range of different measures, initiatives and projects which can have a long-term benefit for the prevention of crime and offending. It is equally clear that comprehensive social strategies are being developed in some areas, as are projects with a direct bearing on the 'early years'. Nevertheless, these are characterised by a lack of a coherent national policy, vary greatly across regions and depend on the contribution of voluntary organisations. Further, the projects themselves may not be evaluated in any systematic way.

It is clear that there is a distinct lack of information in a number of fields relating to children and young people who offend. For example, notwithstanding the work of Anderson *et al.* there is a lack of information on the life experiences of children and in particular in relation to their involvement in and desistence from delinquent activities. The experience of children as victims is also an area which could benefit from further research. Indeed the separation of children and young people into distinct categories of 'offender' and 'victim' may well conceal the commonality of their experience in terms of the social and environmental context.

Developments driven by rights and equal opportunties

Current legislation, including the Children (Scotland) Act, embodies the principles and philosophy of the United Nations Convention on the Rights of the Child. What has been emphasised in the 'rights' literature and in debate has been Article 12 promoting the right of children to have a say in decisions affecting them.

Equally important, though, is the need to recognise that the convention equally emphasises 'provision' rights (Montgomery 1995). These mean that children have a right to be provided with the social, economic and environmental circumstances necessary to promote healthy growth and development. Policies and programmes relating to young people increasingly resort to the statement that problems of alienation and marginalisation are not the result of some deficit in young people themselves but reflect social and economic deficit which must as of right be rectified. The commitment in the criminological literature to recognising the social and environmental influences on youth behaviour is mirrored by the current preoccupation with the promotion of rights for young people. Again, there is a degree of convergence here.

The absence of any substantial body of knowledge about female offending and involvement of members of ethnic minorities in crime is a glaring omission. The development of measures which are gender and ethnically sensitive is accordingly impeded (Asquith 1996).

Juvenile justice: the way forward

The search for new means of dealing with children who commit offences has to be seen not simply as part of the review of measures but more as an element of a search for a new philosophy or paradigm on which justice for children and young people should be based. Current debates throughout Europe, including the UK, suggest that 'justice' in relation to the young offender has to be seen in association with either 'restorative' justice (Walgrave 1996) or social justice. But what is clear is that there is a recognition of the need for a closer articulation of preventive strategies with wider social policy concerns.

As stated above, it does appear to be the case that there is convergence in understanding of the factors which are associated with delinquency and other child and youth related variables such as child abuse, ill health, low educational attainment and so on. In that respect, policies which address themselves to the common risk factors have the potential to affect positively a number of areas of children's lives. If there is to be a shift towards truly preventive strategies based on the need to recognise the social and familial context in which children and young people find themselves, there are a number of implications for those responsible for developing policy.

One is that a shift in political vision has to be made from short-term and supposed immediate gains to one in which long-term investment in the lives of our children is accepted. This is the imperative which derives from the literature on the significance of early intervention in the lives of children and requires a rethink about the way in which resources for crime prevention are to be allocated.

Second, the acknowledgement of the increasing marginalisation and alienation of our children and young people requires that there be an acceptance of policies and programmes which are committed to integration and social inclusion. The French notion of 'insertion' which underpins a number of French strategies both in the crime field and the social field more generally, best illustrates the true potential of integrative or inclusive strategies for young people, implying as it does an approach in which all aspects of young people's lives are taken into consideration in the attempt to integrate them or include them in mainstream social and political life. This involves recognition of their social, employment, health, educational, housing and financial needs amongst other things (see Asquith 1995 for a review of integrative and inclusive strategies in member states of the Council of Europe). Strategies which fail to acknowledge the young person's social environment will inevitably fail and will reinforce alienation, marginalisation and exclusion.

Third, this chapter has highlighted in many ways the positive long-term potential of early intervention in the lives of young children. There is clear and unequivocal evidence not only that early preventive strategies can reduce delinquent behaviour but that they can also inhibit those general risk factors which anticipate other behavioural problems experienced by children and young persons as they mature. The reduction of delinquency and criminal activity has to be seen in relationship to a general concern for the mental and physical health of our children as a means of promoting, in the long term, the mental and physical health of the community.

Fourth, any search for alternative means for dealing with crime by children and young people must be based on a commitment to a rights based approach. This will not only involve offering young people greater opportunities to have a voice in social and political life (though that is in itself important) but will also promote the acceptance of alterations in the social and political environment in which they live 'as of right'. Commitment to the realisation of rights as conceived in the UN Convention on the Rights of the Child which the UK ratified in 1991 will foster a commitment to social change in the interest of promoting enhanced life opportunities for children and young people. The potential of the UN Convention in promoting radical change in the life experiences of children and adults who relate to them should not be underestimated.

Fifth, the search for alternative means of preventing crime by children and young people should be based not simply on the results of research into particular strategies but on a coherent philosophy. All too often changes in juvenile and criminal justice are piecemeal, incremental and lacking in integrity and coherence. The search for alternatives should benefit from current debates in Europe on the nature of juvenile justice and in particular should be based on a clear statement of aims and objectives. The articulation of a clear basis for change in approaches to preventing crime by children is important in the presentation of a coherent and integrated system.

No claim is being made here that preventive strategies based on a recognition of the social and familial contexts of children and young people's lives is the only means of preventing delinquent and criminal behaviour. Rather, policies and strategies which ignore the contribution of social and familial factors will not in and of themselves substantially reduce offending behaviour.

References

Anderson, S., Kinsey, R. and Smith, C. (1990) *Cautionary Tales: A Study of Young People and Crime in Edinburgh.* Centre for Criminology, University of Edinburgh.

Asquith, S. (1995) *Survey Analysis of Provisions for Young Offenders in member states of the Council of Europe.* Council of Europe.

Asquith, S. (1996) Children who kill children. *Childhood 3,* 1, 99–116.

Asquith, S., Buist, M., Loughran, N., Montgomery, M. and McCauley, C. (1995) *Children, Young People and Offending in Scotland.* Report to the Criminal Justice Research Unit, The Scottish Office.

Bradshaw, J. (1990) *Child Poverty and Deprivation in the UK.* London: National Children's Bureau.

Cappelaere, G. (1994) *Children's rights and Juvenile Justice – Riyadh Guidelines.* University of Ghent.

Cohen, N. (1995) What causes crime? *Independent on Sunday.* 4 June.

Farrington, D. (1994) Early developmental prevention of juvenile delinquency. *RSA Journal,* 22–34.

Garbarino, J. and K. Kostelny (1996) Children and violence: trauma in the American war zone. In S. Asquith (ed) *Children and Young People in Conflict with the Law.* London: Jessica Kingsley Publishers.

Graham, J. (1993) Crime prevention policies in Europe. *European Journal of Crime, Criminal Law and Criminal Justice 1,* 2, 126–142.

Graham, J. (1996) The organisation and functioning of juvenile justice in England and Wales. In S. Asquith (ed) *Children and Young People in Conflict with the Law.* London: Jessica Kingsley Publishers.

Junger-Tas, J. (1994) *Delinquent Behaviour Among Young People in the Western World.* Ministry of Justice.

King, M. (1995) The James Bulger murder trial: moral dilemmas and social solutions. *International Journal of Children's Rights 3,* 2.

Kirkbride, J. (1995) Flogging Bill falls in the first round. *The Daily Telegraph.* 8 June.

Kyvsgaard, B. (1991) The decline in child and youth criminality: possible explanations of an International trend. In A. Snare (ed) *Youth Crime and Justice.* Oslo: Norwegian University Press.

Kilbradon Report (1964) *Report of the Committee on Children and Young Persons* (Scotland). HMSO.

Levy, A. (1994) The end of childhood. *Guardian,* 29 November.

Levy, A. (1995) *Scotsman,* 12 June.

Loughran, N. (1995) A review of the research literature. In Asquith *et al.* op cit.

McCalpine, J. (1994) Caught on video nasty. *Scotsman,* 2 November.

Mills, H. (1995) Police Chiefs call for new policies on crime. *Independent on Sunday,* 15 May.

Montgomery, M. (1995) An audit of policies and practices. In Asquith *et al.* op cit.

Naysmith, S. (1995) Do genes predispose people to crime? *Scottish Child,* June/July.

Qvortrup, J. (1994) Childhood matters: an introduction. In J. Qvortrup, M. Bardy, G. Sagritta and H. Wintersberger (eds) *Childhood Matters.* Aldershot: Avebury.

Roberts, Y. (1993) Teaching children to be bad. *New Society and Statesman,* 3 December.

Rutter, M. and Smith, D. (1995) *Psychosocial Disorders in Young People.* Chichester: Wiley.

Utting, D., Bright, J. and Henricson, C. (1993) *Crime and the Family: Improving Child Rearing and Preventing Delinquency.* London: Family Policy Studies Centre.

Walgrave, L. (1996) Restorative justice: a way to restore justice in Western European systems. In S. Asquith (ed) *Children and Young People in Conflict with the Law.* London: Jessica Kingsley Publishers.

Waller, I. (1991) An international perspective with special reference to Canada. Paper presented at International Seminar on Crime and Social Policy. NACRO.

CHAPTER 6

Children's and Young People's Participation in Decision-Making
The Legal Framework in Social Services and Education

Ruth Sinclair

Introduction

The past decade has seen major changes to the legal framework relating to children and young people in England and Wales. The two most important public services to children – social services and education – have both been the subject of substantial and far reaching new statutory regulation, the most important being the Education Reform Act 1988, the Education Act 1993 and the Children Act 1989. Relating specifically to children's participation in decision-making, the landmark decision in the Gillick Judgement in 1985 established that parents have diminishing rights to make decisions on behalf of their children as they mature. Most significant in establishing the principles governing the way in which children in our society are treated, is the United Nations Convention on the Rights of the Child, adopted by the UN in 1989 and ratified by the United Kingdom government in 1991.

Yet this package of legal changes does not all carry the same message. At a time when the principle of consulting children has gained broad acceptance, it is within the legislative framework governing the provision of education that the rights of the child are most conspicuous by their absence.

In this chapter we shall examine the current legal frameworks for involving children in decisions that affect them, contrasting in particular the position of children within the education system with that pertaining in other situations. Before that, it is worth restating briefly the benefits to be gained from the participation by children and young people in making decisions.

Children's and young people's participation in decision-making

Participation by young people can be supported for reasons of principle and reasons of practice. First and foremost the participation by children in matters which affect them is a recognition that children are individuals who have opinions and views of their own, which cannot be represented, necessarily, by parents or professionals. The issue is simply the basic right of the individual to be consulted in decisions that affect them. In relation to children this means that adults decide with rather than for children, increasing the child's right to self-determination as he or she progresses towards adulthood.

Second, participation by children leads to better decision-making. Research into the decision-making processes of social workers suggests that when children and young people are involved decisions are more likely to be based on accurate and complete information, are more likely to be implemented and are more likely to have beneficial outcomes (Thoburn 1992; Hodgson 1996).

Third, a failure to listen to children can have damaging consequences. This was illustrated most painfully in Cleveland in 1987. The inquiry into the unprecedented rise in the diagnosis of sexual abuse concluded: 'There is a danger that in looking to the welfare of the children believed to be the victims of sexual abuse the children themselves may be overlooked. The child is a person and not an object of concern.' (Butler-Sloss 1988). A failure to listen to children was also an important element in the abuse by staff in residential care and boarding-school settings, abuse which continued over many years and involved a great number of children (see Berridge and Brodie, this volume). Inquiries into these scandals noted in particular the lack of any complaints procedure which could have enabled children to seek help (Staffordshire CC 1991; Leicestershire CC 1992; Bramen, Jones and March 1992). These reports demonstrate clearly that the right of children to participate is closely linked to their rights to protection, an issue which is fully addressed in the report of a working group convened by the Gulbenkian Foundation, *One Scandal Too Many* (Caloustre Gulbenkian Foundation 1993).

Fourth, involving children in decision-making enhances their sense of responsibility. Inherent in the transition from childhood to adulthood is the giving and taking of greater levels of responsibility. The more children and young people are encouraged to participate in decisions, the more prepared they will be to exercise their growing responsibility appropriately. This is true whether we are talking about the child as an individual or as a member of a group

Participation is a broad concept. It embraces more than the rights of the individual child to be consulted in matters which affect him or her personally. It is also about collective participation – about developing a sense of involvement in a community, whether that is within the locality, or a Children's Home or a school (Henderson 1995). The benefits from such an approach are well illustrated in a recent publication which reviews all forms of group living for children (Kahan 1994). This contains many examples of the ways in which young people have responded positively to being involved in the running of their living unit:

> Participation of children and young people is fundamental not only to the openness in the daily life of the establishment, but also to their acceptance of the necessary structure and 'rules of the house'. When they are involved...they will have an investment in good standards for behaviour, for the environment and the development of 'their home'. This can also be a very effective way of ensuring that the establishment is child-centred and not, as sometimes happens, run for the convenience of the organisation or the staff. (Kahan 1994)

Whichever concept of children's participation in decision-making is employed, it is very important to distinguish between consulting with children and abdicating to them the sole right (and with it, the responsibility) to make decisions. Many of those who oppose or feel uneasy about consulting children do so on the grounds that children should not be allowed to have their own way. Such a view is a misrepresentation, possibly a mischievous misrepresentation, of both the Children Act 1989 and the UN Convention on the Rights of the Child. Giving children and young people the right to express an opinion and to have their views taken into account is not the same as giving them the final say when important decisions are made, especially when those decisions affect others. Judgements will still need to be reached but these should be based upon an accurate reflection of the child's wishes and feelings about the matter.

In this section we have demonstrated that the rationale for children's participation is much broader than that presented by the single perspective of children's rights. However that perspective is the foundation for understanding the position of children in our society today. Any discussion of the current legal frameworks for encouraging children's participation is best seen within the principles laid down by UN Convention on the Rights of the Child.

UN Convention on the Rights of the Child

The Convention was adopted by the United Nations in November 1989 and ratified by the UK Government in December 1991, albeit with minimum publicity. Although the Convention does not carry the same legal weight as national legislation, it is binding on those States which ratify it. The Convention contains 41 substantive Articles covering three main sets of rights: the child's right to protection from abuse and exploitation; the right to the provision of services; and the child's right to participate in decision-making (Newell 1993).

In this way the Convention recognises that children should be accorded equal value as adults, but because of their age they are vulnerable and in need of protection. However this protection has to be balanced with giving children increased independence and enabling them to take on greater responsibility as they mature. This responsibility is best developed by giving the child increasing opportunities to participate in matters which affect them and by recognising the rights of children as active and emergent citizens (Asquith and Hill 1994).

It is the third category, the rights of the child to participate, which is the particular focus of this chapter. Here we shall highlight just one – Article 12. First a cautionary note. While focusing on this one Article it is important to see the Convention as an indivisible whole: all of the rights contained therein are interdependent, each building upon the other and none taking precedence over another. So in emphasising the child's right to participate we must also remember, for instance, the right to privacy (Article 16) and the right to freedom from exploitation (Article 36).

Article 12

1. States Parties shall assure to the child who is capable of forming his or her own views the right to express those views freely in all matters affecting the child, the views of the child being given due weight in accordance with the age and maturity of the child.

2. For this purpose, the child shall in particular be provided the opportunity to be heard in any judicial and administrative proceedings affecting the child, either directly, or through a representative or an appropriate body, in a manner consistent with the procedural rules of national law.' UN Convention on the Rights of the Child (1989)

It can be seen that Article 12 clearly establishes that children, as individuals in their own right, have views and opinions that must be taken seriously; that we cannot assume that others (parents or professionals) can present the views of children, even if they believe that they are acting in 'the child's best interest'. The Article goes on to specify that the views of the child should be heard in any administrative or judicial proceedings which affect them.

So how do the actions of the UK Government measure up to their commitment to act in accordance with the Convention? The Convention requires that two years after ratification each State should report to the UN Committee on the Rights of the Child, detailing their achievements in implementing the Convention (Article 44). Within the UK the Department of Health has been given lead responsibility for ensuring progress towards implementation of the Convention and the report was duly submitted to the UN Committee early in 1994. An independent critique of the application of the Convention to law, policy and practice in Britain was prepared by the Children's Rights Development Unit (CRDU 1994).

After due consideration of the submissions from States Parties, the Committee can issue a Report setting out their observations on the State's achievements, including recommendations for changes. Such a Report relating to the UK was issued in January 1995 (UN 1995). This pointed to the Children Act 1989 as one of the positive achievements of the Government, but it was critical of education legislation in its failure to reflect the principle of the 'child's best interests' and the right of children to be consulted on decisions which affect them. We explore the basis of the Committee's conclusions by looking in more detail at the legislation in these two areas, starting with the Children Act.

The Children Act 1989

The Children Act 1989, which was implemented in England and Wales in 1991, goes much further than any previous legislation in giving to children and young people the right to be involved in decisions which affect them, most notably in relation to Family Court proceedings and involvement with social services departments. The Act places a clear and specific statutory duty on social services departments and the Courts to ascertain the wishes and feeling of the child and to take these into account when making decisions.

Children's rights are enhanced in other ways. Social services departments are required to establish and make known a complaints procedure that is accessible to children and which includes independent representatives. All children who are party to public (but not private) law proceedings can have access to their own legal representation and the services of a guardian ad litem, recognising that children have views which are separate from those of other parties to the case. For the first time children have been given qualified rights to refuse to submit to medical or psychiatric assessment or examination. The criterion for exercising this right is that of 'Gillick competence', namely that the child is judged to have 'sufficient understanding'. The importance of this right is the control that it gives to children, placing the onus on professionals to ensure that the value of any assessment or examination is clearly understood and articulated.

Also for the first time children have been given limited rights to initiate proceedings in the Family Proceeding Court. Children 'of sufficient understanding' can seek leave from the Court to apply for a Section 8 Residence or Contact Order – that is, an Order which determines where the child shall live or with whom they shall have contact. It is this section of the Act that has been so misrepresented in the mass media as children being able to 'divorce' their parents, with veiled suggestions that children will be able to blackmail their parents in order to have their own way. In reality this part of the Act only offers limited, if important rights to the child. The child has first to ask if the Court will be prepared to hear his or her case. Before any such request is granted, the Judge will take due consideration of the child's 'age and understanding' and whether, in his or her judgement, the circumstances of the case merit a hearing. Such requests are unlikely to be granted for frivolous reasons. Nor do these Orders take away parents' parental responsibility towards their children.

As well as the actual statutory duties set out in the Act, the total Children Act package comes with several sets of Regulations (such as Children's Homes Regulations 1991) and nine Volumes of Guidance. Although the Guidance does not carry the same legal force as the Statute or the Regulations, they are issued under Section 7 of the 1970 Local Government Social Services Act so that local authorities are required to seek to achieve these standards. It is often in the detail of the Guidance that the principle of the participation by children and young people is most fully articulated. For instance, in expanding on the Children's Homes Regulation 7(2)(b) on maintaining a home in good order, the Guidance says 'Children resident in the home should have a say in the decor and upkeep of the home if they wish to, and particularly in the decoration and personalisation of their own rooms' (Vol 4, para. 1.73). Enabling children to participate in the everyday decisions, as well as at the significant moments in their lives, all builds towards a developing sense of responsibility and membership of the community. This is made very clear in the section in the Guidance which deals with maintaining Good Order and Discipline.

> It is essential that children should be consulted and their wishes and feelings ascertained in matters concerning them. Good order is much more likely to be achieved in homes where children are routinely involved in decision making about their care. They should be encouraged to accept responsibility for their own care, appropriate to their age and understanding. (Children Act Guidance Vol. 4, para. 1.88)

When given the opportunity to express their views, it is clear that young people share these aspirations. A recent study which reported interviews with over 60 young people in residential care shows how realistic young people are when asked for suggestions about the services they receive. Moreover this report highlighted again the relationship between the participation of young people in running the home and their levels of self-esteem (Willow 1995).

The Children Act therefore presents clear statutory requirements on which have been built Guidance about involving children and giving them a voice. Such legislative requirements are only the first step; what matters is the way in which these are put into practice. There is now evidence that young people are routinely invited to attend planning or review meetings where decisions are made about their future (Sinclair and Grimshaw 1995). This is also a growing practice in child protection case conferences (Lewis 1992; Corby, Millar and Young 1992). Review meetings may not always be appropriate for younger children and their views will have to be ascertained in other ways. There are also real questions about how comfortable even older children find these occasions, and whether the bureaucratic nature of many current reviews is conducive to genuine participation by the child (Freeman et al., Chapter 16 of this volume; Fletcher 1993; Sinclair, Garnett and Berridge 1995; Triseliotis *et al.* 1995).

While the day to day practice of involving children may well need further developments in social work practice, the Children Act has brought forth a genuine commitment on the part of social services departments to the philosophy of working in partnership with young people. How does this compare to the current climate within education?

Education legislation

Undoubtedly there are individual schools and members of staff who would welcome the opportunity to involve children, both in decisions which effect them as individuals and in the broader running of the school. Indeed many schools have developed such child-centred approaches; however this is not supported by the statutory framework in which schools operate (Hodgkin 1995). This past decade has seen enormous changes in schools in England and Wales; in the way in which they are governed, in the way in which pupils are allocated places, in funding and financial management, in the assessment of standards and not least in the curriculum that is taught. Not all these changes have been once and for all. Many, as with the National Curriculum, have been subject to further changes and revision as earlier flaws have become exposed. Despite the opportunities presented by these legislative changes, no attempt has been made to include reference to the participation by pupils within these new statutory frameworks. Indeed the 1988 Education Reform Act abolished the previous right of pupils to be appointed as school governors.

This is not to say that the education service has been immune to the Government's pledge, under its Citizen's Charter initiative, to enhance the voice of the consumer of public services. However the Government is clear that the consumers of the education services are not children, but their parents: hence the guarantee of standards of education services is the Parent's Charter.

Given the heightened profile of the principle of involving children with the passage of the Children Act and the ratification of the UN Convention, it is somewhat surprising that similar principles were not adopted in the enactment of the Education Act 1993. From the debates in Parliament during the passage of the Bill, it appears that this was not due to oversight, but rather a perception by government ministers that children should be the passive recipients of education, rather than involved members of a school community. When questioned in the House of Commons why the Education Bill did not contain similar rights on children's participation as were present in the Children Act, the minister responded:

> The answer is that the (Children) Act ranges much more widely on welfare issues, inter-personal relations and the child's existence in a social environment, whereas the Bill deals with more strictly

educational matters. It is at least arguable that there is a difference between taking full account of a young person's attitudes and responses in a social and welfare context and asking the child to make a judgement, utter an opinion or give a view on his or her educational requirements. (Hansard 1993a)

Neither did the Government see any necessity to ensure that the obligations of the UN Convention were replicated within this education legislation:

My advice is that there is no conflict between the Bill and the UN Convention. Article 12 of the Convention states that the child shall in particular be given the opportunity to be heard in any judicial and administrative proceedings affecting the child. We believe that the Children Act should cater for that. Therefore I believe that my noble friend's amendment is unnecessary to bring us into the ambit of Article 12. (Speech by Lord Henley, Hansard 1993b)

This narrow interpretation of children's participation was apparent in the Education Department's deliberations prior to ratification of the Convention, when a minister confirmed that the education clauses were already being met (DES 1992). But here the minister was referring solely to that part of the Convention which deals with the child's right to the provision of education (Article 28). No consideration was given to the child's right to be consulted, in 'all matters affecting the child' and in any 'administrative proceedings', as guaranteed by Article 12. A similar very limited perspective of the relevance of the Convention to education was apparent in the First Report of the UK Government to the Committee on the Rights of the Child (Department of Health 1994).

How does this lack of statutory support for children's participation in decisions about their education manifest itself in practice? We look first at the involvement of individual pupils in decisions which affect them and then look at the involvement of young people as members of their school community.

Excluding the voice of the child and young person at school
The quotation above from Lord Henley would seem to imply that there are no important administrative procedures relating to the child at school. This is clearly not the case. The procedures involved in allocating a child a school place and in the exclusion of a child from school are examples of key decisions which have a major impact upon the child. Given the rapid increase in exclusions in recent years, from both secondary and primary schools, it is especially important that these decision-making processes involve children and young people (for a summary of trends in exclusions from school see Brodie 1995). Yet the new statutory arrangements governing these procedures do not give children the right to express their views. The right to consultation about such decisions lies with parents (DFE 1994c). Surely the decision to exclude a child from school

is a clear example of the sort of situation that can benefit from involving those most directly affected by the decision? As we saw above this is likely to lead to a better informed decision; greater efforts in achieving a workable solution; and a greater likelihood of commitment to a better outcome.

A more recent example of the failure of education ministers to ensure that children have the opportunity to express their opinion concerns the statutory regulations on the provision of sex education. The changes created by the Education Act 1993 in the legal position on sex education in schools were further elaborated in DFE Circular 5/94 (DFE 1994b). Biological aspects of sex education are now included within the National Curriculum at all key stages and are therefore compulsory in maintained secondary schools. However, an Order under section 241(4) of the 1993 Act prohibits the teaching, as part of the National Curriculum in science, 'of any material on AIDS, HIV, and any other sexually transmitted diseases, or any aspect, other than biological aspects, of human sexual behaviour'. Also under this section of the Act parents have the right to withdraw their children from any part of the school's programme of sex education that is not required by the National Curriculum. There is no requirement to ask children or young people what their views might be; nor is there any requirement for the parents to give any explanation for their decision or to seek any alternative instruction for their children. Moreover, this Order allows parents to remove any of their children from such classes, whatever their age, including those over 16.

One would hope that parents would only take a decision which so directly affects their child after they had taken full account of the child's opinion. However it was in recognition of the possible divergence of views between parents and their children that the Gillick Judgement confirmed that as children mature they have increasing rights to self-determination in matters such as this. 'The parental right yields to the child's right to make his own decisions when he reaches a sufficient understanding and intelligence to be capable of making up his own mind' (Lord Scarman 1986).

It is to be regretted that this principle was not followed when framing this Order on sex education.

A further source of difference between the Children Act and the Education Acts is the omission from the later of a statutory right for children to 'make representations' or to make a complaint regarding any aspect of the education service. There is little evidence that the complaints procedures in social services departments are abused through inappropriate or malicious complaints (VCC 1994). There may be some concerns about the best way to achieve an appropriate balance, ensuring there is independent representation without creating mechanisms which are over-elaborate and formal, and which can drown out the voice of the child; however these have not dented the commitment by social services departments to enable children to make a complaint that is treated seriously.

Membership of the school community

As well as the missed opportunities to ensure that children have the statutory right to express their views in the specific situations set out above, there are more general ways in which participation by children in their school is important. Just as we noted earlier the importance of giving residents in children's homes the opportunity to be involved in the minor as well as the major decisions in their lives, so too a school is likely to be a more ordered community when children feel they are active participants whose views are taken seriously.

This point was forcefully made by Lord Elton in his report on discipline in schools. 'Head teachers and teachers should encourage the active participation of pupils in shaping and reviewing the school's behaviour policy...to foster a sense of collective commitment to it' (Elton Report 1989). One way of encouraging participation in the development of such policies is through a School Council. Lord Elton also saw the value of such bodies but warned that to be effective they needed to be more than a token gesture:

> Our impression is that where they (School Councils) exist that pupils are likely to make responsibly use of them... Setting up a Council that works, involves a commitment by staff to listen to what pupils are saying and to take their views seriously. We believe that commitment is worth making. (Elton Report pp.143–144)

The recent pack of six Circulars relating to 'Pupils with Problems' contains Guidance from the Department for Education on Pupil Behaviour and Discipline (DFE 1994c). In the opening paragraph of this Guidance there is acknowledgement of recognised good practice in maintaining discipline – 'It builds on the Elton Report'. Although the Circular does contain some very limited reference to pupils' involvement in discussing 'whole-school behaviour policies' as recommended by Elton, this appears rather peripheral and somewhat tentative. 'Schools can also nurture a greater sense of responsibility in pupils, and greater commitment to the aims of the school, by encouraging them to discuss the aims and rules of the school' (para. 21).

Neither does the reference to Schools Councils in the next paragraph appear particularly encouraging. The Circular concludes with an Annexe which sets out 14 possible phases in the development of whole-school behaviour policies; nowhere in this is participation by pupils mentioned. Of course good schools will involve their pupils, but it would have encouraged others to do so, if this had been either a statutory requirement or a more central theme in the Circular.

Positive guidance on listening to the child and young person in school

The approach of central government to young people's participation in the educational sphere is not all negative. Indeed the lack of reference to involving pupils in the Circular on Behaviour and Discipline is in contrast to the positive guidance in the Circular on Pupils with Emotional and Behaviour Difficulties. One can only speculate why this might be so. Could it relate to perceived characteristics of the pupils and the nature of their 'problems'; or is it because implementation of this later Circular requires an interdisciplinary approach, one which includes working with colleagues in social services who may wish to apply Children Act principles of partnership and participation by children and young people.

This disparity between the participative philosophy promoted by the Children Act and neglected in education legislation is exemplified in the case of Education Supervision Orders (ESO). ESO were introduced in the Children Act to offer support and supervision to young people who were failing to attend school. Before making an ESO under the Children Act the Court is required to ascertain the wishes and feelings of the child – yet no such consultation is required in making the decision to exclude a child from school a procedure governed by education legislation.

Another area of educational provision which requires a multi-disciplinary approach is the assessment of Special Education Needs (SEN). Here also the new framework promotes participation by the child or young person in a positive way. The 1993 Education Act required the Secretary of State to issue Regulations together with a Code of Practice on the Identification and Assessment of Special Educational Needs. These were passed in April 1994 and implemented in Autumn of that year. While the Regulations do not lay down any statutory duty to consult with the child during assessment, this is contained within the Code of Practice. As with Children Act Guidance, the Code of Practice is regarded as the standard which the LEA and the school should reach; any failure to do could be challenged in the Courts.

Although most of the Code is directed to the role of the parents, the rationale for involving the child is clearly spelt out in the Code, as can be seen in the following extract:

- *practical* – children have important and relevent questions. Their support is crucial to the effective implementation of any individual education programme

- *principle* – children have a right to be heard. They should be encouraged to participate in decision-making about provision to meet their specila education needs.

(Department for Education 1994a, para. 2.35).

The Code recognises that positive pupil involvement may take time and offers suggestions for achieving this. At this stage it is still too early to have any evidence of how the Code is operating in practice and whether young people do feel they are an active part of the process. However the experience of Children Act suggests that clear enabling guidance does bring about changes in attitude that have positive effects on practice.

Conclusion

The theme of this chapter has been the current statutory framework in England and Wales for enhancing the participation by children in the services that they receive. In this we have contrasted the very different attitudes emanating from the Department of Health and that of the Department for Education, which have resulted in much more limited statutory rights for children in schools to be consulted on matters which affect them than is the case for children in relation to family court proceedings or as users of social services.

A statutory framework does not, in itself, ensure good practice in effective consultation with young people. Indeed the use of a legislative framework as a mechanism for changing practice is unlikely to work without a complimentary strategy of professional development. Nor does the lack of a statutory right mean that children may not be involved and in many schools this will certainly be the case. A statutory right may be little more than a formality in situations where there is already a belief that working in partnership with children is both more respectful and more effective. Where that is not the case, the protection offered by legislation is necessary; it sets the minimum standards that are acceptable and acts as a spur to the development of good practice.

References

Asquith, S. and Hill, M. (eds) (1994) *Justice for Children*. Dordrecht: Martinus Nijhoff Publishers.

Braman, C., Jones, J. and March, J. (1992) *Castle Hill Report Practice Guide*. Shropshire County Council.

Brodie, I. (1995) Exclusions from School. *Highlight* No.136. London: National Children's Bureau.

Butler-Sloss (1988) *Report of the Inquiry into Child Abuse in Cleveland 1987*. CMD 412, London: HMSO.

Calouste Gulbenkian Foundation (1993) *One Scandal Too Many*. London: Calouste Gulbenkian Foundation.

Children's Rights Development Unit (1994) *UK Agenda for Children*. London: CRDU.

Corby, B. Millar, M. and Young L. (1994) Power play. *Community Care 1039*, 24.

Department for Education and Science (1992) Press Realease, March 1992.

Department for Education (1994a) *Code of Practice on the Identification and Assessment of Special Educational Needs*. London: DFE.

Department for Education (1994b) *The Education Act 1993: Sex Education in Schools*, Circular, May 1994.

Department for Education (1994c) *Pupils with Problems*. Circulars, 8/94 to 13/94. London: DFE.

Department of Health (1994) *First Report of the UK Government to the Committee on the Rights of the Child.* London: DoH.

Elton, Lord (1989) *Discipline in Schools: Reports of the Committee Enquiry.* London: HMSO.

Fletcher, B. (1993) *Not Just a Name.* London: Who Cares?/National Consumer Council.

Gillick v West Norfolk and Wisbech Area Health Authority and another High Court (1984) 1 All ER 365; Court of Appeal (1985) 1 All ER 533; House of Lords, *The Times*, October 18 1985.

Hansard (1993a) House of Commons, 26 January 1993, Col. 1108

Hansard (1993b) House of Lords, 20 April 1993, Col. 1547

Henderson, P. (ed) (1995) *Children and Communities.* London: Pluto Press.

Hodgkin, R. (1995) Schools and community. In P. Henderson (ed) *Children and Communities.* London: Pluto Press.

Hodgson, D. (1996) *Young people's participation in Social Work Planning: A Resource Pack.* London: National Children's Bureau (forthcoming).

Kahan, B. (1994) *Growing up in Groups.* London: NISW.

Leicestershire CC (1992) The Leicestershire Inquiry, Andrew Kirkwood QC: The report of an inquiry into aspects of the management of children's homes in Leicestershire between 1973 and 1986. Leicester: Leicestershire County Council.

Lewis, A. (1992) An overview of research in child protection work. In J. Thoburn (ed) *Participation in Practice.* Norwich: UEA.

Newell, P. (1993) *The UN Convention and Children's Rights in the UK.* National Children's Bureau, London.

Sinclair, R. Garnett, L. and Berridge, D. (1995) *Social Work and Assessment with Adolescents.* London: National Children's Bureau.

Sinclair, R. and Grimshaw, R. (1995) *Planning and Reviewing under the Children Act: Shaping a Framework for Practice.* London: National Children's Bureau.

Staffordshire CC (1991) Levy, A. and Kahan, B. *The Pindown Experience and the Protection of Children.* Stafford: Staffordshire County Council.

Thoburn, J (1992) *Participation in Practice – Involving Families in Child Protection.* Norwich: University of East Anglia.

Triseliotis, J. Borland, M. Hill, M. and Lambert, M. (1995) *Teenagers and the Social Work Services.* London: HMSO.

United Nations Committee on the Rights of the Child (1995) *Concluding O-bservations of the Committee on the Rights of the Child: United Kingdom of Great Britain and Northern Ireland.*

Voice for the Child in Care (1994) *An Evaluation of the Independent Person Service in London.* London: Voice for the Child in Care.

Willow, C. (1995) *A Word in Edgeways.* London: National Children's Bureau.

PART 2

Child Protection

CHAPTER 7

The Legal and Social Construction of Significant Harm

Pauline Hardiker

Background

Significant harm is a major site in the 1989 Children Act where the boundaries between state intervention and family life are redrawn. Some of the reasons why these boundaries were seen to be in need of redrawing include (Adcock *et al.* 1991):

- the findings of the 1984 Short Report which recommended codification and amendment of child care law (House of Commons 1984)

- Child Death Inquiries, e.g. Beckford (London Borough of Brent 1985), Carlile (London Borough of Greenwich 1987), Henry (London Borough of Lambeth 1987)

- the Cleveland Report (1988)

- research findings which concluded that the needs of children in care were not being met, and that a rescue approach predominated over a preventive one (Department of Health and Social Security 1985a).

Masson (1994) argues that:

> the proper balance between the family and the state, which ensures that children are adequately protected but that the family is free from unwarranted intervention, is the ultimate goal of child protection legislation. Achieving such a balance depends on recognising the value of families to children, establishing procedures which involve families in decisions about children, and setting appropriate standards for intervention. The Children Act 1989 sought to create such a system. (p.170)

The Act aimed to do this through three mechanisms:

1. Imposing duties on local authorities to promote the upbringing of children by their families.

2. Establishing the principle of partnership between families and local authorities.

3. Setting a clear, single standard for compulsory measures of care, i.e. the significant harm test.

The context in which the balance between judicial and welfare criteria is altered was clearly expounded in the Review of Child Care Law (Department of Health and Social Security 1985b). Though the new Act identified the child's welfare as a paramount consideration, the circumstances in which this was to be taken into account were to be strictly circumscribed in public law. The Review considered whether '...a simple welfare or 'best interests' test should be now adopted where the state, in the shape of the local authority, is in conflict with parents' (p.6).

> 2.13. We are firmly of the opinion that it should not and that in cases where compulsory committal to local authority care is an issue the present balance between the welfare of the child and the claims of his parents should be maintained. Taken to its logical conclusion, a simple 'best interests' test would permit the state to intervene whenever it could show that the alternative arrangements proposed would serve the child's welfare better than those proposed by their parents. But 'the child is not the child of the state' and it is important in a free society to maintain the rich diversity of lifestyles which is secured by permitting families a large measure of autonomy in the way in which they bring up their children. (p. 6)

The Review argued that broad criteria provide insufficient protection against unwarranted interventions where parents are 'good enough' and they provide insufficient guidance to bound the discretion of courts and practitioners.

The threshold criteria for establishing significant harm were an important lever by which state intervention in family life was to be circumscribed. The next section explores the meaning of the term significant harm and the processes by which it is established.

Significant harm

Significant harm is a new term which first appeared in the Review of Child Care Law (Department of Health and Social Security 1985b, pp.102–103). Its origins, though, reflect categories in the 1969 Children and Young Persons Act S1 (2) (a) (b) (bb), (Department of Health 1986). The argument in the Review (p.103, 15.12), was that

> (In) our view the primary justification for the state to initiate proceedings seeking compulsory powers is actual or likely harm to the child (15.13).

> The present description of harm in Section 1 (2) (a)…identifies several different types: neglect or impairment of health, neglect or prevention of 'proper development', and ill-treatment.

These terms specify that 'harm' consists of a substantial deficit in or detriment to the standard of health, development and well-being which can reasonably be expected for the particular child. The standard is not to be the best that could possibly be achieved, because this would open up those floodgates identified above. This definition of harm was considered to provide sufficient protection for families, '…indicating the degree to which they must have fallen short of acceptable standards, while covering the same circumstances as are at present covered in the harm-based grounds' (15.19, p.104).

Significant harm is a civil concept which was first used in relatively lay terms in the Review of Child Care Law Interim Discussion Papers (Kleinig 1978; Department of Health and Social Security 1986). The concept was the subject of legal debate in the House of Lords Committee proceedings on the Children Bill (Hansard 1989). For example, it was contended that the word 'significant' is redundant because all harm is significant to a greater or lesser extent. There were concerns that the phrase 'significant harm' would become vulnerable to considerable litigation and, hence, delay in proceedings.

The concept appears to have taken on a life of its own as the legislation has been implemented. As it is a legal cornerstone of the legislation, it is important to understand the ways in which it is put into operation by lawyers and social workers. The next sections, therefore, illustrate 'significant harm' in practice.

Stages in establishing significant harm

The only means by which compulsory measures of care can be imposed is through care proceedings (S.31). There are three stages in the process:

1. Stage I (S31 (2) (a))
   The court is satisfied that the child concerned is suffering, or is likely to suffer, significant harm.

   - Harm means ill-treatment (physical, sexual, emotional, social, other) or the impairment of health and development (physical, intellectual, emotional, social or behavioural development; physical or mental health).
   - Significance turns on what health or development can be reasonably expected for this child in comparison with a similar child.

2. Stage II (S31 (2) (b)): source of harm
   The court is satisfied that the harm or likelihood of harm is attributable to the care given to the child not being what it would be reasonable to expect a parent to give to him, or the child's being beyond parental control.

   Once an acceptable standard of upbringing for the child has been decided, substantial deficit in that standard should be shown; minor shortcomings or deficits should not trigger the possibility of compulsory interventions unless they may have serious and lasting effects on the child.

3. Stage III (S31 (11)): care or supervision orders
   There is a presumption against intervention, since the benefits of making an order have to be set against those of making none (Hogget 1989). This decision is to be aided by applying the welfare checklist, but only after the thresholds at Stages I and II have been established. The welfare checklist criteria include:

   • the wishes and feelings of the child
   • the child's physical, emotional and educational needs
   • the likely effect on the child of any change in circumstances
   • the age, sex and background of the child
   • the harm suffered or at risk of suffering
   • the capability of parents or others of meeting the child's needs
   • the range of powers available.

Therefore, it has to be determined that an order will meet the child's welfare and that the gain is sufficient to justify compulsory intervention.

Legal constructions of significant harm

A selective review of some legal judgements relating to significant harm is now undertaken. When the Children Act came on the Statute Books, several commentators anticipated that care proceedings would be the subject of considerable judicial interpretation (Masson 1990). Freeman (1990) said: 'each of these elements (i.e. the minimum threshold criteria for a care order) will require considerable judicial exegesis. Almost every word will require interpretation and analysis' (p.135).

What is significant harm?

Significant means substantial, considerable or noteworthy. Freeman (1990) argued that significant is a lesser standard than serious or severe. This is one aspect of legal interpretations which aver that the seriousness of, say, injury to the child (ill-treatment) should not determine the outcome of care proceedings. For example, White (1994) reported that in one case a care order was not made because the more serious allegations could not be substantiated; the logic underlying this was that the more serious the allegation, the more convincing was the evidence needed to balance it (p.329). The judge decided the threshold criteria were satisfied, though, because the mother had failed to seek proper medical assistance. 'There seems to be a perceptible move away from the balance of probabilities as the proper standard of proof to some higher standard' (ibid). Spencer (1994) suggests that the trial judge was influenced by a particular theory about the standard of proof: 'Although in civil cases the balance is that facts are proved on the balance of probabilities…given the seriousness of the nature of the allegations and the personalities and relationships involved, it is to be a proportionately higher standard of probability than otherwise for a less serious allegation (p.161).

Spencer concluded that in practice this judgement means that, the worse danger the child is in, the less likely the courts are to remove her from it (ibid.). Morgan (personal communication) challenges Spencer's conclusion because it is not helpful in child protection. For example, if a court cannot find evidence to identify a sex abuser, it can reach a lesser finding, i.e. that sexual abuse occurred while in the care of this person. The perpetrator does not have to be identified in order to establish significant harm. The threshold criteria for a Care Order may thus be met. However, failure to identify the perpetrator may make long-term planning for the child difficult, such as making Contact Orders. The 'is likely' threshold is a general rule test.

The timing of 'is' suffering

The word 'is' indicates that *past* harm is not a threshold for establishing significant harm unless it is likely that it will be repeated (Masson 1990). None the less, the meaning of 'is' has been the subject of much legal debate. *Re M* has become a celebrated case in which one of the issues hinged on the interpretation of the timing of 'is suffering': the date of the original ill-treatment, the date of the care proceedings hearing, the period immediately before the process of protecting the child was put in motion, or some notion of a continuing process (Fortin 1993; Whyebrow 1994a, 1994b; Masson 1994).

When M was four months old his father brutally murdered his mother. When the case came to court, the Judge held that Section 31 (2) was satisfied because M had been permanently deprived of the love and care of his mother; this state of affairs was attributable to his father's unreasonable care (Masson 1994 p.171).

The Court of Appeal's decision to fix the time for this test as the date of the hearing '…realigns the balance between the family and the state in a way which substantially weakens the family's power to withstand state intervention'

(Masson p.171). Masson suggests that the Court of Appeal's decision deprived the 'is suffering' condition of any effect. For example, if a child is being accommodated prior to care proceedings, it would be very difficult to argue that he/she is suffering at that time.

The issue is, however, more complex than this. 'Is suffering' has to be seen as a continuous situation starting immediately before the process of protecting the child was begun and involving judgements about the various alternative arrangements suggested for the care of the child. In this case, these included the imprisoned father's request for a Care Order and adoption, the murdered mother's cousin's (Mrs W) request for a Residence Order and the need to make new placement arrangements. Lord Mackay stated that '…unless there is evidence that a child is being positively harmed by a failure in the family, the state should not interfere' (Mackay 1989 p.508).

These judgements are clearly shaped by partnership arrangements between families and local authorities; Masson (1994) argued that the House of Lords decision in Re M has weakened the position of the family where there are child protection concerns. The thresholds should not be considered outside of arrangements for care by other family members. The Lords endorsed the reasoning of the first Judge, reversed the Court of Appeal's decision and made a Care Order on the understanding that M would remain with Mrs W.

Morgan (personal communication) agrees that 'is suffering' should be applied when the court application is made, if the local authority has taken protective steps. If the local authority has not taken protective steps, the criterion can be applied later.

A similar child

Section 31 (10) of the Children Act states: 'Where the question of whether harm suffered by a child is significant turns on the child's health or development, his health or development shall be compared with that which could reasonably be expected of a similar child.'

Masson (1990) and Freeman (1990) both suggested that the reference is to a similar child and not to a child of similar parents; the standard of care relates to that which can reasonably (not 'best') be expected to be given to similar children. Similar relates to physical attributes rather than to social and environmental background.

Freeman argued that this language obfuscates and overlooks the essential individuality of families and their problems. For example, a deaf child cannot easily be compared with other deaf children because there are so many variables.

> If he has asthma or brittle bones he may need more care, or a different type of care than 'normal' children. The standard is objective: the parents' quality of care must equal that of hypothetically reasonable parents. (Freeman op. cit. p.152)

The reasonableness criterion makes no allowance for parents who, for one reason or another, are incapable of meeting the reasonableness hurdle. (ibid.)

Disadvantaged or disabled parents may find it difficult to care reasonably for 'this' child but they are expected to seek and co-operate with supplementary parenting arrangements. 'Reasonable parents do not suffer disability, any more than they suffer from alcoholism, drug addiction or...poverty. All parents come to the judgement seat on an equal footing, however unequal they are in the world outside the court' (ibid.). Morgan (personal communication) suggests that the reference to 'a similar child' should be explored through a needs-led assessment. What would be reasonably expected of parents should be weighed against parents' capacities, otherwise the test may be importing social class assumptions.

The role of cultural factors

The legislation, guidance and regulations convey a stance of cultural pluralism, but operating this is not straightforward. One argument is that cultural factors are relevant in respect of Stage III, i.e. decisions about making an order and choice of placement using the welfare checklist, but irrelevant at Stages I and II (Freeman 1990, Bainham 1991). Factors such as poverty and environment should not be taken into account in determining what it is reasonable to expect in parenting a 'similar child'. The legislators wanted to determine a unified moral standard for state intervention in family life but there is no consensus, say, on what constitutes acceptable disciplinary measures by parents. Second, the cultural context shapes the very understanding of harm and its significance. For example, Freeman (1990) discusses the *Re H* case, in which the mother of a family of Vietnamese boat people displayed repeated instances of neglect, ill-treatment and bizarre cruelty towards her children. The judgement considered: the reasonable objective standards of the culture in which the children had hitherto been brought up; minimal acceptable standards of child care in England; in Chinese culture, as applied to the lower social and cultural levels of society in rural Vietnam. Experiencing the hazards of being a family of Vietnamese boat people may also have a bearing on definitions of harm. Third, Freeman (1990) suggests that the 'reasonable' condition avoids a totally relativist position; for example, it is not reasonable for parents to refuse a blood transfusion for their child on grounds of religion and culture.

Many sociologists argue that cultural factors shape and sometimes determine the very definition of a problem, the construction of events and the capacities for all parties to work in partnership (Poster 1978; Hardiker and Curnock 1984). Freeman (1990) says that the Children Act reflects '...a deliberate shift in policy away from coercive intervention into family relationships on broad welfare considerations and towards the establishment, with the threshold criteria of standards of legality, of a doctrine of fair opportunity' (p.134).

Fortin (1993) reminds us that achieving a balance between over-aggressive state intervention and maintaining a proper respect for family autonomy is '...probably as unlikely as finding the end of a rainbow' (p.156).

Social constructions and significant harm

The Children Act redefines the boundaries between state intervention and family life, and social workers are key actors in this process. The Department of Health (1993) provided a textbook definition of the process in the context of child protection.

> In practice the decision about whether the assessed risk for the child is best managed on an entirely voluntary basis of work with families or requires the additional authority and framework of a court order will depend on a multiplicity of factors. These include the nature of the harm suffered or likely to be suffered, the surrounding circumstances, the parents' willingness to accept responsibility and to co-operate with the helping agencies and, where their care does not adequately meet the child's needs, an assessment of their ability to change. (p.13)

It is the social worker's task to consider all these aspects and this is part of the process of socially constructing significant harm (Seden, Hardiker and Barker 1996). Legal judgements and arguments obviously consider significant harm from one end of the telescope, whereas social workers address it from another angle.

Hardiker and Barker (1994) explored significant harm in relation to a purposive sample of 12 cases during the first year of implementation of the Children Act. The typical family pattern was that of young parents with very young children. In general, the families lived in socially disadvantaged circumstances and the majority of them were previously known to the Social Services Department. In six cases, the major problem was defined in terms of physical abuse and injury; in one case, the problem definition was sexual abuse and in four cases it was vulnerable parenting and neglect; in one case, the problems included physical abuse, sexual abuse, delinquency and social isolation.

The dimensions of significant harm were:

	No of Cases
Ill-treatment and impairment of health and development	5
Impairment of health and development	1
Ill-treatment	3
Ill-treatment and impairment of development	3
	N=12

The harm was typically multi-dimensional and considered to be significant. The Welfare Checklist was used in all cases and Orders were made in ten of them (eight Care Orders and two Supervision Orders).

The determination of significant harm and the need for state intervention occurs in different ways in child protection practice, and some examples are now explored. The first three examples indicate some congruence between legislative intent, the letter and the spirit of the law and social work practices. In the fourth case, the courts appear to be custodians of legislative practice; in the fifth case, social workers' strategies are perhaps pushing the spirit of the law to its limits.

Deciding whether and when the thresholds have been crossed

It is not always easy to decide when the thresholds have been crossed, especially when a child is reaching normal developmental milestones.

Ms R was in care and gave birth to Jill when she was nearly 16. Concerns began to be expressed about Ms R's care of Jill when she was eight months old; Jill seemed to be 'failing to thrive' and experiencing poor standards of care. Ms R had a relationship with a known sex offender who sometimes had sole care of Jill. The health visitor had difficulty in making contact with Ms R. Jill was found to have a small horse-shaped bruise on her left cheek which was thought to be consistent with a finger-mark. Two child protection packages were devised. The social worker said, 'ill-treatment or impairment of health and development were not obvious. I would visit and the baby seemed fine but everything else I saw made me concerned. Ms R was indicating non-verbally six months ago that she wished she had never had this child.'

In spite of poor standards of care, the baby reached her developmental milestones. An Emergency Protection Order was made because the child was left with her grandparents, her parents were not keeping in contact with her and no one knew when they were returning. The Social Services Department were becoming increasingly worried because they were losing control of where Jill was and how she was being looked after. Eventually a Care Order was made. The social worker said 'the gap between the initial child protection registration and care proceedings might have been shorter had significant harm been clearer'.

Do all parents come to the judgement seat on an equal footing?

As Freeman argues, the 'reasonableness' criterion makes no allowance for people who, for whatever reason, are incapable of meeting the reasonableness hurdle. Disadvantaged parents must compete in the same race as those who are more advantaged. The next example suggests that it is not always easy for parents to come to the judgement seat on an equal footing if they experience multiple disadvantages in their own lives. 'Good enough' parenting still has to meet the needs of 'this particular child'.

Mrs H is 35, has learning disabilities and is being treated for depression. She has five children under the age of ten. The eldest child is the subject of an educational statement and is currently suspended from school. The second eldest child (D), aged 7, is microcephalic, his weight is below the third centile and there is a query about his failure to thrive; he has learning difficulties and has had an educational statement. There are no major concerns about the third child, though there are concerns about the two youngest ones.

The family had been known to the Social Services Department for ten years. There had been several child protection packages and care proceedings. Two years previously, the children returned home subject to Care Orders (Children and Young Persons Act 1969 S.1 (2) (a)) which were subsequently varied to Supervision Orders. These Supervision Orders lapsed. Mrs H requested custody of her children following divorce proceedings. Supervision Orders were requested and granted (Matrimonial Causes Act 5.43)

These Supervision Orders were extended under the Children Act (Schedule 3 para. 6 (3). The thresholds for significant harm were met in respect of D:

- harm is defined in terms of impairment of health and development
- harm is significant because D's weight is below the third centile and he is possibly failing to thrive
- he is suffering and is likely to suffer significant harm
- the harm is attributable to the care his mother gives him.

Mother faced the stresses of feeding, budgeting and keeping the house warm. She had no informal support networks. A package of family support services was mobilised.

The welfare checklist was used and it was thought that a Supervision Order would meet D's welfare needs and that statutory intervention was justified. There were concerns about the physical and emotional care of the children, the level of their supervision and the standard of housing conditions. The social worker said: 'There have been a lot of concerns for a very long period. It is very hard to maintain the status quo and the level of care at a fairly acceptable level.'

It was thought that there was a positive quality in the relationship between Mrs H and her children; ill-treatment was not considered to be a dimension of the harm. The significance of the harm was not difficult to establish because the concerns were there in such a degree. The thresholds and welfare criteria were thought by the social worker to be useful because they focused on different areas and were more specific than the previous ones.

The situation illustrates some of the most profound dilemmas in child protection. There must be limits to which services can enable severely disadvantaged parents to come to the judgement seat on an equal footing.

Cultural factors

It was shown above that cultural factors shape the very ways in which cases are constructed and that a stance of cultural pluralism may oversimplify complex issues. The A case illustrates some of the complexities.

Mrs A is 34, Asian, Muslim and lives alone with her three children. Her husband lives in India and has not been granted an immigration permit. Mrs A had lived with her parents but there were problems and she moved with her children to the Homeless Unit. They were subsequently rehoused and Mrs A was left to cope on her own.

1. There were concerns about Mrs A's parenting capacities.

2. Mrs A had mental health problems, including depression and obsessional behaviour.

3. Mrs A's father helped in many ways but the strain eventually became too much for him.

4. Family support services were mobilised.

5. The family thought Mrs A was 'possessed' and this prevented her from being 'normal'.

6. Eventually, care proceedings were started, the threshold criteria were met and Care Orders were made.

Cultural factors in interaction with Mrs A's mental health difficulties were associated with a protracted assessment (Hardiker and Curnock 1984). As the social worker said, with the wisdom of hindsight:

> The situation was allowed to *drift* too long before any action was taken. It was a year before the problems were understood and addressed. At face value, the children were not seen to be at major risk but further assessment highlighted this. Furthermore, we have to look at everybody in the family and this also led to drift. The Act works better in respect of extended kin but in this case the grandparents were scared of the mother and reluctant to assume responsibility.

Mrs A planned to go with her children to India to see their father. An *ex parte* Prohibited Step Order (S8) was obtained and port stop procedures implemented because it would be the monsoon period when sickness and diarrhoea are common. This would make the girl who was failing to thrive very vulnerable and at higher than average risk of becoming ill.

A stance of cultural pluralism does not obviate the need to individualise personal and social dynamics in these complex situations.

Courts leading the way

Courts may play a proactive role in the construction of significant harm. In a case of sexual and physical abuse and delinquency, the dimensions of significant harm were considered separately in respect of four children in a family; the court found more indicators than the social worker at various stages. At the final court hearing, specific thresholds were identified in relation to each child and Care Orders were made.

The social worker observed: 'I am happy for the Magistrates to find evidence of harm. The Social Services Department's focus needs to be clearly on the needs of the children and plans for the future.' This is a good example of ways in which the due process of law can individualise issues in relation to each child.

Proactive use of 'significant harm'

Social services departments are sometimes very proactive in constructing significant harm. There were concerns that a new-born baby being accommodated was 'in limbo' and lacked the security of a permanent home. A change of foster home had also been necessary, the baby was not thriving and was losing weight. The social workers were uncertain how to overcome the family's ambivalence about having her home.

It was a brainwave when it was suggested that the baby could be considered at risk of significant harm on grounds of physical ill-treatment, and impairment to her mental health and to her social and emotional development. It was thought that the threshold criteria would be met and this possibility was used as a 'lever' in negotiations to achieve work agreements and deadlines with the mother in a programme of rehabilitation.

The social services department started from the baby's needs and looked around for a lever which might overcome the family's resistance to having her home or agreeing to a permanent alternative.

There was close liaison with solicitors but no certainty that magistrates would agree with this use of the Act. It was a good example of the creative and flexible thinking needed in operating the changed legal situation.

The child's progress on all the threshold criteria had improved considerably by the time of the Case Conference, and proceedings were not taken as harm was not considered to be significant.

Social Work Processes

The social construction of significant harm has been illustrated through examples of crossing the thresholds, equality before the law, addressing cultural issues, courts leading the way and the proactive use of the term 'significant harm'. These constructions were underpinned by social work processes, i.e. a series of interactions between families and practitioners directed toward achieving an agreed goal (Compton and Galaway 1989, p.370; Hardiker and Curnock 1984; Hardiker and Barker 1981, 1991). In the context of the 1989 Children Act, these processes were underpinned by new requirements: the concept of parental responsibility, working in partnership with parents and with extended kin, mobilising family support services, more precise legal requirements, increased paperwork, a swifter pace of work and the need to make more precise assessments (Hardiker and Barker 1994).

Conclusion

'Concern with family violence has been a weathervane identifying the prevailing winds of anxiety about family life in general' (Gordon 1989, p.2).

This chapter illustrates some ways in which child protection concerns are a weathervane identifying changing balances between state intervention and family autonomy (Parton 1991). Significant harm is a major lever by which state interventions and family autonomy are balanced. There are three stages in the process before the state intervenes compulsorily in family life.

It is obviously difficult to evaluate whether the right balance between state interventions and family autonomy has been struck and this will continue to be a topic of legal and social debate (Levy 1994). These debates need to be vigilantly scrutinised.

References

Adcock, M., White, R. and Hollows, A. (eds) (1991) *Significant Harm*. Croydon: Significant Publications.

Bainham, A. (1991) Care after 1991 – a reply. *Journal of Child Law* April/June, 99–104.

Ball, C. (1990) The Children Act 1989: origins, aims and current concerns. In P. Carter, T. Jeffs and M. Smith (eds) *Social Work and Social Welfare Yearbook 3*. Buckingham: Open University Press.

Children Act 1989 (1989 C41). London: HMSO.

Cleveland (1988) *Report of the Inquiry into Child Abuse in Cleveland 1987*. Cm 412. London: HMSO.

Compton, B. R. and Galaway, B. (1989) *Social Work Processes*. Belmont: Wadsworth, Fourth Edition.

Department of Health (1993) *Children Act Report*. London: HMSO.

Department of Health and Social Security (1985a) *Social Work Decisions in Child Care: Recent Research Findings and their Implications.* London: HMSO.

Department of Health and Social Security (1985b) *Review of Child Care Law: Report to Ministers of an Interdepartmental Working Party.* London: HMSO.

Department of Health and Social Security (1986) *Review of Child Care Law Interim Discussion Papers.* London: HMSO.

Fortin, J. (1993) Significant harm revisited. *Journal of Child Law 5,* 2, 151–192.

Freeman, M.D.A. (1990) Care after 1991. In D. Freestone (ed) *Children and the Law: Essays in Honour of Professor H.K. Bevan.* Hull: Hull University Press, 130–171.

Gordon, L. (1989) *Heroes of their Own Lives: The Politics and History of Family Violence.* London: Virago Press.

Hansard (1989) *House of Lords Official Report: Children Bill – Committee (Fourth Day)* (Col. 333). London: HMSO.

Hardiker, P. and Barker, M. (eds) (1981) *Theories of Practice in Social Work.* London: Academic Press.

Hardiker, P. and Barker, M. (1991) Towards social theory for social work. In J. Lishman (ed) *Handbook of Theory for Practice in Social Work.* London: Jessica Kingsley Publishers.

Hardiker, P. and Barker, M. (1994) *The 1989 Children Act: Social Work Processes, Social Policy Contexts and 'Significant Harm'.* Leicester: University of Leicester, School of Social Work, Research Report.

Hardiker, P. and Curnock, K. (1984) Social work assessment processes in work with ethnic minorities – the Doshi family. *British Journal of Social Work 14,* 1, 23–47.

Hoggett, B. (1989) The Children Bill: the Aim. *Family Law,* 217–221.

House of Commons (1984) *Children in Care: Second Report from the Social Services Committee, Session 1983.* London: HMSO.

Kleinig, J. (1978) III Crime and the concept of harm. *American Philosophical Quarterly 15,* 1, 27–36.

Levy, A. (ed) (1994) *Refocus on Child Abuse: Medical, Legal and Social Work Perspectives.* London: Hawksmere.

London Borough of Brent (1985) *A Child in Trust: The Report of the Panel of Inquiry into the Circumstances Surrounding the Death of Jasmine Beckford.* London Borough of Brent.

London Borough of Greenwich (1987) *A Child in a Responsible Society. Kimberley Carlile.* London Borough of Greenwich.

London Borough of Lambeth (1987) *Whose Child? The Report of the Panel Appointed to Inquire into the Death of Tyra Henry.* London Borough of Lambeth.

Mackay, Lord (1989) Perceptions of the Children Bill and beyond. *New Law Journal,* 505–508.

Masson, J. (1990) *The Children Act 1989: Text and Commentary*. London: Sweet and Maxwell.

Masson, M. (1994) Social engineering in the House of Lords: re M. *Journal of Child Law 6*, 4, 170–174.

Parton, M. (1991) *Governing the Family: Child Care, Child Protection and the State*. London: Macmillan Education Limited.

Poster, M. (1978) *Critical Theory of the Family*. London: Pluto Press.

Seden, J., Hardiker, P. and Barker, M. (1996) Child protection revisited: balancing state intervention and family and assessing through social work processes. *Child and Family Social Work 1*.

Spencer, J. (1994) Evidence in child abuse cases – too high a price to pay for too high a standard? Re M (A Minor) (Appeal) No 2. *Journal of Child Law 6*, 4, 160–161.

White, R. (1994) A case of significant harm? *New Law Journal*, March 4, 329–330.

Whyebrow, J. (1994a) Care, supervision and interim orders. *Journal of Child Law 6*, 4, 177–181.

Whyebrow, J. (1994b) Re M: past, present and future significant harm. *Journal of Child Law 6*, 2, 88–92.

CHAPTER 8

Families', Social Workers' and Police Perspectives on Child Abuse Investigations

Lorraine Waterhouse and Janice McGhee

The management of child abuse in the United Kingdom has evolved since the mid 1970s to a nationally co-ordinated system which includes local area review committees to co-ordinate policy and interdisciplinary co-operation. All areas now have procedural guidelines for the different professions concerned with children's welfare, child protection registers to identify children at risk of harm and multi-disciplinary case conferences led by social work/services departments as a forum to assess risk and formally identify children in need of registration. There is an increasing co-operation between the law enforcement, health and social work agencies most recently exemplified by the moves towards joint interviewing of children and their parents by police officers and social workers. These procedural guidelines and the numerous governmental circulars on child abuse have been the consequence of inquiries into the deaths of children at the hands of their parents and/or guardians (see for example the Beckford Inquiry; Blom Cooper 1985). The Cleveland DHSS (1988) and Orkneys (1992) inquiries provided further impetus for the development of investigatory techniques which will provide evidence admissible within an adversarial court system.

These twin forces have increasingly shifted the emphasis in social work/services departments away from the universal principle of welfare established in the Kilbrandon and Seebohm Committees to a concern with the detection and identification of children at risk of physical and sexual abuse. This has inevitably led to an allocation of resources to match the requirements for assessment and surveillance where public accountability remains uppermost. Services with a preventive or social education focus have become a secondary priority, especially within statutory agencies where legal responsibilities to investigate are located. This chapter explores the impact of these twin forces on professional practice and the significance of this for the relationship between social workers, other professionals and families subject to investigation.

The identification of child abuse

Child protection registration in modern practice acts as a gateway to services which might not otherwise be available to unregistered children. This in turn impacts on professional perspectives leading to a process whereby children in need become defined as abused children and therefore a priority for service. In a UK context of generally poor levels of state child welfare services, especially for under-fives, registration may act as a criterion of eligibility to gain access to limited child care services. This could be an abuse of natural justice and runs the risk of increasing the stigmatisation of children and families already facing disadvantage and adversity. Much of the research on the social circumstances of children who are placed either on child protection registers or in the public care system demonstrates that low income, health problems, chronic unemployment, poor housing and poor parental education are characteristic (Creighton 1984; Packman, Randall and Jacques 1986; Holman 1988; Kolvin *et al.* 1990; Loney 1992). One consequence of this emphasis on abuse as a trigger to service provision is to operate an apparently rational principle of selectivity based on a higher threshold of need against a background context of widespread disadvantage in the lives of many children in our society.

This principle of selectivity operates on the assumption that abusing and non-abusing families can be distinguished. Empirical research has shown that the circumstances of children coming into public care, many of whom have allegedly been abused, are not significantly different from those remaining at home (Packman *et al.* 1986). This is further supported by Packman's finding that many of the children initially refused admission to public care were subsequently admitted.

Research which attempts to define the social and personal factors discriminating between abusing and non-abusing parents or guardians tends to identify circumstances that are generally associated with families in adversity. The main recipients of social work services are frequently families in the most disadvantaged circumstances. Other research reviewing children placed on child protection registers has also confirmed that the incidence of serious physical injury remains low (Gough 1993; Pitcairn and Waterhouse 1993; Gibbons, Conroy and Bell 1995). Registered children may be facing difficult family situations which are disturbing to them. However, physical abuse is not necessarily a reliable discriminator for identifying children most in need of scarce services. Dingwall (1989) makes the point that it is not always clear whether the children who are registered have indeed been abused. Differences, if any, in child rearing patterns between registered and unregistered children remain unknown, although Quinton and Rutter (1988) have shown that, in the absence of serious abuse or neglect, family discord is a key variable in childhood disturbance and poor adult outcomes.

Despite the increased reporting of sexual abuse and the widespread acceptance that many significant numbers of children experience sexual misuse, sometimes from a very young age, there is a lack of systematic research on both severity and nature. Waterhouse, Dobash and Carnie (1994), looking at the criminal records of 500 convicted offenders, provide some insight. They found the level of abuse was severe and ongoing, with a significant proportion of the cases involving a form of sexual intercourse. This was sometimes accompanied by violence. Research suggests there is a delay between the onset of the abuse and disclosure with subsequent investigation by the authorities.

Parents' and social workers' perceptions of child abuse investigations

Research has suggested a number of key issues related to parents' and social workers' perceptions and experiences of the child protection system:

- lack of congruence of views
- stigmatisation of parents
- using child protection to secure resources
- undetected risk or harm
- the need for open communication
- anxieties of both parents and professionals leading to misunderstanding.

A number of studies have recently looked at the experience of the child abuse investigation from the perspective of families and professionals involved. Farmer (1993) studied the extent of match and mismatch between the views of social workers and parents during the initial stages of child abuse investigation in 44 cases of children registered for reasons of physical abuse, sexual abuse or a combination of neglect and abuse. She found only 18 per cent demonstrated complete agreement between the social worker and the parent as to whether abuse had occurred, who was culpable and whether the incident/alleged abuse posed a serious risk to the child's future safety and well-being. In a third of cases there was no agreement on any of these factors. Farmer found that parents sometimes questioned the legitimacy of child protection intervention, creating at the outset a gulf between parents and social services which inhibited open and frank communication.

The parents in this study found the procedural requirements of the case conference and registration of the child stigmatising. They felt blame was attributed to themselves as failing parents. Cleaver and Freeman (1993) similarly found that parents felt violated and ashamed by the investigation and were still reviewing what had happened to them 18 months later. The parents claimed family relationships rarely returned to their previous state and they remained profoundly suspicious of social workers. Brown (1986) also noted in her study of parents whose children had been referred to Social Services because of allegations of abuse that the surveillance function of registration was uppermost for these families. These views are further reinforced by preliminary findings from Thoburn, Lewis and Shemmings (1991) who found that parental participation in child protection case conferences occurred in only a fifth of cases. This has the effect of reducing the opportunity for parents to express their views and to gain information. Professional groups other than social workers appeared the more reluctant to have parents attend. (See also Thoburn this volume).

Problems of stigmatisation are not solely the province of parents accused of abuse. Dempster (1993) interviewed 34 women whose children had been referred to the social work department for incidents of child sexual abuse where they were clearly identified as the non-abuser. She found the women to have experienced trauma on discovery of the abuse, leading to acute feelings of powerlessness, guilt and betrayal. These women looked to the social services for support and recognition of their distress but apparently experienced a response characterised by suspicion that they may have colluded with the abuse of their child.

Involvement in the child protection system may however bring benefits from access to services. Farmer (1993) found many social workers viewed registration as the key to accessing scarce resources for families which would not otherwise have been available. The benefit arising from increased access to resources intended as helpful may be diminished by a method of allocation which emphasises compulsion and may be perceived by parents as controlling rather than supportive. Clark (1993), drawing on an Australian sample, argues against child protection procedures being used as a gateway to securing resources for families already facing social adversity. This simply serves to misrepresent the problem of poverty which the majority of her sample experienced. Families themselves cite material deprivation as a major deleterious influence on their children (Magura and Moses 1984). It also contributes to parental anxiety, depression and stress which in turn can contribute to parenting difficulties and child behaviour problems.

These studies are interesting in light of the emphasis in the Children Act 1989 in England and Wales and the Children (Scotland) Act 1995 on partnership between families and professionals involved in their lives. Procedural practice which is primarily concerned with detection and monitoring could in some instances serve to drive a wedge between parent and professionals to the detriment of children. These very procedures arising from the practices of local authorities in the field of child protection may be applied indiscriminately in all cases, leading to defensive practice and loss of appropriate discretion in decision-making. Procedures can never be a substitute for sound professional judgement, nor a remedy for a dearth of community health and child care services. However it is also true that professional perceptions of the causes of abuse may not always take account of the full scope of the problem and therefore influence their expectations at investigation.

Children at risk of emotional abuse or experiencing psychological difficulties appear to remain largely undetected by the child protection system in part because of the problems of definition, recognition and proof in the legal context. Research has shown that emotional abuse can have serious consequences for the psychological well-being of children, with continuing detrimental effects if the abuse persists (Bagley and King 1991). This group of children are equally in need of help yet in the absence of any kind of injury remain unlikely to gain access to resources under criteria which stress physical or sexual abuse.

Even when children are registered for physical or sexual abuse, serious psychological problems may go undetected. In a study (involving the authors) of 43 children registered for physical abuse a standardised check-list was administered to measure behavioural problems in the children (Rutter 1967; Richman, Stevenson and Graham 1984). These items have considerable predictive value in discriminating children with neurotic or anti-social disorders. The majority of children scored highly on the Rutter or Richman scales, indicating emotional difficulties were significant regardless of the level of abuse. The level of physical injury was unrelated to the degree of behavioural disturbance in the children. Social workers' assessment and intervention, however, continued to focus on the physical risks to the child's safety and they appeared unaware of the level of psychological disturbance present in these children.

The problem of child abuse was mainly defined as the poor parental handling of children. What appears to have been ignored by social workers was the contribution of the child's behavioural difficulties to the parent–child interaction. Mothers frequently complained of behavioural problems in their children and reported difficulties in managing their behaviour. Social workers, whilst acknowledging the potential relevance of some of the mother's concerns, often failed to recognise the central significance of behavioural problems as a possible contributor to the alleged abuse. Consequently social workers frequently did not take the mothers' concerns seriously and as a result children were not offered direct help in their own right. This group of children may, therefore, have a strong claim on child care services not only because of physical abuse but because of the risk to their psychological status.

This would suggest that good communication is central to the relationship between social workers and parents especially in this context, where, in the absence of gross indicators, assessment of risk is mainly dependent on parental accounts of child care practice and observation of the family environment. Brown (1986) found that parents often felt the social worker ignored or diminished their concerns. Parents sometimes tested the social worker's degree of interest by raising minor problems in the first instance as a prelude to discovering whether they were likely to get help in more major areas. Broader studies of client perceptions of social work help (Sainsbury 1975; Lishman 1978) stress the importance of openness, clarity and informality in the exchange between clients and social workers as the precursors to an honest and frank discussion of difficulties.

The need for open communication is further reflected in Brown's study where parents experienced a lack of clarity about professional expectations of them as parents, and about the role of the social worker, especially when encountering social services for the first time. Pitcairn and Waterhouse (1993) found parents feared their children would be removed from them and taken into public care. This may be a serious misperception by parents of the perspective which social workers bring to child care assessment and decision making. Vernon and Fruin (1986) found that social workers were reluctant to admit children to public care and adopted a 'wait and see' policy in the hope that admission could be avoided. Packman et al. (1986) endorsed this finding when she observed that children in similar circumstances were more likely to be admitted into public care when other professionals, especially the police, reported serious difficulties.

The combined anxiety parents may experience about the aims of social workers and the fear of losing their children may inhibit parents seeking help. Lishman (1978) in her small study of families attending out-patient child psychiatric services concluded parental functioning was impaired through heightened anxiety and energies diverted from working collaboratively on problems to covering up or hiding family troubles. Cleaver and Freeman (1993) in a study of health, police and social service files found a similar dynamic in cases of suspected child abuse. They further found that professionals feared that each investigation might become a potential child abuse scandal. The combined anxiety of parents and professionals can lead to mis-attributions on the part of both at a critical stage of the investigation. Consequently normal parental behavioural responses to stressful encounters may be construed as potentially indicative of abuse.

Uncertainty about the function of social work as support or policing of families causes anxiety in social workers who have duties in law to protect children from harm. Awareness of the policing role may lead parents to hold back out of fear and social workers to focus on the alleged abuse rather than the pressing mundane daily concerns of parents.

This may contribute to professional concern emphasising disciplinary strategies, particularly in child physical abuse where parental control strategies are often perceived as aggressive and overly controlling. Physical chastisement has been shown in non-abusing families to be routinely used as a method of behavioural control (Newson and Newson 1976), and this may have reinforced the notion of a continuum of physical disciplinary strategies where in an abusive situation normal limits may have been exceeded.

In Pitcairn and Waterhouse's (1993) study of parents whose children were registered as potentially at risk, difficulties in the control and management of the children clearly emerged. Surprisingly the nature of these difficulties as reported by the parents reflected a failure to discipline the children consistently and routinely, even when the parents were clear that some intervention on their part was necessary. Lax disciplinary strategies appeared to predominate for parents, whilst social workers' framework remained fixed on the idea that excessive discipline was central in parent–child relationships in the context of alleged abuse. Misunderstanding of this aspect of the problem may lead to inappropriate solutions which fail to influence the daily management of the child in a positive way, especially for parents overwhelmed by the demands of parenting young children. It is perhaps ironic that one of the main conclusions Fisher et al. (1986) drew in their study of young people in residential care is the wish on the part of care professionals for parents to exert more parental control and discipline while parents look to residential child care staff to carry out this task on their behalf.

Children's perceptions of child abuse investigations

Children's views have been largely under-researched. Roberts and Taylor (1993), one of the few studies in this area, investigated the perceptions of 84 sexually abused children who underwent child protection investigations. They explored with the children whether the investigative process in itself compounded the original abuse. Of the 35 children who explicitly responded, 17 concluded that the abuse itself was the most distressing event. As one child said, 'the worst part was it actually happening.' Similarly the vast majority of children were ultimately relieved that they had told about the abuse mainly because this resulted in it stopping. A 16-year-old male commented 'I'm glad I told – stopping it was the most important.'

Farmer (1993) confirmed that the main motivation for children reporting abuse is the wish for it to cease. The children had little idea beforehand what telling would precipitate, and both parents and children became concerned when swept along by the forces of investigation. This was often in the context where a child had told an adult other than the non-abusing parent, the children experiencing further powerlessness in the face of official action.

Roberts and Taylor (1993) and Murray (1995) observed that children were still subject to multiple interviewing in relation to alleged abuse. This caused distress to children due to the invasion of their privacy and the repetition of events to a range of professionals. However there was no concomitant involvement of the children in professional decision-making. Farmer (1993) found that children were rarely invited to attend case conferences and some children felt excluded from the conference deliberations, as highlighted by one child who said, 'it was as if everyone was talking behind my back' (p.48). Few children appeared to know that their names were on a child protection register but those who did know were very embarrassed at being publicly singled out and were afraid their friends would find out.

A further source of anxiety for abused children was the fear of not being believed, particularly in the context of a criminal prosecution. Where a prosecution had not resulted in a criminal conviction, children felt this public outcome suggested that they had not told the truth (Murray 1995). Roberts and Taylor (1993) describe a similar phenomenon as exemplified in the words of a 15-year-old, 'It was not proven. The procurator fiscal told me they knew it was true but that wasn't any consolation. I was so angry I couldn't sleep.'

Roberts and Taylor (1993) conclude from their discussions with children that, despite the fact that some children had difficult court experiences or unpleasant medical examinations, the overwhelming message from the children to other children is to tell about the abuse. They counsel a highly individualised response focused on the needs of each particular child, with professionals willing to listen to how the child makes sense of his/her experience and its outcomes for them.

Police views on child protection investigations

The past 20 years have seen an increasing role for the police in child protection investigation and inter-agency collaboration. *Working Together* (Home Office 1986) stressed that police involvement in child abuse investigation stems from an overriding consideration of the welfare of the child and not only from their traditional responsibility to protect the community. They bring their own professional perspective which is concerned to marshal evidence and secure prosecution.

It is interesting in this context that Brown (1986) found that five out of the eight families in her study where police were involved in the child protection investigation felt they had been dealt with by police officers in a sensitive manner which did not increase their feelings of guilt. Burman and Lloyd (1993) in their study of police specialist units for the investigation of crimes of violence against women and children in Scotland found the move toward joint police and social work investigations did cause confusion for the child and their family in some cases.

A study by Waterhouse and Carnie (1991) identified very different roles and responsibilities adopted by social workers and police officers in child protection investigations despite the increasing emphasis on joint interviewing. They found social workers were primarily concerned to predict child care risk, while police officers concentrated on the likelihood of a crime having been committed. Social workers mainly focused their involvement on women and children whilst police officers concentrated on male perpetrators. Burman and Lloyd (1993) similarly showed that the police were primarily concerned with gathering evidence and that they expressed concerns about social workers asking leading questions or discussing the alleged crime with the perpetrator, fearing contamination of evidence which could affect subsequent legal proceedings. Burman and Lloyd identified the possibility that social workers are becoming 'police aides' assisting in criminal investigation. In our view this points to the risk that social workers may fail to give full attention to the welfare aspect of their child care role.

Despite this difference in orientation, professionals reported that collaborative working relationships developed although professional boundaries were maintained (Waterhouse and Carnie 1991; Burman and Lloyd 1993). The views of families on interdisciplinary child protection investigations have not been studied in any depth despite recent research interest on professional views in this area (Hallett and Birchall 1992).

Conclusion

Hallett (1993) compared European and UK practices in relation to child protection and stressed the need to strike a balance between the paramountcy of the welfare of the child and the notion of justice within the wider community. In the UK an increased emphasis is being given to the investigation and surveillance of children and their families. The development of child protection procedures as a gatekeeping mechanism to allocate scarce resources for children in need may have distracted attention from the need for comprehensive, high quality child care services within the community for all children.

Concentration within social work on the investigation of alleged child abuse has resulted in the development of complex procedural guidelines and the expectation of inter-agency co-operation epitomised in the joint police/social work investigative interview. Whilst this brings the benefits of standardisation, minimising the need for a child to re-tell events to numerous adults, there remain questions about how well such broad guidelines can substitute for professional judgement about a child's individual circumstances. Standardised procedures of investigation and surveillance may serve to undermine an emphasis on the individual child and family's welfare, especially if intervention is experienced by families as policing and control rather than support and prevention.

It is clear from research that parents feel stigmatised by processes associated with case conferences, child protection registers and police investigations. Parents felt blamed for real or apparent failures in raising and protecting their children, which could inhibit frank communication. Parents' own concerns about their child's behaviour appeared to be minimised by social workers, which could seriously limit professional assessment. Social workers tended to concentrate on over-chastisement, ignoring the psychological status of the child. True partnership is, therefore, curtailed, with possible detrimental consequences for children.

Parents' overwhelming anxiety in the context of a child protection investigation remains the fear of the removal of their child into public care. Social workers' overwhelming anxiety is that every child protection investigation may become a child abuse scandal. These differing preoccupations may serve to exacerbate difficulties in communication and confirm parents' perceptions that the emphasis is on investigation rather than support. Children's anxieties revolve around a fear of being disbelieved, especially when this may lead to prosecution of the alleged abuser. Despite this worry, children involved with social work services were in the main relieved that they had told about the abuse.

Much of the standardised procedures and guidance resulting from criticisms of social work practice in well-publicised inquiries depend on good inter-professional co-operation. The links between social work and police have been strengthened by their joint involvement in child protection investigation. However, despite improvements in liaison, difficulties still remain in reconciling the differing responsibilities for prosecution and welfare.

Child protection investigation and subsequent registration may be inadvertently separating out the deserving and undeserving poor, the latter being drawn into a system of social control and monitoring which may fail to address their primary needs for employment, good housing and adequate educational opportunities. It may also stigmatise and devalue the caring and supportive role of child care within social work. Perhaps the question for the future is not just how we can find those children who are likely to be seriously injured or abused by their carers but how all children in need can be supported and protected in our society.

References

Bagley, C. and King, K. (1991) *Child Sexual Abuse: The Search for Healing.* London and New York: Tavistock, Routledge.

Blom-Cooper, L. (1985) *A Child in Trust: The Report of the Panel of Inquiry into the Circumstances Surrounding the Death of Jasmine Beckford.* London: Borough of Brent.

Brown, C. (1986) *Child Abuse Parents Speaking: A Consumer Study: Parents' Impressions of Social Workers and the Social Work Process.* Bristol: School for Advanced Urban Studies, University of Bristol.

Burman, M. and Lloyd, S. (1993) *Police Specialist Units for the Investigation of Crimes of Violence Against Women and Children in Scotland.* Scottish Office Central Research Unit. Edinburgh: Scottish Office

Clark, R. (1993) Discrimination in child protection services: the need for change. In L. Waterhouse (ed) *Child Abuse and Child Abusers: Protection and Prevention.* London: Jessica Kingsley Publishers.

Cleaver, H. and Freeman, P. (1993) Parental perspectives in suspected child abuse and its aftermath. In D. Gough (ed). *Child Abuse Interventions. A Review of the Research Literature*. Public Health Research Unit. University of Glasgow. London: H.M.S.O.

Creighton, S.J. (1984) *Trends in Child Abuse*. London: NSPCC.

Dempster, H. (1993) The aftermath of child sexual abuse: women's perspectives. In L. Waterhouse (ed) *Child Abuse and Child Abusers: Protection and Prevention*. London: Jessica Kingsley Publishers.

Department of Health and Social Security (1988) *Report of the Inquiry into Child Abuse in Cleveland* (Butler-Sloss). London: HMSO.

Department of Health and Social Security (1986) *Child Abuse – Working Together*. London: HMSO.

Dingwall, R. (1989) Some problems about predicting child abuse and neglect. In O. Stevenson (ed) *Child Abuse: Public Policy and Professional Practice*. Hemel Hempstead: Harvester Wheatsheaf.

Farmer, E. (1993) The impact of child protection interventions: the experiences of parents and children. In L. Waterhouse (ed) *Child Abuse and Child Abusers: Protection and Prevention*. London: Jessica Kingsley Publishers.

Fisher, M., Marsh, P., Phillips, D. and Sainsbury, E. (1986) *In and Out of Care: The Experience of Children, Parents and Social Workers*. London: Batsford/BAAF.

Gibbons, J., Conroy, S. and Bell, C. (1995) *Studies in Child Protection: Development After Physical Abuse in Early Childhood*. London: HMSO.

Gough, D. (1993) *Child Abuse Interventions. A Review of the Research Literature*. Public Health Research Unit. University of Glasgow. London: HMSO.

Hallett, C. (1993) Child protection in Europe: convergence or divergence? *Adoption and Fostering 17*, 4, 27–32.

Hallett, C. and Birchall, E. (1992) *Co-ordination and Child Protection: A Review of the Literature*. Edinburgh: HMSO.

Holman, B. (1988) *Putting Families First*. Basingstoke: Macmillan.

Kolvin, I., Miller, F.J.W., Scott, D., Gatzanis, S.R.M. and Fleeting, M. (1990) *Continuities of Deprivation?' The Newcastle 1000 Study*, ESRC DHSS Studies in Deprivation and Disadvantage. Aldershot: Avebury.

Lishman, J. (1978) A clash in perspective. *British Journal of Social Work 8*, 3, 301–311.

Loney, M. (1992) Child abuse in a social context. In R.W. Stainton, D. Hevey, J. Roche and E. Ash (eds) *Child Abuse and Neglect: Facing the Challenge*. London: Batsford with The Open University.

Magura, S. and Moses, B.S. (1984) Clients as evaluators in child protective services. *Child Welfare 53*, 2, 99–112.

Murray, K. (1995) *Live Television Link. An Evaluation of its Use by Child Witnesses in Scottish Criminal Trials*. Scottish Office, Central Research Unit.

Newson, J and Newson, E. (1976) *Seven Year Olds in the Home Environment.* London: Allen and Unwin.

Packman, J., Randall, J. and Jacques, N. (1986) *Who Needs Care ? Social Work Decisions about Children.* Oxford: Blackwell.

Pitcairn, T. and Waterhouse, L. (1993) Evaluating parenting in child physical abuse. In L. Waterhouse (ed) *Child Abuse and Child Abusers: Protection and Prevention.* London: Jessica Kingsley Publishers.

Quinton, D. and Rutter, M. (1988) *Parenting Breakdown: The Making and Breaking of Intergenerational Links.* Aldershot: Avebury.

Richman, N., Stevenson, J. and Graham, P.J. (1984) Pre-school to school: a behavioural study. In R. Schaffer (ed) *Behavioural Development: A Series of Monographs.* London and New York: Academic Press.

Roberts, R. and Taylor, C. (1993) Sexually abused children and young people speak out. In L. Waterhouse (ed) *Child Abuse and Child Abusers: Protection and Prevention.* London: Jessica Kingsley Publishers.

Rutter, M. (1967) A child's behaviour questionnaire for completion by teachers: preliminary findings. *Journal of Child Psychology and Psychiatry 8,* 1–11.

Sainsbury, R. (1975) *Social Work with Families.* London and Boston: Routledge and Kegan Paul.

Scottish Office (1992) *The Report of the Inquiry into the Removal of Children from Orkney in February 1991.* Edinburgh: HMSO.

Thoburn, J., Lewis, A. and Shemmings, D. (1991) *Family Involvement in Child Protection Case Conferences.* Discussion Paper 1, University of East Anglia Social Work Development Unit.

Vernon, J. and Fruin, D. (1986) *In Care: A Study of Social Work Decision Making.* London: National Children's Bureau.

Waterhouse, L. and Carnie, J. (1991) Research note: social work and police response to child sexual abuse in Scotland. *British Journal of Social Work 21,* 373–379.

Waterhouse, L., Dobash, R.P. and Carnie, J. (1994) *Child Sexual Abusers.* Edinburgh: The Scottish Office Central Research Unit.

CHAPTER 9

Partnership-Based Practice in Child Protection Work

June Thoburn, Ann Lewis and David Shemmings

Introduction

This chapter considers the nature of social work practice with families whose children are, or are suspected to be, in need of protection. A review of the literature on social work in child protection suggests a move has taken place along a continuum towards practice which is essentially forensic, focusing on investigation and assessment, and away from practice which has a child and family welfare focus and concentrates on the provision of support or therapy, with assessment of the protection needs being integrated with the other aspects of the work.

The increasing emphasis on a forensic and investigatory approach went alongside a child welfare philosophy which concentrated on short-term practice designed either to keep children at home or return them safely home as quickly as possible, or to place them permanently with substitute families. The research studies which influenced the Children Act 1989 and the Regulations and Guidance accompanying it (DH 1985; DH 1991a, 1991c) and the Children Act itself indicated the need for a better integration of investigative and supportive practice. Although the word 'partnership' does not appear in the Act itself, it is repeatedly found in the Guidance, including the Guidance on working with children in need of protection (DH 1991b, p.43).

> This guide emphasises the importance of professionals working in partnership with parents and other family members or carers and the concept of parental responsibility. The involvement of children and adults in Child Protection Conferences will not be effective unless they are fully involved from the outset in all stages of the child protection process and unless from the time of referral there is as much openness and honesty as possible between families and professionals.

More recently the Department of Health (1995) has issued a further guide giving more practical assistance to policy makers and managers as well as practitioners on how to design and provide family support services which are based on the principle of working in partnership with family members in all cases where this does not directly impede the provision of adequate protection for the child. Four main reasons why the Department believes that working in partnership with children and parents should be aimed for are listed in the guide:

- A more co-operative working relationship is likely to lead to a more effective service in safeguarding the child's welfare
- Family members have unique knowledge about their difficulties but also their strengths
- Family members have rights as citizens to hear what is said about them and to have a say when important decisions are made about them
- Being involved in this way may help parents and children to feel less powerless and to function more competently.

Not only are children in need of social services and their families to be consulted about the sorts of services which they believe will alleviate their own difficulties, but the Schedules to the Act and The Challenge of Partnership (DH 1995) encourage child protection and family support workers to include parents and older children as individuals or as members of self-help groups in discussions about the detail and nature of the protection and support services to be made available in their areas. Turning to specific cases, the Department of Health guidance on the Children Act clarifies that in child welfare and child protection cases, although the child's welfare must always be the first consideration: 'Parents are individuals with needs of their own. Even though services may be primarily offered on behalf of their children, parents are entitled to help and consideration in their own right' (DH 1989, p.8).

The requirement to attempt to work in partnership remains even in the more serious cases when a Local Authority has parental responsibility for a child in care, since a Care Order does not extinguish parental responsibility and the Local Authority may only take away so much of the parents' responsibility as is necessary in order to secure the welfare of the child. Thus even when a Care Order has been made in child protection cases, the Local Authority is required to consult and involve the parents and attempt to work co-operatively with them in the interests of the child. However, legal powers to limit parental rights apply for only a small minority of children who come to the attention of social workers because of child protection concerns. Recent studies have shown that between 75 and 80 per cent of children about whom a child protection conference is held remain living at home with at least one parent and with no statutory order in force (Dartington 1995). In the study which this chapter describes, almost 50 per cent of the children were living for the greater part of the six month period after the abuse allegation with at least one parent who was alleged to have been involved in the maltreatment. Thus, for the majority of cases an approach which made no attempt to work co-operatively with the parent having twenty-four hour care of the child would be likely to increase the risks to the child rather than diminish them.

The legal and ethical mandate to attempt to work in partnership is unambiguous. The extent to which this mandate is, or indeed can be, carried out in the early stages of child protection cases is however less clear. This Chapter considers the extent to which social workers are succeeding in working in partnership with children in need of protection and their families. It will concentrate on a Department of Health funded study focusing on this issue, the fieldwork for which was conducted just as the 1989 Act was being implemented (Thoburn, Lewis and Shemmings 1995a, 1995b) but also draws on insights from a study nearing completion of a cohort of 'significant harm' cases entering the protection system in 1993–4 (Brandon, Lewis and Thoburn 1996). The emphasis is on social work practice, since it is social workers who are given the major responsibility for assessment and service provision when children are believed to be in need of additional support and protection. However, social work practice cannot be separated out from the formal child protection process which involves members of other professions, and guidance suggests that longer-term support and therapy should normally involve a multi-disciplinary core group seeking to work in partnership with family members.

Research on partnership-based practice

A bibliographic search of the British evaluative or practice literature on partnership and child protection might lead one to believe that child protection work is synonymous with child protection conferences. Lewis (1992) summarised the large number of evaluations of pilot projects to invite parents to initial or review conferences which took place between 1989 and 1991. These studies appear to have reassured a somewhat sceptical professional world that parents did wish to take part in these meetings and that the results were generally viewed by parents and professionals alike as helpful and in the interests of the children. However, with one or two exceptions they gave little information about the involvement of the young people, and about other aspects of the work before and after the conference. Few studies have been undertaken of the involvement of family members, either individually or as members of self-help groups, in the design of child protection services or information leaflets, although it is known that this happens in some authorities.

Before proceeding to a detailed examination of issues specifically relevant to family involvement, it is useful to draw from these studies and the more recent ones reviewed by the Dartington team (1995), a picture of the type of work covered in the United Kingdom by the 'child protection' label. There is considerable agreement that children identified as possibly in need of protection services are, apart from a small proportion of investigations resulting from inaccurate or malicious information, children who are 'in need' of support services under the terms of Section 17 of the Children Act. Most are poor, badly housed, living in deprived areas where levels of unemployment are high. They are more likely than the population as a whole to live with a single parent or a parent and step-parent; marital disputes often involving violence are more frequently part of family life and parents and children are more likely than the norm to have mental or physical health problems or disabilities.

Cleaver and Freeman (1995), who looked at a cohort of cases where suspicion of abuse was notified to the child protection system, concluded that most of the families could be allocated to three main groups, and our two studies would support the usefulness of this categorisation. The likelihood of successfully working in partnership will be greater in some types of cases than in others. The largest group were already well known to social workers and other professionals because of multiple and interlocking problems, and were pushed into the child protection system, often for the second, third, or fourth time, by an event or incident not necessarily connected with previous causes for concern. An example from our studies would be a family where the level of physical and emotional care of the children had caused concern to teachers, social workers and the GP for some time, and was evident in the children's behaviour, but which came into the child protection system because of sexual fondling by a baby-sitter. The second group, which they describe as 'acute distress' families, are those who in better times had been coping adequately, but who were rocked by either one devastating blow or a series of sometimes unconnected events. In our partnership study, a succession of miscarriages and still births and the consequent grief reaction of the mother, a teacher, led to marital conflict and the emotional neglect and excessive physical punishment of the children. Families in these two groups will often be asking for a service, and partnership-based practice can be possible if agreement can be reached about the aims of the work and the methods to be used.

The third group identified by Cleaver and Freeman were the 'single issue' families where the family was often not known to have problems until a child protection referral (often an allegation of sexual abuse) was made. If there was agreement between parents and social workers that abuse had occurred and about who was responsible for it it was usually possible to engage the family in the work. The study by Thoburn *et al.* (1995) suggests that parents who are accused of abusing a child but deny any involvement, especially if there is no clear evidence to substantiate the allegation or allocate responsibility, are never likely to be able to work in partnership with professionals seeking to implement a protection plan. They might however be kept fully informed, treated with courtesy and involved in drawing up a plan which provides adequate monitoring but is not overly intrusive in family life.

It was with these considerations in mind that frameworks for analysis for our study were constructed which required the nature of the case to be taken into account before a conclusion was reached as to whether an appropriate degree of partnership had been achieved. Each case was allocated by the researchers to a 'best', 'middle' and 'worst' scenario grouping in terms of the likelihood of partnership based practice being feasible and also to consider gradations of success in the light of these difficulties.

Arnstein's ladder of citizen participation, adapted from a community development focus for use with individual cases, proved helpful in the construction of a continuum of family involvement along which we could rate each case (Arnstein 1969). 'Successful partnership' was identified by 'respect for one another, rights to information, accountability, competence and value accorded to individual input. In short each partner is seen as having something to contribute, power is shared, decisions are made jointly, roles are not only respected but also backed by legal and moral rights' (Family Rights Group, 1991, p.1). This definition does not suggest that power must be shared equally in order for partnerships to be established, but does imply some sharing of power between social workers and family members. At the other end of the scale were cases where family members were not involved at all or were placated or manipulated. In the middle of the continuum were cases where family members were kept fully informed and their opinions sought on some aspects of the case but where they did not become involved in the work nor appear to influence the decisions. In some cases this was the choice of the family members themselves since they did not share the professionals' views about the existence or seriousness of problems.

Although the extent of participation was our main outcome measure, a protocol was devised for the assessment of interim outcomes for the children at the six month stage, since it would be inappropriate to allocate a case to the 'successful outcome' group in terms of partnership if this appeared to be associated with a poor outcome for the child.

The study focused on agency policies and social work practice from immediately prior to an allegation or suspicion of maltreatment to either case closure or six months after the initial Child Protection Conference. A cohort of 220 consecutive cases which reached Child Protection Conferences was identified from parts of seven authorities. The research team rated attempts to work in partnership with the parents (including parents who were no longer living in the family home and those who were believed to be responsible for the maltreatment as well as those who were believed not to have been implicated); the children and young people who were old enough to be involved in the work and decision-making at least to some extent; and a small number of close relatives who played an important part in the protection of the children. In total 385 family members could have been involved in the work.

Data were collected from social workers, parents, a small number of young people and from case files. Seventy-seven Child Protection Conferences were observed and some managers were also given questionnaires to complete. More detailed illustrative material was collected from a small sample of 33 cases where the parents and some of the children were interviewed, mostly on two separate occasions. This material was complemented by questionnaires completed by family members so that we had the views of 120 family members from 79 of the cohort families as to whether they considered themselves to have participated in the work. Table 1 gives details of the sources of data.

Table 9.1 Sources of data on the 220 cases

Families in cohort	220
Families included in interview sample	33
Potential family member participants	385
Data adequate for rating participation	378
Main parent/parenting pairs	220
Non-resident parents in sample	77
Children aged 10+ in sample	72
Number of family members from whom there was direct evidence of participation	120

Conferences resulted in 62 per cent of the index children (the oldest child in the family who was believed to have been maltreated) being recorded on the child protection register. All categories of abuse and neglect were included in similar proportions to the national picture. The full range of severity of abuse was included with 30 per cent of cases involving serious physical injury, life-threatening neglect or penetrative sexual abuse.

The extent of partnership in 220 cases

From the data available it was possible to draw conclusions about the extent to which family members were involved in a) the work as a whole, and b) the main decisions which were taken. It was concluded that only 2 per cent were full 'partners' in the protection process and 14 per cent were rated as participating to a considerable extent. Thus only one in six participated or were partners. This proportion was the same even if only the main parent(s) were included. At the other end of the scale, 13 per cent of the total and 7 per cent of the main parents were rated as 'not involved at all', 'placated' or 'manipulated'. The older children were slightly more likely than the parents to participate in the social work process and the detailed decisions about how the investigation and initial assessment should be undertaken. They were less likely than their parents to participate in the conference and in decisions about the protection plan.

Since such a small proportion was rated as participating to a substantial extent, a less rigorous rating scale of 'involved', 'involved to a limited extent or at some time', and 'not involved' was used for purposes of analysis. A more encouraging picture then emerges with 42 per cent of the main parents and 39 per cent of the children aged ten or over being rated in the 'involved' group; almost half of the main parents and just over half of the older children being involved to a limited extent or at some time; and 7 per cent of the main parents and 10 per cent of the older children not being involved at all.

A similar though slightly less positive picture emerges for the 73 main parents from whom we have direct information, with 33 per cent considering themselves to have been involved; 44 per cent involved to some extent or at some time and 23 per cent not at all. This suggests that, if anything, the researchers have been over- rather than under-generous in their ratings. Although not invariably the case, it was most likely that if parents were involved in the work this would also be the case for the children.

A protocol was devised for rating the interim outcome for the children at the six month stage (see Thoburn *et al.* 1995 for details). Sixty-five per cent were rated as having good or moderately good interim outcomes; in a quarter of cases there appeared to be no change; and in 10 per cent the outcome for the child at the six month stage appeared to be poor. There was a highly significant association between the main parent being involved and the child having a good or moderately good interim outcome. This should reassure those who have expressed concerns that attempts to work in partnership with parents might have a negative impact on the child's welfare. This positive conclusion drawn from the quantitative analysis was strongly supported by the interview data. The following quotes are from cases where a high level of partnership was in evidence.

PARENT: 'It did turn out to be helpful. She [social worker] was very helpful. She was a nice woman. She would say what she was doing as it happened, so we knew.'

12-YEAR-OLD BOY: 'They were talking about me and mum and everyone else so I wanted to hear what they were talking about – what they were saying and whether it was correct or not. It was the meeting that mum and I went to so that they could decide whether or not she was good enough to keep me.'

The characteristics of partnership-based practice

When scrutinising the data in an attempt to identify any variables which appeared to be associated with working in partnership we considered the characteristics of the family; variables about the child and the abuse; variables about the agency procedures and policies; and the work of the individual social workers. As a result of overlapping variables and small numbers in each cell our analysis was mainly descriptive and the tests of significance must be treated with some caution. The details are available elsewhere (Thoburn *et al.* 1995a and 1995b) and this chapter ends with a descriptive account of the nature of practice which appeared to be associated with working in partnership.

In general, although some parents and children had such severe problems that it was not possible to involve them at all, these were very few in number. Even when the degree of difficulty in a case was such that a poor outcome for child or a parent was almost inevitable some workers managed to involve some of these parents and children in the work. We concluded that in the majority of child protection cases a skilled and determined worker would be able to involve parents and older children, and move towards working in partnership as the case progressed. The proportion of cases where family members were involved or were partners would have been higher had opportunities not been lost by insensitive or unskilled workers or agency policies which undermined parents who were willing and able to participate in plans to help and protect their child. In short, whilst failure to work in partnership can sometimes be attributed to aspects of the case itself (our worst scenario cases), differences between cases where family members were informed, involved and consulted and those where they were not seemed almost always attributable to either the agency policy and procedures or the social work practice or both together.

Agency policy and practice
The timing of our study meant that we had a ready-made quasi-experimental situation, since agency policy varied, particularly in respect of the routine invitation of parents to initial child protection conferences. Whilst we set out to go beyond most previous studies and look at the whole of the process and not just the conferences, our study in a sense vindicates the emphasis which other researchers have placed on them. If there was one single practice which aided or impeded family member involvement it was the inclusion of parents as valued participants and not just attenders at conferences. This was partly because of the contribution they made to the effectiveness of the conference, but also because their involvement at conferences changed the way all other aspects of the case were handled. Other aspects of agency policy and procedures which figured highly in cases in our two studies in which family members participated or were partners were:

- An emphasis on the provision of a range of clear verbal and written information about the protection process, including information about where the family might go for additional assistance and support, and facilities to help them to attend (eg transport, the provision of interpreters or baby-sitting). (Information was rarely available for children and young people and those with a communication difficulty but this deficit is now being remedied in many authorities.)

- An insistence by managers and social workers themselves that time must be available for careful preparation before meetings and for the offering of appropriate advice and support to the family members who were going to attend interviews, medicals or conferences.

- Help for each family member in preparing what they wanted to get across to the conference, whether or not they would be attending in person; and clarity about who would give the views of family members who were not present.

- The interviews with parents who attended conferences suggest that training for chairs of conferences and for all conference attenders should be required so that they can practice less destructive ways of saying things which might be hurtful or shocking when those concerned are present. Most of the chairs of conferences where parents were present for all or most of the meeting were enthusists for this practice and had devised ways of proceeding which parents appreciated. Negative comments about chairs and other professionals were more likely if parents attended for only short parts of the conferences.

- Encouragement to family members to bring a supporter with them to important meetings and guidance about how to choose, pointing out some of the pitfalls, such as the potential problems if friends hear information which they had not previously known.

- A high priority placed on recruiting social workers and managers who believe in the importance of involving parents and children in their work. Most social workers do, but some are more equivocal. On the basis of the evidence available from a range of sources, 60 per cent of the workers were rated as strongly committed to working in partnership; 38 per cent moderately so and three (2 per cent) not at all.

- Provision of receptionists and reception facilities which are comfortable and welcoming; message-taking facilities which are efficient and reliable; and interview and meeting rooms which are suitable for the purpose.

- Most important of all, however, was a policy which reassured workers that when they saught to work in partnership they would have the backing of managers, (and preferably also of the Social Services Committee and the Area Child Protection Committee), and that the resources essential to make partnership based practice a reality would be made available.

Social work practice

Parents fell into two groups. A significant minority of around a third found themselves caught up in the child protection system but did not want help for themselves although they might have wanted it for their children. Once this had happened, they wanted the process to make sure they knew what was going on and to be treated in an open, honest and efficient way. Around two thirds, however, did want help before and after the conference, whether or not the child was registered, and for them, the quality of the relationship was of central importance.

Some wanted help but not from a particular social worker whose attitudes and approach at the time of the allegation or in the past they had found unhelpful. Others however developed a relationship of trust over the crisis of the referral and were upset and resentful at having to have a new worker, especially if the change was hurried or they were left without a worker until one could be allocated. The least desirable option for those who knew they and their children needed help was to be passed from investigating team to assessing team all of whom kept their emotional distance, doing a competent job except for the one ingredient which parents and children valued most: being cared about as individuals and having their strengths acknowledged even if their inadequacies and vulnerabilities had to be exposed. The lucky ones managed to retain one skilled and caring worker throughout or eventually reached a long-term team worker who started to provide the help they had been asking for from the first mention of abuse or even long before. If evidence of skilled and caring work and appropriate practical help was not provided early enough, family members did their best to outwit the assessors and get themselves off the books as soon as possible and without having received the help they knew they needed. On hearing some of these accounts, corroborated often by what we read in the files, we could believe that a new model (or a variation on an old theme) of social work practice, 'the deterrent model', had been added to the child protection repertoire. If we make involvement with social services a sufficiently unpleasant and unhelpful experience they won't come back.

Clearly case allocation systems are needed, but if partnership means anything there must be some flexibility about the timing of a change of worker and the possibility of the worker who undertook the investigation remaining if it will be difficult for a parent or child to establish trust in a new worker. Equally a request for a change of worker should be taken seriously and acted upon if trust really has broken down or not been established.

In broad terms, if a longer-term service was needed after the child protection conference, successfully working in partnership was dependent on the allocation of a key worker who offered continuity and a supportive or therapeutic relationship as well as marshalling and co-ordinating the packages of help and any monitoring of the child's well-being. This mother clearly lacked such a sense of continuity:

> For me, it was a bad experience. I don't think Kevin benefited, and having different social workers' faces each time and going through it all over again wasn't good. He wasn't happy about them coming round again. He was more worried that Alan (his step-father who was accused of physically abusing him) might be put away.

If this element of continuity and co-ordination was in place, our study suggested that additional workers could with advantage be brought in alongside the key worker to provide short-term specialist assessment or therapeutic services. Family centres or specialist children's services teams appeared to be particularly effective. They could work with different family members or the family as a group and also had a range of practical and recreational resources at their disposal.

Conclusion

We conclude from our studies that working in partnership with parents and children is either not achievable or not appropriate in some child protection cases. However, in the majority, social work practice and agency policy which makes a serious attempt to engage family members can succeed in doing so. There were examples of skilled and caring social work even in some of the more unpromising cases as well as in those where help was sought and welcome. However, the actual methods used by those who succeeded in working in partnership appeared less important than the values and personality of the worker and such characteristics as reliability and honesty. Efficiency, technical competence and attention to procedures without evidence of caring was not valued by those who needed help and led to comments such as 'all she was interested in was doing a good job – following the procedures', and 'we were just another job lot'. The parent and young person quoted earlier give a more positive picture and convey the consistent message from our two studies of child protection work that partnership, caring and competence are inextricably intertwined.

References

Arnstein, S. (1969) A ladder of citizen participation. *Journal of American Institute of Planners 35*, 4, 215–224.

Brandon, M., Lewis, A. and Thoburn, J. (1996) The Children Act definition of significant harm: interpretations in practice. *Health and Social Care in the Community*.

Cleaver, H. and Freeman, P. (1995) *Parental Perspectives in Cases of Suspected Child Abuse.* London: HMSO.

Dartington Social Research Unit (1995) *Child Protection and Child Abuse: Messages from Research.* London: HMSO.

Department of Health (1989) *The Children Act 1989: Principles and Practice in Regulations and Guidance.* London: HMSO.

Department of Health (1985) *Social Work Decisions in Child Care.* London: HMSO.

Department of Health (1991a) *Patterns and Outcomes in Child Placement.* London: HMSO.

Department of Health (1991b) *Working Together under the Children Act 1989.* London: HMSO.

Department of Health (1991c) *The Children Act 1989: Guidance and Regulations.* London: HMSO.

Department of Health (1995) *The Challenge of Partnership in Child Protection.* London: HMSO.

Family Rights Group (1991) *The Children Act 1989: Working in Partnership with Families.* London: Family Rights Group.

Hardiker, P. (1991) *Policies and Practice in Preventive Child Care.* Aldershot: Avebury

Lewis, A. (1992) An overview of research. In J. Thoburn (ed) *Participation in Practice: A Reader.* Norwich: UEA.

Thoburn, J., Lewis, A. and Shemmings, D. (1995a) *Paternalism or Partnership? Involving Families in the Child Protection Process.* London: HMSO.

Thoburn, J., Lewis, A. and Shemmings, D. (1995b) Family participation in child protection. *Child Abuse Review 4.*

PART 3

The Continuum of Out-of-Home Care

CHAPTER 10

Respite Accommodation
A Case Study of Partnership
Under The Children Act 1989

Jane Aldgate, Marie Bradley and David Hawley

Accommodation

'Accommodation' is a new term in child welfare law in England and Wales. It refers to out-of-home placements for children where the arrangements are made entirely voluntarily between parents, children and social workers. The Children Act 1989 repealed former legislation relating to voluntary arrangements, which placed sanctions on parents removing children from local authority care after six months. It also allowed for the first time for planned periods of respite care, of up to 90 days in total, to be included as a single placement episode. It is this short-term form of accommodation which is the subject of the research findings given in this chapter. Accommodation can be of any duration, from one day to several years. Longer-term arrangements would generally be assumed to include an element of shared care with parents. Any placements where it was thought that parental contact would be detrimental to children's welfare would come under a different part of the Act relating to care proceedings. But even here, parental responsibility would not necessarily be extinguished entirely but rather be controlled: 'Parents should be expected and enabled to retain their responsibilities and to remain as closely involved as is consistent with their child's welfare, even if that child cannot live at home either temporarily or permanently' (DH 1989, p.2).

Accommodation needs to be seen in the context of the underlying philosophy of the Act: to keep children within their families, wherever possible; to uphold parental responsibility; and to effect a partnership with parents and children. This partnership recognises and values families' needs and their rights to be involved in decisions about placing children away from home. There is also recognition of the importance of maintaining continuity for children separated from their parents, even for brief periods.

Upholding parental responsibility

Accommodation reflects the Children Act philosophy that being a parent is an important contribution to citizenship. Parents are valued in their role of bringing up children. Further, it is normal for families to experience periods of stress which are beyond their capacities. Most families find support within their own networks of family and friends but some families do not command such resources, and should be able to turn to the State when they need help. By providing timely supportive and non-stigmatising services, more intrusive interventions may be prevented at a later stage (Hardiker, Barker and Exton 1995).

The Act recognises that support services should be broadly conceived and may necessitate the judicious use of out-of-home placements. This represents a significant change of emphasis from previous legislation where there was a narrow definition of preventive work, with the aim principally to diminish the need to receive children into care. This resulted in considerable stigmatising of 'in-care' services which were seen as a last resort. Research evidence from the 1980s showed that children growing up in the care system often lost contact with their families (Millham *et al.* 1986) and left care ill-prepared for an independent adult life (Stein and Carey 1986; Triseliotis 1980).

This evidence on outcomes was complemented by that from several studies which suggested that parents did not receive help when they needed it at an earlier stage, and that even when children were removed compulsorily from home, parents still wished to fulfil their parental responsibilities. The overall conclusions of research from the mid 1980s was that there were 'potentialities for using short-term respite as a means of preventing the permanent break-up of families by offering temporary relief care' (DHSS 1985, p.16).

The research evidence was incorporated into various government-backed papers reviewing child care law, culminating in the White Paper 'The Law on Child Care' (DHSS 1987) which preceded the Children Act 1989. This stressed that placements away from home should be used 'as a means of providing support to the family and reducing the risk of family breakdown' (DHSS 1987, p.6). The recommendation about using short-term out-of-home placements was firmly incorporated into the Children Act 1989 by introducing the use of accommodation to replace voluntary care. Accommodation was deliberately placed within the clauses of the Children Act 1989 which outline duties to support families in the community, rather than in a separate section referring to out-of-home placements. The term 'care', which had become so stigmatised, would be retained only in cases where children were compulsorily looked after by the local authority away from home. The regulations and guidance accompanying the Children Act 1989 spell out the changes which the law intends and give the rationale for those changes:

> The Act gives a positive emphasis to identifying and providing for the
> child's needs rather than focusing on parental short-comings in a

negative manner. The responsibility on local authorities to provide accommodation for children in need who require it – because, for example, the parents are prevented from providing appropriate care during the illness of one parent – replaces 'reception into care' with its unhelpful associations of parental shortcomings. Where, for example, parents who usually provide good and devoted care for their child need a break, the provision of additional help in the home or suitable accommodation for the child for a short time should be seen as a service to the child and family without pressure or prejudice. Children accommodated are 'looked after' by the local authority in partnership with the parents. The Act also emphasises that partnership with parents should not become weaker if it becomes necessary to provide the child with accommodation. (DH 1991b, p.16)

Promoting partnership with parents and children

As suggested in the chapter by Hill and Aldgate in this volume, partnership is a pivotal concept of the Children Act 1989. The offering of short-term accommodation as a service to families necessitates arrangements that enhance partnership. Similarly, involving children in planning for accommodation and giving them a choice of placement can enhance their feeling of control over their lives. The law is emphatic that children who are to be accommodated should be consulted, according to their age and understanding. What is meant by 'consultation' is open to debate, as will be discussed later in the chapter.

Continuity for children

Much of the criticism of out-of-home placements for children cited in research relates to children's loss of connections with their families once they are placed (see DHSS 1985; DH 1991a). The Children Act takes a holistic approach to child development, recognising that significant influences on children's development relate not only to kinship but must also include dimensions such as race, culture, religion and language. Further, preserving continuity of education may be highly significant for older children. School may sometimes be the one stable factor in the life of a child whose family is in transition. School also represents a significant link with the familiar for children separated from their parents.

New research on respite accommodation – an overview of the findings

The need for more information about the use of short-term accommodation was addressed in a four year study funded by the Department of Health and undertaken by Aldgate, Bradley and Hawley at the Universities of Oxford and Leicester The study was in two parts. The first part reviewed 13 examples of respite accommodation services for children other than those designated 'disabled'. It concluded that effective respite accommodation was being offered by social services departments and voluntary agencies to a wide range of families under stress. There was evidence of schemes providing respite accommodation to children of all ages. The second part of the study traced the progress of 60 families through a period of respite accommodation, mainly in two city local authorities, looking at expectations, progress and outcomes from the perspective of children, parents, carers and social workers.

Both parts of the study gave much useful information about the value of the service and its meaning to those who used it. The study found that respite accommodation illustrated the use of family support services to prevent family breakdown. Short-term respite accommodation aimed to keep children in their family of origin, preserving for them the ordinary but important continuity of childhood. It was used for families under stress – stress which came from within and without the family. At the beginning of the study, parents were experiencing problems related to income, housing, health, and the care and day-to-day management of their children. They also felt unconfident about their parenting skills, had low self-esteem and little support from families and friends. By the end of the study, parental self-esteem had improved, as measured on a standard test. As importantly, parents felt more in control of their lives. Their preoccupation with their own chronic health problems had shifted and they had a more realistic view of their abilities and lives. Over half the parents began to address their social isolation by the end of the study. Around one-third of the parents commented on the fact that establishing links with carers helped them feel more part of the community.

The service linked parents and children with carefully selected carer-families who generally lived in the same neighbourhood. The carers learned to work in partnership with parents by providing a family placement that did not threaten parental responsibility in any way. It was very much a service which aimed to help parents and children at the stage when they asked for help.

The research suggests that, for a respite accommodation service to work well, there needs to be a synthesis of several components. The social worker has two important roles – as a direct service provider and as an enabler. Social workers offer the resource of respite care – they also bring parents the opportunity of reflecting on their needs, and of using counselling and support to look at how they might use their strengths most effectively to promote their children's welfare.

The manner in which the service is offered is as important as the service itself. Decisions about placements are made jointly between parents and social workers, each contributing their own expertise. Emphasis is placed on parents taking the lead in decisions about their children, and on social workers giving parents the information on which to base those decisions. Every effort is made to help parents to feel in control in the decision-making. Carers also reinforce the service and the process build parents' self-confidence. Mutual respect and agreement between participants about the aims of the placement enables children to benefit and enjoy their time away from home.

Respite care can be offered as either a discrete service or as part of a package of services. It is seen by users to fulfil one or more of the following purposes:

- to provide relief from the normal stresses of being a parent
- to provide children with relief from stressful family living
- to help manage children's behaviour
- to provide a link with the community for families living in social isolation
- to help with relief from the stress of living in continuing poverty
- to offer an alternative to admission to full time accommodation
- to provide a relief for sick parents
- to provide early diversion from potential physical abuse
- to build parents' self-esteem as parents
- to offer a different and relaxing experience for children.

Characteristics of the study families

Though each family and each arrangement was highly individual in its own way, they shared common features. Many of the families were headed by a single parent, generally the mother. Parents were not especially young, most were between 25 and 40 years old. Many parents were alone following the breakdown of long-standing relationships. The majority of parents were not in paid employment and nearly all of them were living in poverty, dependent on income support. They were similar in social circumstances to families of children who come into the care system reported in earlier research (DH 1991a). Most of the families were rather socially isolated and had few people on whom they could depend in social, emotional and practical ways. While they often lived quite close to their extended families, they did not have especially strong links with them. The lives of the majority were dominated by high levels of chronic physical illness, stress-related illness, anxiety and depression. Mrs Maidment was a good example. Aged 28, she had two children aged seven and nine. The family lived in an inner-city bedsit and were waiting to be rehoused. She said: 'It is hard on them, since he [husband] left. I get very low sometimes and a bit ratty, and there's nowhere much for them to play. It's a godsend, it gives me a break and they have a lot of fun. I'm glad to see them again.'

Partnership in action

The remainder of this chapter draws on the study findings to highlight the key practice and organisational issues for the setting up of respite accommodation in partnership with parents and children. As will be shown, it mattered greatly to parents that their sense of parental responsibility was fully recognised. Parents were bedevilled by insecurity about their parenting. Social worker and carer actions and attitudes were significant factors in empowering parents to use the services constructively.

Throughout the study, we were impressed by the commitment of parents to their children and their wish to improve the quality of life for the family. Short-term accommodation was most often sought for relief from the day-to-day demands of bringing up children in social and economic deprivation, which made the task that much harder. A break for themselves, knowing that the children were well cared for, was what most parents hoped for from the arrangements. The children's enjoyment of the visits was an important but complicated matter for parents. It also brought worries about the possibility of children feeling dissatisfied with home. 'I was very nervous at first, in case Stuart thought I didn't want him, and I wondered if [the carer] would cope. He'd never been away before. He had a great time. In fact, I wondered if he liked it better there.'

Families thought highly of the services they received, and commented particularly on the quality of the work of the carers, their approachability and practical sensitivity: 'Well, they [the carers] were really good. They never looked down on me – never. She was sort of ordinary but special. I always felt like Becky's mum and I knew I could always talk to her.'

One of the greatest difficulties, however, was associated with the earliest contact with the agency. Needing help but not knowing about 'support services' meant many parents waited a long time before talking to the agency. Getting to the point of actually being considered for services was another sizeable hurdle: parents frequently felt that they had to be 'desperate' before help would be offered. Once parents had been accepted for the service, the support and help offered was very positive but the research suggests that agencies are a long way from providing the needs-led family support service envisaged by the Act: 'I saw three different social workers before anyone really listened. I said I'd murder him if they didn't give me some help – but I didn't want to lose him, I've never hurt him. Then she told me about it [short-term breaks]. It's been brilliant.'

Ongoing support and advice from social workers was generally highly valued. Parents worried a great deal that seeking outside help might undermine their own confidence and coping ability as parents, that needing help would be seen as indicative of their failure as parents, that their children might feel rejected by them and prefer the care they receive elsewhere. Parents usually found social workers approachable, helpful, honest and reliable in the process of making the arrangements and in their meetings afterwards. This attitude was a firm foundation for partnership. One mother commented on the social worker: 'Oh! she really did seem to understand. She offered the right amount of help at the right time – any different and it would have taken away my confidence. I did worry that they would think I was a bad parent.'

Children's understanding and experience of respite accommodation

In the study, we observed and talked to children between the ages of one and 15 years. Children who were old enough to talk to us about their experiences of short-term care were usually free and articulate in doing so. Some of the younger children could make use of (and sometimes initiated!) guided play – usually structured around telling a story about a visit to the carer family – to give a sense of their feelings about the breaks. Talking to parents about their understanding of the child's experience was also useful, especially in the complicated area of the interrelating of children's and parents' needs. It was a measure of social work preparation and parental concern that children were usually quite clear about what the arrangements were, and why they had been made. Some children saw the purpose of the arrangements as first and foremost to give their parent a break, and children's ability to see the long-term benefits for all the family was impressive. Others accurately saw the primary reason for the arrangements as being to give themselves a break from stressful circumstances at home while most felt the breaks to be for the benefit of both parent and child. There was considerable congruence between children's perceptions and the stated aims in social workers' recording of plans. Paula, aged eight: 'It's so my mum can have a rest and maybe go out a bit, but it's lovely going there, once I got used to it.'

All of the children found that talking about the arrangements as part of their preparation, helped them to think about what it might be like, and what might be, and feel difficult for them when they went. The preparatory visits to the carer's home were the most important factor in reassuring the children and in helping them to feel less worried about being away from home. They were especially reassured by tangible evidence that there was a place for them in the carer's home. Asked what helped to reassure him about the arrangements, Simon, aged six, said: 'It was when I saw the bed that was meant for me that I knew it was all right.'

This little boy had assumed he would have to share a bed, since this was what he was used to at home. Having an idea of family routine, which would nevertheless take account of their special needs and wishes, was also reassuring to children. Such attention to detail also reassured parents that their parental responsibility was not threatened in any way and was a significant aspect of a partnership approach to the service. Tom, aged seven:

We went to tea, me and Jenny, and mum. We had sandwiches and cake. Only I don't like egg, I was really worried. I thought what would I do if it was only what I didn't like? But she asked me – don't you like egg? Then she asked if I'd like cheese instead, and what else did I specially not like?

Despite the generally excellent and invaluable preparation, homesickness was nevertheless a universal problem for the children and reminded us of the importance of recognising the significance of any change for children.

KATHY, AGED 10: 'Oh! it was hard, it's not the same. You can't just go to the cupboard and get something to eat when you like. I felt lonely. Now it's great, now I'm used to it.'

RESEARCHER: Did you miss being home?'

MEGAN, AGED 8: 'Well, no. Maybe. I did miss mum…and David…and everyone.'

RESEARCHER: 'Did you worry about being away from home?'

SAM, AGED 5: Oh, yes! I couldn't think where she was (mum) and if she was all right.'

Having someone to talk to beforehand helped the children to think about and to cope with their feelings. Knowing how contact could be made between carer and home was also helpful. Few families had phones at home, so this needed to be thought about – especially for the early breaks. Most of the children felt that their carers would understand and be sympathetic to their feelings, and would be approachable if they were needed. On the whole, children found it most helpful to have some private time and place to recover their equilibrium, with background support from the carer. Rosie, aged nine: 'I like to be by myself, and think a bit, when I'm sad. She [carer] knows though.'

Finally, what children enjoyed and commented on most frequently about their stays was the quality of care they received. The kindness and consideration they experienced from the carers, and the opportunity to relax and play, were much more frequently mentioned than material advantages. Joey, aged 11: 'They're all right…kind, you know. And they play with me.'

Most of the children seemed to have talked freely to their parents about their experiences. Where children had the opportunity to talk to social workers, they were surprised and pleased about this consultation. 'I was glad to talk about it. I was a bit surprised when they asked me, you know. Well, I thought, I have to go, don't I? But she really did ask what I thought, and what I wanted.'

This last comment illustrates the achievement of a balance between adult responsibility and the process of consultation. The child recognised that accommodation was going to happen but valued her participation in both choosing the carers and the fact that her views were included in the decision-making.

Implications for practice

The delivery of respite accommodation demands careful attention to details of practice and organisation of services. The study findings suggest that the following issues among others may be important when arranging respite.

Acknowledging family worries in the decision-making

The decision to use any short-term accommodation is usually a complex one. This applies as much to respite as to full-time arrangements. Parents and children have worries about what it will entail. Parents sometimes worry that children may see the request for short-term accommodation as a letting go of care and responsibility, in a way that may undermine the relationships between parents and children. Parents also worry that other people may see it this way too, including professionals. Parents are anxious that the experience of spending time in another home, where life is seemingly more fortunate and less stressful, may mean that their children come to prefer this home and these parents. Not least, there are sometimes the difficult feelings of envy for parents – what about me? All of these anxieties are difficult to voice, particularly if parents feel that such fears will influence how they are seen and the service they will receive. When these worries are acknowledged and discussed, the stability and the success of the arrangements seems to benefit.

No hidden agendas

Bearing in mind the anxiety of parents and children, several other points must be satisfactorily addressed before the discussion and exploration of arrangements can begin. Parents and children must have a clear idea of what short-term accommodation is and what it is not. This should include reassurance that arrangements are purely voluntary and parents retain full responsibility throughout. At no time in the future should the experience of accommodation be used against parents in court proceedings. To do so would be a betrayal of parental trust and would undermine the concept of a service freely given and received.

A partnership rooted in reality

Recognising that the service should be offered in a spirit of partnership, it is important that families know what is realistically available, and what choice is open to them within that. If families understand that restrictions in choice of placement are to do with limitations in provision, then they are likely to respond more positively. Even if choices are limited, every attempt should be made to give both parents and children some choice of placement. This will enhance parents' sense of empowerment, and help older children to feel some control over the new challenge that faces them. Parents and children should also be able to refuse the service, if after negotiations they feel it is inappropriate for them.

Written agreements

Written agreements exemplify partnership by spelling out what is expected of all parties. They may be as effective in allaying fears of social workers who worry about children drifting into long-term unplanned placements as they are in clearly spelling out for parents when placements will end. The research suggests that agreements must be written simply, in parents' first language if possible. If parents cannot read very well, agreements can be tape-recorded.

Choice as an empowering tool

Where user families can be given some choice in the selection of the carer family with whom they will be linked, this does much to confirm a sense of partnership in the making of the arrangements, and strengthens commitment to their success. A useful model is that of child-minding, where families come to the agency and ask for information about carers, then make their own selection. While in practice it may not be possible to offer the same range, providing choice should be considered in the longer-term developments of the scheme. From the experience of the study families, families find it most helpful to meet two or three families. A greater range may be confusing, time-consuming and counter-productive for everyone concerned. Parents need to know why these families have been selected for them.

Meetings with carer families

The meetings to help with selection are best held in the carers' homes, so parents and children can get a good sense of what it feels like to be there. Where possible, decisions should be made within a clearly defined period, say perhaps a week. However, where such choice is not possible, the sharing of this limitation in an appropriate way can still endorse the sense of a working partnership by allowing parents to deal with the reality of the situation.

Placement arrangements

The Children Act 1989 draws attention to the importance of factors relating to ethnic origin, cultural background and religion. The regulations advise that

'...other things being equal and in the great majority of cases, placement with a family of similar ethnic origin and religion is most likely to meet a child's needs as fully as possible and to safeguard his or her welfare most effectively' (DH 1991c, p.11).

For some children, the continuity of these very important dimensions of their own family life will be the most important considerations in making short-term arrangements. However, it may be that other factors are considered more significant by the child and the family. Keeping other links such as proximity to friends, school or neighbourhood, or finding a carer family who can take all members of a sibling group, may be more important. The pertinent issue is that the decision rests with the family and is made on the basis of informed discussion with them.

Individuality and continuity

Nevertheless, there will be times when the possibilities for meeting ethnic, cultural and religious needs of some children are restricted because there are no carers available from similar groups. When this is the case, the family needs to know this and to be helped to make the best decision for the child in the light of such a shortage. Carer families with different cultural, ethnic or religious backgrounds can sensitively understand and value these aspects of the child's family life, and there should be an emphasis on this in training. They should also be actively helped and supported to make provision for the observation of and contact with the cultural, ethnic and religious elements of children's experience. The Guidance and Regulations are helpful in stressing that:

> None of the separate factors involved should be abstracted and converted into a pre-condition which overrides the others or causes any of them to be less than fully considered....different factors will obviously vary in importance in relation to different children or in relation to the same child at different times'. (DH 1991c, p.7)

Understanding and communication

Spanning all the particular details of the arrangements, the research firmly suggests that it is important to attend to the details of expectations about family life in both families. A degree of common ground in culture, lifestyle and life experience will ease communication and transitions between the two homes. Added to this, carers who have experience of regarding parents as a natural and central feature of their work with children – child-minders, playgroup leaders, nursery workers and playscheme leaders, for example, are likely to communicate well with parents. Partnership is best expressed in the tangible events of every-day life which provide common ground between families. Every-day issues such as discipline, rewards, eating, playing, bedtime and pocket-money provide the ground for common values. The guiding principle is the safeguarding of continuity in the children's lives as far as possible. Additionally, and as importantly, children must know that their experiences are being thought about and that they will be taken care of by adults who are concerned about them and who have taken the trouble to find out about their needs and wishes.

Working in partnership with parents – addressing the power imbalance

The rhetoric of partnership is seductive, but, as the respite accommodation study suggests, effective partnership comes from careful well-thought-out social work practice. Partnership implies an equal and informed meeting of the people concerned with making decisions – the participants. It is important to bear in mind that the participants have different roles and different levels of power in the process of discussion and negotiation, and will be affected by different constraints.

In the making of short-term respite accommodation arrangements, research showed that in addition to parents and children the participants may include several professional workers – a social worker for the scheme and usually a social worker for the family and the carers. Others may be involved if they have a key part in the welfare of a particular family, for example medical social workers, health visitors or teachers.

While there is a situation of inevitable asymmetry between the participants in terms of their needs and their control of resources, and differences in the kind of power they have, this need not result in inequality in the social work undertaken with families. The research showed that parents need to know that they will be listened to without pre-judgement, that information about resources is honestly presented, and that they are told about any limitations of resources.

The research on respite accommodation found that the key elements of a constructive partnership include the recognition of differences and constraints, and a readiness to recognise and build on the strengths of children and their families. It requires making sure that the process is clear, showing thoughtful planning in all aspects, including the timing and location of meetings, the time scale of the process, the use of jargon-free language. Accountability to the users is a primary responsibility, including open access to files.

Locating short-term accommodation within family support services

In the last decade, much UK child welfare social work has become preoccupied with the investigation of suspected child abuse. This has led to an imbalance between the provision of support services and child abuse investigation. But as the recent Department of Health studies show, much effort is placed on investigative enquiries with little follow-up of either protective or supportive services (DH 1995). This approach has been criticised by the Audit Commission who recommend a diversion of resources to family support. Achieving such an aim is not easy. It would be a brave Director of Social Services who would refuse to investigate suspected abuse. Nevertheless, there does need to be a shift towards offering a wider range of family support services, of which short-term accommodation is one in a range of options. A way forward may be to experiment with local initiatives, as happened with the schemes in the study. The respite accommodation study showed that an early response to family stress can provide simultaneously a protective and a supportive service. Nor was there any evidence to support the myth that if families are offered accommodation, they will take advantage and abandon their children to long-term placements. Indeed, the contrary was evident. Out of 60 placements, only two turned into long-term arrangements. Parents showed themselves capable of responsible and responsive behaviour. For them a service which offered family support was indeed the best option. Their only complaint was that there was not enough of it.

References

Department of Health (1989) *An Introduction to the Children Act 1989.* London: HMSO.

Department of Health (1991a) *Patterns and Outcomes in Child Placement.* London: HMSO.

Department of Health (1991b) *The Children Act 1989 Guidance and Regulations Volume 2 Family Support.* London: HMSO.

Department of Health (1991c) *The Children Act 1989 Guidance and Regulations Volume 3 Family Placements.* London: HMSO.

Department of Health (1995) *Protecting Children – Messages from Research.* London: HMSO.

Department of Health and Social Security (1987) *The Law on Child Care and Family Services.* London: HMSO.

DHSS (1987) *The Law on Child Care and Family Services.* London: HMSO.

Hardiker P., Barker, M. and Exton, K. (1995) *The Social Policy Context of Child Welfare.* London: Commission for the National Society for the Prevention of Cruelty to Children.

Millham, S., Bullock, R., Hosie, K. and Haak, M. (1986) *Lost in Care.* Aldershot: Gower.

Stein, M. and Carey, K., (1986) *Leaving Care.* Oxford: Basil Blackwell.

Triseliotis, J. (1980) *Growing up in foster care and after.* In J. Triseliotis (ed) *New Developments in Foster Care and Adoption.* London: Routledge and Kegan Paul.

CHAPTER 11

Short-Term Foster Care

Clive Sellick

Introduction

The development of short-term or temporary foster care, especially between 1948 and 1991, has had little direct legislative or research scrutiny. Yet throughout this period its place has been central to the provision of services to children separated from their families in the public care system. As Rowe and her colleagues remarked in their extensive study of the beginning and ending of placements over two years in six local authorities: 'The day to day, bread and butter work of fostering is still the placement of younger children needing care for a brief period during a family crisis or to give relief to hard pressed parents.' (Rowe, Hundleby and Garnett 1989, p.79).

As the number of children looked after in public care has fallen (from 92,270 to 59,834 – or by 35 per cent – in England and Wales between 1981 and 1991), so the proportion of those placed in foster care has risen. For example, 65 per cent of all children looked after by local authorities between April 1992 and March 1993 were fostered. This figure increases to almost 90 per cent for children aged under ten years. Most of these fostered children spend very short periods of time in care: less than 14 days for about 50 per cent of those children who are aged one to nine years (Department of Health 1994a p.37).

Legislation

In spite of the widespread use of short-term foster care its only legal definition in England and Wales is in respect of respite care. Indeed for a brief period following the abolition of an eight week statutory time limit (Department of Health 1988) short-term fostering was left without any legal definition at all. The Children Act 1989 Guidance and Regulations in respect of Family Placements define short-term placements as those which occur within a period which does not exceed one year, where no single placement lasts for more than four weeks and where taken together these placements do not exceed 90 days (Department of Health 1991, p.48).

However the Regulations also lay down in considerable detail practice guidelines in respect of the Approval and Review of all foster carers, the Foster Care Agreement they must enter into, and the supervision arrangements including support which should be made available to them by the approving fostering agency. Much of this guidance is of particular relevance to short-term foster carers who, for example: 'can play an invaluable role in promoting both successful contact and reunification. But the extent to which they will be able to do this, in practice, depends on the recruitment, training and support which are available to them.' (Department of Health 1991, p.66).

Research

The research literature, whilst growing, is still quite limited and refers to special aspects or kinds of fostering. They include:

- Jassal (1981) who conducted a small-scale study of 20 short-term foster carers in one English city. He focused on the carers' reactions when children left their care, specifically the intellectual and emotional impacts.

- Hope (1983) conducted a small research project of 35 short-term foster carers in Wiltshire. She looked at factors which influenced the usage of these carers by social workers.

- Shaw and Hipgrave (1983) considered a number of major issues which arose from two research studies: a pilot project of a specialist fostering scheme in one East Midlands social services department, and a subsequent national survey of 45 specialist schemes in 44 local authorities and voluntary organisations throughout the United Kingdom except in London. This was updated in 1988 by the completion of questionnaires by three-fifths of all social services and social work departments.

- Berridge and Cleaver (1987) conducted a study of breakdowns in 530 short-term, intermediate and long-term foster placements in three constrasting agencies: a county council, a London Borough and a voluntary organisation. They studied social work case notes and also interviewed the various participants of ten cases in the county council.

- Westacott (1988) studied a Barnardos bridging foster care scheme. Mainly school aged children under 12 years old were referred to it by local authorities for specialist temporary care in preparation for new permanent families. Foster carers in this scheme also provided care for children after a permanent placement broke down, either on a planned, emergency, or respite care basis.

- Aldgate, Pratt and Duggan (1989) and Bradley and Aldgate (1994) studied the use of respite care to prevent long-term family breakdown by conducting a nationwide study of relevant services and by evaluating the use of local authority respite accommodation. The experiences of the key participants: children, parents and carers were considered.

- Sellick (1992) interviewed short-term foster carers in four local authorities and two independent fostering agencies, in order to identify and evaluate their support needs.

- Waterhouse (1992) examined the experiences and attitudes of short-term foster carers from two local authorities towards birth family contact.

- Part (1993) evaluated the questionnaire responses of 75 children of foster carers in a Scottish region in respect of their experiences and views of being part of a foster family.

The only study to look at short-term fostering in general examined all short-term foster care placements over a 12 month period in a northern English city shortly before the implementation of the Children Act (Stone 1995). It confirmed that foster care is primarily a very short-term service with 70 per cent of children returning home to their families within three months. The study also raised concerns about the number of children who were placed with short-term foster carers in emergency situations without either clear plans or aims; moves from one temporary placement to another; and those often older children who do not return home quickly.

Little wonder that at the end of the 1980s major figures in the field remarked that short-term foster care 'is one of the least researched types of fostering' (Triseliotis 1989, p.10) or that 'this whole area remains remarkably uncharted' (Berridge and Cleaver 1987). More recently Thoburn writes in the Foreword to Stone (1995) that: 'leaving aside specialist schemes, short-term foster care was, in the 1980s, the most neglected aspect of child and family social work both by researchers and by those who wrote about practice'. However, when viewed together these studies do tell us a good deal about the changing nature of the temporary fostering task, the skills and qualities required of competent foster carers and, in turn, what they value or seek from social workers and social services departments in respect of status and support.

Tasks and skills

Whilst the use of short-term fostering is extensive so too is the range of tasks undertaken by the foster carers. Indeed in the absence of a comprehensive legal definition of short-term foster care it is these tasks which define the nature of contemporary, time-limited foster care practice. Such tasks include:

- receiving children at very short notice during family crises
- offering periods of planned or unplanned respite care
- applying court conditions in respect of children on remand
- assisting children to return home or to move on to other carers or to semi-independent living
- recording, reporting and reviewing their work.

All of these tasks presuppose a number of features which have always been associated with short-term care such as offering sympathetic and high quality care to children who may be distressed, damaged and disruptive; working closely with social workers and others such as medical, psychological, teaching and legal personnel; and encouraging frequent parental and other family contact. By its very nature therefore short-term foster care has always required foster carers to provide in combination high standards of physical and emotional care to children, a responsive and sympathetic service to their families and accountability to social workers and fostering agencies.

However, the Children Act 1989 has had a significant impact upon the practice and lives of short-term foster carers, especially through its emphasis upon contact between foster children and their families and the need for foster carers to work alongside social workers. A recent government funded study into Contact Orders (Department of Health 1994b) highlighted the detailed arrangements expected by both courts and local authorities regarding contact. It found that contact arrangements for individual children were often highly complex and required substantial inputs from local authorities. Foster carers are normally in the front line of such contact arrangements and these may have a considerable impact upon their own domestic and family routines. Contact may be frequent, even daily in some cases. Also, there may be several relatives involved as well as parents. In order to be both meaningful and effective such contact tends to occur at the busiest times in a foster care household: at meal-, bath- and bedtimes. Visits by professionals such as social workers, Guardians *Ad Litem* and psychologists to supervise, observe and treat children and their families places further demands upon foster carers and their families. Even when contact takes place elsewhere, foster carers are still involved in the practicalities and have to deal with the emotional effects associated with the preparation, transportation and return of children.

The Children Act also requires foster carers to play an important role through their participation in drawing up foster placement agreements and attending a range of meetings, conferences and reviews as well as training events and support groups. The placement of withdrawn and aggressive children is another component part of short-term foster care practice. The full impact of the harm they have suffered may not be known until after they have been placed. Even where the local authority has provided details of the child's background it is often short-term foster carers who will be the first to hear directly from a child about previously unknown information concerning neglect or abuse. The foster carer will need to support that child and at the same time go on working with the relatives who may be responsible for the harm the child has suffered.

In order to perform these varied and complex tasks effectively in their daily, face to face work with children, families, social workers and other professional staff, short-term foster carers need to acquire a range of skills. The particularly helpful summary cited by Howe (1987) is a good place to start in making sense of a skills base which can be applied to foster care as well as to social work. In his review of client studies of social work effectiveness, Howe talks of the need to be both responsive and systematic. Later studies make much the same case and so too do earlier descriptions of casework and counselling practice. Responsive foster carers who learn to understand why parents feel vulnerable, become angry, avoid difficult and painful issues and let their children down can develop skills of advocacy and negotiation. Equipped with these skills foster carers will speak up for a child, make a case to parents and social workers to alter contact, contribute purposefully to the making of a placement agreement and help their own children and partners to understand the behaviour of foster children and their families.

Systematic foster carers will learn to develop observation and assessment skills as their experience of caring for children and participating in contact arrangements grow. They will also use skills of recording what they have seen and heard in order to communicate this with parents, social workers and other professionals in both formal and informal settings.

Fostering as supplementary care

Foster care is increasingly used in the UK as a means of supplementing the parental care of children of families in crisis. This helps to explain the current emphasis on frequent family contact, voluntary placements and a collaborative working relationship between parents, social workers and foster carers. Elsewhere greater emphasis is placed upon the concept of substitute foster parenting. This is particularly true in countries which have suffered major social upheaval associated with war or political change such as Japan (NFPAJ 1993) and much more recently Uganda (Tuhaise 1993) and Romania (Lowe 1993). Elsewhere supplementary care has progressed further than in the UK. In Sweden, for example, foster carers play a significant role as providers of support to families in need and this has led to a significant decrease in the use of compulsory care measures (City of Goteburg 1994).

The written accounts of recent British research contain optimistic reports from parents and foster carers of the use of supplementary care. One study which examined the use of short-term family based breaks for children in need reported that parents 'commented on the friendliness and supportiveness of the carers, their generosity, and their non-judgmental approach which seemed to restore their self-esteem and confidence as parents' (Bradley and Aldgate 1994, p.27). Earlier, Ryburn (1991) related this to the preparation and assessment process of potential foster carers which if conducted in a manner which, empowers carers and encourages them to empathise with parents, frees them 'from an inherently judgemental process themselves [so] they are freed in turn to see birth families in ways that are less judgemental' (Ryburn 1991, p.79).

In another study into the support needs of short-term foster carers one well-supported foster carer reported that:

> There's a huge argument for shared care. It's a challenge. It's good news for keeping children in their own homes and saying when life gets too difficult for the parent or the child they can just 'phone somebody up, not do it through great official channels, and say 'can you have so and so for the weekend cause I need a break?' It seems to me so sensible, absolutely reasonable, such a good way of avoiding taking kids into care all the time, of allowing them to maintain contact and for them to control when they've had enough. (Sellick 1992, p.96)

This ethos of voluntariness, family support and service does however carry some risk where there is no judicial oversight. The phenomenon of drift identified by Rowe and Lambert (1973) and that discovered by Berridge and Cleaver in which 28 per cent of the children in their study were still with their short-term foster carers six months after placement and 14 per cent for a year or more (Berridge and Cleaver 1987) should be guarded against. However at the other extreme a local authority policy which attempts to ring-fence its workforce of short-term foster carers by preventing individual carers from seeking to adopt particular children is equally unacceptable. The Court of Appeal recently upheld an appeal by a foster carer against a local authority's wish to move a child in her care to proposed adopters as she wished her own adoption application to be considered in respect of the child (Cullen 1994).

Support

All these positive developments have placed considerable burdens upon the lives of foster carers operating at the sharp end of child care practice. These burdens can be considerably lightened by the provision of a range of supports to foster carers which sustain them in their work. A range of realistic and reliable financial support; regular training which is informed by the foster carers' own expressed needs; available and responsive respite arrangements; sensitive and informed specialist advice from psychological, educational and medical staff and the mutual support of other carers and from family placement and family social workers are crucial. Social workers should develop a rapport and a working relationship with foster carers, provide immediate and accessible support related to each child in placement and advocate and liaise on the carer's behalf and help foster carers develop their practice.

Yet foster carers report that their work is often inadequately supported by local authority practice. Most local authorities still pay their approved foster carers less than the National Foster Care Association's minimum recommended allowance and wide discrepancies remain across the country regarding the type and amount of payment. Neighbouring authorities may pay as much as double the rate for children of the same age (NFCA 1994b). Many local authorities still operate discretionary, slow and cumbersome schemes for compensating carers for loss or damage to their possessions as a result of their fostering. Few have responsive schemes which provide legal defence costs for foster carers alleged to have abused children in their care (Triseliotis, Sellick and Short 1995). Not one short-term foster carer out of 18 in Sellick's study had anything positive to say about finance or insurance provided by local authorities. These foster carers did not feel sufficiently rewarded nor recognised by the allowance they received. Most had experienced delayed payments especially when children first arrived or where children and young people had caused damage, often extensive, to their homes or possessions.

Deficiencies in support to foster carers from social workers and in particular their practice of partnership are still lamented by many carers. For example, Waterhouse (1992) reported that:

> Foster carers perceived themselves as having low status and little information or influence; many respondents did not perceive themselves as part of an active team working together with social workers and parents to find a satisfactory outcome for a child. This was borne out in the way contact plans and decisions were made by the agencies, with little involvement and nurturing of the foster carers. (p.43)

In the report of the second in a series of recent Government inspections of six local authority fostering services (Department of Health 1994c) the different expectations of foster carers in respect of their link worker and the child's social worker were particularly marked. Foster carers had low expectations of the support they would receive from children's social workers, 'who were seen as difficult to contact, slow to respond and often poor at ensuring the necessary administration was undertaken to enable foster carers to receive appropriate resources' (p.23). In other words, to refer back to Howe (1987) children's social workers were neither responsive nor systematic. By contrast foster carers were generally content with the service and support they received from their link social worker. A cautionary note should be struck, however, in the light of an inquiry report following the conviction and life imprisonment of a foster carer for the indecent assault and manslaughter of one child and the grievous bodily harm and wilful ill-treatment of another child in her care (Derbyshire 1990).

This report warned against link social workers over-identifying with foster carers. Collusion is best avoided, when there is a partnership between social workers and foster carers based on a shared sense of purpose, mutual respect and negotiation. From this basis they can work together in ways which acknowledge each other's role, tasks and authority. A foster carer in a recent study illustrated how even when she disputed a decision she could still acknowledge the responsibility of a social worker:

> I might not agree with what the department are saying but I can see why they are doing or saying it and I accept this and we agree to differ. There's no bad feeling because ultimately, at the end of the day, they are responsible and if anything happens to that kid it's their heads which will be on the block. (Sellick 1992, p.64)

Written agreements and training are tangible devices which support a partnership model. Reference has already been made to the importance of foster carers showing empathy to parents if they are to offer an effective and sensitive service. The latest NFCA training package which emphasizes the importance of parental involvement is particularly helpful in this respect (NFCA 1994a). However less formal training sessions where social workers and foster carers participate together can be equally effective:

> Tackling the complexities of family contact, learning how to negotiate a placement agreement, or how to contribute purposefully to a case conference or review, can be fruitful developments which spring from the process of social workers and foster carers working together in a training session. Role playing a sensitive contact visit where a social worker plays a foster carer and a foster carer plays a parent can be the stuff of effective and supportive training. (Triseliotis et al. 1995, p.108)

Well-supported foster carers are more likely to weather the storms of fostering and to experience fewer placement breakdowns with the associated human and financial costs involved. Berridge and Cleaver (1987) for example found that frequent visits by social workers to foster carers were associated with fewer breakdowns. Two fifths of the short-term foster carers in their study were visited at least fortnightly and in these the breakdowns were only at a rate of 10 per cent compared with almost 25 per cent of the remainder. In other words, support, 'keeps carers, cuts costs and prevents placement breakdowns' (Triseliotis et al. 1995, p.98).

Conclusion

Time-limited fostering which supplements and supports parental care and which seeks to avoid long-term family breakdown is the commonest placement for children who need to be looked after away from home. As the providers of this form of care foster carers need to consolidate old skills and develop new ones if their good practice is to be maximised. Children and young people have always required sensitive, consistent and high standards of physical and emotional out-of-home care and their parents and other relatives should always have been welcomed, encouraged and supported by foster carers. Nowadays considerably more is demanded of short-term foster carers both as care givers or sharers and as full participants in children's services teams. They need to negotiate, advocate, liaise and communicate and in order to do so they need to be trained, advised, paid and generally supported in ways which sustain them and develop their practice. Most are still members of a volunteer workforce motivated by their desire to care for children yet for all that are key players in the game of prevention and reunification in child care.

References

Aldgate, J., Pratt, R. and Duggan, M. (1989) Using care away from home to prevent family breakdown. *Adoption and Fostering 13*, 2, pp.32–37.

Berridge, D. and Cleaver, H. (1987) *Foster Home Breakdown.* Oxford: Basil Blackwell.

Bradley, M. and Aldgate, J. (1994) Short-term family based care for children in need. *Adoption and Fostering 18*, 4, pp.24–29.

City of Goteborg (1994) *Alternative options provided for children in foster care. Different forms of placement in Sweden.* Paper presented at the European Foster Care Conference. Berlin. September 1994.

Cullen, D. (1994) Legal notes, re: C 1994. *Adoption and Fostering 18*, 3, 40.

Department of Health (1988) *Boarding Out Of Children (Foster Placement) Regulations.* 1988. London: HMSO.

Department of Health (1991) *The Children Act 1989. Guidance and Regulations. Volume 3. Family Placements.* London: HMSO.

Department of Health (1994a) *Children Act Report 1993.* London: HMSO.

Department of Health (1994b) *The Children Act 1989. Contact Orders Study.* London: HMSO.

Department of Health (1994c) *Inspection of local authority fostering service.* London Borough of Redbridge Social Services Department. Social Services Inspectorate London East Inspection Group.

Derbyshire and Nottinghamshire County Councils and the Southern Derbyshire and Nottingham District Health Authorities (1990) *Report of the inquiry into the death of a child in care.*

Hope, K. (1983) *Variations in the use of short term foster parents and factors which might influence their usage.* CQSW Dissertation. South Glamorgan and Gwent Institutes for Higher Education.

Howe, D. (1987) *An Introduction to Social Work Theory.* Aldershot: Ashgate.

Jassal, B. (1981) *Short-term Foster Parents: Reactions to Foster Children Leaving their Care.* Masters Degree Dissertation. University of Birmingham.

Lowe, M. (1993) Romania – moving towards family based care. *Adoption and Fostering 17*, 1, 21–25.

National Foster Care Association (1994a) *Choosing to Foster – the Challenge to Care.* NFCA.

National Foster Care Association (1994b) *Foster Care Finance.* NFCA.

National Foster Parent Association of Japan (1993) *Outline of Foster Care in Japan.* Paper presented at the International Foster Care Conference. Dublin. July 1993.

Part, D. (1993) Fostering as seen by the carers' children. *Adoption and Fostering 17*, 1, 26–31.

Rowe, J. and Lambert, L. (1973) *Children Who Wait.* London. Association of British Adoption Agencies.

Rowe, J., Hundleby, M. and Garnett, L. (1989) *Child Care Now: A Survey of Placement Patterns.* London: BAAF.

Ryburn, M. (1991) The myth of assessment. *Adoption and Fostering 15*, 1, 76–80.

Sellick, C. (1992) *Supporting Short-Term Foster Carers.* Aldershot: Avebury.

Shaw, M. and Hipgrave, T. (1983) *Specialist Fostering.* London: Batsford.

Stone, J. (1995) *Making positive moves. Developing Short-Term Fostering Services.* London: BAAF.

Triseliotis, J. (1989) Foster care outcomes: a review of key research findings. *Adoption and Fostering 13*, 3, 5–16.

Triseliotis, J., Sellick, C. and Short, R. (1995) *Foster Care: Theory and Practice.* London: Batsford.

Tuhaise, C. (1993) *Child Fostering in Uganda: A Solution or an Additional Problem?* Paper presented at the International Foster Care Conference. Dublin. July 1993.

Waterhouse, S. (1992) How foster carers view contact. *Adoption and Fostering 16*, 2, 42–47.

Westacott, J. (1988) *Bridge to Calmer Waters.* London: Barnardos.

CHAPTER 12

Children's Perspectives on Long-Term Foster Care

Colette McAuley

This chapter discusses a prospective study which focused on the views of children entering long-term foster care in Northern Ireland. The importance of the perspective of the child has been strongly reinforced by recent legislation. The Children Act 1989 (England and Wales) and the Children (NI) Order 1995 in Northern Ireland gave the strongest recognition to date of the right of children to be consulted in any major decisions relating to the their upbringing. This was further reinforced by the United Nations Convention on the Rights of the Child.

Following on from this legal imperative, it seems reasonable to expect that managers, practitioners and indeed researchers need to be actively endeavouring to ensure that children's views are sought and considered in decisions affecting their lives. Where children are entering new care episodes it would be particularly valuable to ascertain their views and, if possible, not just once but over time.

Context of the Children's Study

Throughout the 1980s foster care had been the preferred placement option for children needing substitute care in Northern Ireland. There had also been a steady growth in its usage. On 31 March 1989 there were 2783 children in care, i.e. five per 1000 population under 18 years old at that time. Of the number of children in care 55 per cent were in foster care on that date. This reflected similar trends in the usage of foster care in England during this period.

In 1987 the Department of Health and Social Services (NI) commissioned a study of long-term foster care, the results of which have already been reported (Kelly and McAuley 1992). Alongside this, a study of the emotional and social development of the children during the fostering episodes was carried out by the author (McAuley 1996). This is known as the Children's Study. The perspective of the children concerning their close social relationships was a key element and will be used as the basis of discussion in this chapter.

The Children's Study

This was a prospective study of children across Northern Ireland during the first two years of their fostering placements. The children were selected on the basis that they were:

- 4–11 years old at the time of placement
- placed in a new foster placement (i.e. where the child and the family had no previous relationship)
- placed in a planned long-term placement (i.e. where the social work plan was that the child would be expected to remain there for at least one year)
- placed with non-relatives.

The four Health and Social Services Boards which cover Northern Ireland referred to the study all children who met the above criteria and who were being placed during the last six months of 1988 and the first month of 1989. All of the children who were eligible for inclusion participated in the study.

The children

The above criteria generated a sample of 19 children, living in 16 foster families from across the four Health and Social Services Boards. There were 12 boys and seven girls, most of whom were eight years and over. There were three pairs of siblings included in the sample and five more children had a sibling in the same placement who was not included in the study. Most of these children were the subject of compulsory admissions to care.

The majority of the children had experienced several previous care placements and had been in substitute care over two years prior to the study placements. Most had previously experienced both foster and residential care, although six had only experienced residential care. Two of these children had spent their entire care experience in one residential home continuously for three and six years respectively. Of the three children who had experienced only foster care, one had been placed in four foster homes prior to being placed in the study placement at four years and four months.

According to the social workers, all of the children had experienced abuse and/or neglect. For the majority this had been persistent emotional and physical neglect, accompanied in many cases by emotional and physical abuse. Four of the children had been sexually abused over considerable periods of time and another child disclosed previous extensive sexual abuse during the study placement. The abuse/neglect had been carried out by birth parent(s), cohabitees, older birth siblings or by previous foster carers.

The majority of the children had regular access to their birth parents and siblings prior to and during the study placement. Only two had no contact with any member of their birth families. The reasons offered for lack of contact were that the agency had decided that it would not be in the best interests of the child or that the parent had not requested or taken up offers of access.

All of the children had, in the view of the social workers, developed attachments previously to either someone in their birth family, a previous carer or a significant other. Only one child had not developed a significant attachment to someone in his birth family. Rather he had, for the first time, developed an attachment to a residential carer in his previous placement. Most of the children had exhibited behaviour problems at home and/or at school in the year prior to placement. Again more than half of the children were rated by their social workers as having lower than average educational attainment in that period. Almost half of the children were reported to have had health and/or developmental problems in the year prior to placement.

The children's interviews

The interviews with the children took place at four months, one year and two years into placement where the placement was still intact. Of the 19 children, 15 were still in placement at the year stage and 14 at the two year stage. They were seen in special interview facilities at Queen's University, Belfast to provide a consistent child-orientated environment outside of the foster homes. Interviews with the children were held after interviews with the social workers and foster mothers. All of these were carried out by the author.

Since a major aim of this study was to gain the child's perspective, considerable thought went into the planning of the format of children's interviews. The purpose of the interview, the role of the interviewer and confidentiality issues were addressed at the outset as well as the format and duration of interviews. Age-appropriate explanations were used. Support was provided for the child with the presence of a trusted adult in the next room. Particular attention was paid to the beginnings and endings of interviews. It was assumed that the children would be anxious on arrival and should begin with a relaxing exercise. Further it was felt to be appropriate that the endings should be relaxed and on a positive note (Hill 1985).

Interviews with children had already been included in earlier large British studies of long-term foster care (e.g. Thorpe 1974; Rowe *et al.* 1984). However, these studies had involved one-off interviews of children of a wide age range and in their foster homes for varying lengths of time. Although the authors had made the content of the questions less complex for the children, the interviews were carried out as direct face to face interviews as with adults.

In contrast this study attempted to provide information about children in middle childhood during their first two years of foster placements. Further, it focused specifically on the perspectives of the children. All children of eight years and older were asked about their perspectives on established relationships. Given the recent advances in practice in direct work with children (Aldgate and Simmonds 1988), it seemed sensible to attempt to develop direct work materials for the purpose of the research study. Hence the children's views were sought by means of an interview schedule and the use of feeling faces, feeling cards and response cards and questions illustrated through cartoons. Details of the interview schedule and materials are provided in the full report of the study (McAuley 1996). Again all children in the study were asked to complete an adapted version of the Family Relations Test (Bene and Anthony 1957) to gain their perception of the developing relationships within the foster homes.

The inclusion of direct work materials was highly successful in facilitating communication with children eight years and older. The materials seemed particularly helpful to the children when they were responding on highly sensitive areas of their close social relationships. They volunteered more information than would have been expected from previous studies, particularly regarding their birth families. The children in the study by Rowe *et al.* (1984) offered little information when asked for details of their birth families. The authors did not know whether they found the questions too painful or whether they did not have the information. However, the children in that study had been fostered for several years and few had had any recent contact with their birth families. In the Children's Study generally the children had as much information as the agency did. By interviewing the children at these three stages in the foster placement, developments and changes in their close relationships over this crucial period could be charted. This included attention to both established relationships and developing relationships in the foster home.

The children's perspective on established social relationships

The impact of the move into the foster home on the children's established relationships

A predominant theme emerging from the interviews with the children at the four month stage was the impact of the loss of contact with friends and significant others as a direct result of the move into the study placement. The majority of the children who responded indicated that they felt sadness, loneliness, anger and fear about leaving their last home. What they missed were friends in the children's home, the home where they had lived for many years, brothers and sisters left behind in the home and friends who lived nearby and with whom they played. Furthermore, 15 of the 17 children who had attended school previously had had to change school as a result of moving to the study placement. Over half of these children expressed sadness and/or confusion about leaving their previous schools. Many of the children felt sad at the loss of contact with teachers and friends. A number had already moved schools several times before for the same reason. Perhaps the lower educational attainment of some of these children should be considered in this light. With one exception, there had been no choice of placement available for the children in this study. The shortage of long-term placements also meant that placements offered were usually considerable distances from previous placements and schools.

These findings need to be placed in the context of child development. Herbert (1991) suggests that whereas the main social influences prior to school are the family, in middle childhood teachers, friends and peers become important social influences. In his view the years of middle childhood are notable as a period in which children's interactions in their home and school environment help to shape their personality. Children at this stage tend to choose their friends from those who live in the same neighbourhood or who are in the same class at school. Placing the above findings in this developmental context emphasises the extent to which already vulnerable children in care may well be further disadvantaged by disruptions in relationships. It also highlights the need to plan contact as part of the process to maintain continuity in relationships which the children view as important.

The children's preoccupation with their birth families over time

Another finding which emerged was the preoccupation and identification of the children with their birth families over time. Predominant identification was measured by the children's responses to cartoon versions of four questions devised by Weinstein (1960). They were also asked to complete a cartoon version of the Three Wishes question.

Birth families, and in particular birth parents, predominated in the children's responses to these questions at all three stages. At the year point almost half of the children indicated that they thought about their birth families every day or at least once each week. One girl of eight years whose birth father had died suddenly over a year before said she thought about him: 'Every day and night...worry if I will ever see him again.' She also said that she thought about her mother: 'Every night in bed...how she is getting on...worry about her...same for brothers and sisters...worry about them too...worry most about mum...feel sad.'

Further, five children indicated that they dreamt about their birth families very often or sometimes. One boy aged nine years said: 'I dream about Daddy taking me out...I dream about all of them (birth family) some nights... It's a happy dream...playing football in a field.'

Another boy aged nine years whose mother had died two years previously said: 'I dream about my mother very often...every few nights. I never tell anyone about it. I think over all the things we used to do together.'

Most of the these children had regular contact with birth parents and siblings throughout the two year period of the study. All of those with contact indicated that they were happy about this. Where they had an established positive relationship with birth family members and wanted but did not have contact, they were sad or angry about this. However, the children's preoccupation and identification with birth families was not dependent on the existence of current contact nor upon its level.

When we consider the children's past experiences of abuse and neglect, these findings are all the more dramatic. They had, for the most part, suffered persistent emotional and physical abuse and/or neglect when living with their birth families. Many of the parents had a history of alcohol abuse, some had mental health problems and serious relationship difficulties were evident. On the basis of the histories provided, the findings of this study suggest that children who have experienced emotional and physical neglect and/or abuse by the birth parents may well also have developed relationships with them which the children perceive as important. (Perhaps it is important to note, though, that in this study the children's preoccupation and identification were with parents who did not directly physically or sexually abuse them or where the physical abuse had been minimal.) In general the children's relationships with their birth parents seemed complex, with considerable evidence of them worrying about their parents' welfare. It was as if they sensed the vulnerability of their parents, some of whom had been in substitute care themselves.

The children were also found to be preoccupied by their birth siblings. For the most part they saw them regularly during the placement. That contact was very important to the children and seemed to be closely linked to their sense of family identity. The sense from the children was that they had travelled through troubled times together. Furthermore, where the study child was the eldest, they usually worried about the welfare of the younger siblings living elsewhere as if they were acting almost in a parental role.

The children's view of emotional permission from the birth parents

An important related issue was that several of the children with established positive relationships with birth parents felt they did not have their permission to be fostered: 'They [birth parents] don't want me to be fostered. They want me to be living with them'. 'Cos she [birth mother] thinks I should be with her and they are not my right parents'. This suggests a considerable dilemma for these children. At the four month stage seven of the children did not have the emotional permission of one or both parents. Five did not feel that they had the permission of either parent. At the year stage, four children still felt they did not have permission of one or both parent(s). Without such permission, children reported feeling sad or even angry. Listening to the children concerning this provided a rare glimpse of the complex social and emotional relationships which these children were attempting to manage. Their sadness seemed to reflect the sadness of their birth parents, many of who were not in agreement with their children being in care and especially foster care.

Interestingly, there was some suggestion that older children might reach their own decision as to what might be in their own best interests. One boy of 13 years expressed his feelings about his birth mother's lack of permission: 'I should be with them [foster parents]...I might have a better chance with them cos she [birth mother] drinks. If she was drinking, I would have to go back to [children's home]. I felt lonely when I was in [children's home].'

The children's ability to compartmentalise aspects of their complex social relationships
Perhaps one of the most interesting findings was that the children chose to keep private details of their earlier lives with their parents and contact with their birth families. There were suggestions of a deep loyalty to their parents and a desire not to recall distressful times. They indicated that they would not wish to share these past matters with their foster carers. On the other hand, they did share their current worries and concerns with the foster families, mainly the foster mother. This suggests that children of this age in such situations can compartmentalise close social relationships and choose with whom they wish to share different kinds of thoughts and feelings.

The children's perception of the developing relationships within the foster homes

With the increasing use of foster care and the implicit aim of long-term foster care to provide children with the opportunity to develop longer-term relationships, it is surprising that there is so little research based knowledge available on how children normally develop relationships with new families, nor how this varies with the age of the child and their feelings about previously established relationships.

An adapted version of the Family Relations Test (Bene and Anthony 1957) was used in order to chart the children's view of the developing relationships within the foster families over time. This is a posting exercise and was used to provide a measure of the emotional involvement between the children and members of their new foster families. It was repeated at each of the three stages to chart development over time. The children rated highest involvement with the foster mothers at all three stages. Involvement with the foster fathers appeared to develop more slowly. However by the two year point the rated involvement with foster mothers and fathers was much closer. At the four month stage the children rated highly their involvement with the other children and young people living in the foster homes. This included birth children of the foster carers, unrelated foster children and birth siblings fostered in the same home. However, this rating showed little increase over time and consequently lost its relative position over the two year period. The finding reminds us of the importance of the other family members to a child particularly in the early stages of placement. However, it should also be noted that a considerable proportion of the other children/young people in the foster homes were birth siblings and hence the level of the rating largely reflected the strength of the established relationships with them.

In general, the children's ratings of involvement with the foster families were low at all three stages. This might indicate that the level of emotional involvement with the foster families was at an early stage even by the two year point. An alternative explanation might be that the children's defences were operating in the interviews. However, they did not display undue defensiveness in other parts of the interview.

Overall, the results from this test suggested that the degree of involvement of the children with their foster families was at an early stage even by the two year point. This could have been due to factors in their previous experience, factors in the study placement or, more likely, a combination of both. Given what we have learned from them concerning their wider emotional world, it is not surprising that the development of such relationships by children of this age and with similar experience is likely to be a complex and delicate process.

An interesting finding alongside the above arose from the responses to the predominant identification questions (as discussed in the previous section). At all three stages of interviews almost all of the children chose their foster carers, predominantly foster mothers, as the people in whom they would entrust their concerns. It is likely that the children interpreted this as a daily concern but it is important to know that the children feel they could entrust them to their foster carers from early in placement.

Conclusion

The latest available figures regarding children in care in Northern Ireland indicate that on 31 March 1994 there were 2660 children in care of whom 61 per cent were in foster care (McCoy 1994). All Boards have, over the period 1989 to 1993, increased their percentage of children in foster care (McCoy 1995) and the Regional Strategy target is that 75 per cent of placements should be in foster care. However, these figures tell us little about the care careers of these children nor their experiences of the fostering process. The above study is an attempt to examine more closely the first two years of long-term foster care from the perspective of the child.

Perhaps one of the most important findings was that the children in the study seemed pleased to have the opportunity to share their perspective. Hopefully they were left with a sense that something important about them had been understood (Angold 1994). Their responses provided valuable material to inform future policy and practice concerning foster care. The research tools developed could prove useful to practitioners and other researchers encouraging children to communicate their wishes and feelings.

Undoubtedly the children carried a considerable number of concerns and unresolved issues with them into their new placements. If we start from the premise that a foster placement is an important event in the lives of these children, then adequate resources need to go into preparation of the children and carers for placement. Direct work with the children might include helping them to come to terms with past experiences, ascertaining their wishes regarding fostering, and assessing their emotional readiness to invest in new relationships, apart from simply providing explanations.

The importance to the children of their wider social networks was evident and the impact on them of losing important contacts with family members, friends and others when moving into the study foster placements was regrettably apparent. Whenever possible placement decisions should enable children to keep in close contact with people they value. The impact of changing school also should be particularly borne in mind. Effectively this means that enough placements need to be available to permit these factors to be given consideration. Where there is a shortage of long-term foster placements, agencies need to develop recruitment and support packages which can attract and maintain further carers.

Contact with birth families and significant others should embrace much more than access. Where appropriate, efforts should be made to preserve valued relationships through telephone calls and letters. If these relationships are viewed as important for the children's emotional and social development, contact needs to be actively encouraged.

The children's perceptions of the relationships in the foster families suggested that they were still at an early stage by the two year point. This is an important finding which could be incorporated into the preparation of foster carers. Appropriate expectations could be encouraged and placed in the context of the delicacy and complexity of the fostering process.

The Children (NI) Order 1995 is due to be implemented in the autumn of 1996 and the challenges facing the professions are currently being debated (McAuley and McColgan 1995). The principle that the welfare of the child should be the paramount consideration in court decisions is to be welcomed. The fact that this legislation strongly reinforces the importance of the perspective of the child is particularly welcome. The interviews with the children in this study provide convincing evidence of the need to consult children in care as to their wishes and feelings and convey a glimpse of the complexity of their world.

References

Aldgate, J. and Simmonds, J. (eds) (1988) *Direct Work with Children*. London: Batsford/BAAF

Angold, A. (1994) Clinical interviewing with children and adolescents. In M. Rutter, E. Taylor and L. Hersov (eds) *Child and Adolescent Psychiatry* (Third Edition). Oxford: Blackwell Scientific Publications.

Bene, E. and Anthony, E.J. (1957) *Manual for the Family Relations Test*. Buckinghamshire: National Foundation for Education Research.

Herbert, M. (1991) *Clinical Child Psychology: Social Learning, Development and Behaviour*. Chichester: Wiley.

Hill, P. (1985) The diagnostic interview with the individual child. In M. Rutter and L. Hersov (eds) *Child and Adolescent Psychiatry* (Second Edition). Oxford: Blackwell Scientific Publications.

Kelly, G. and McAuley, C. (1992) *A Foster Care Study*. Department of Social Studies, The Queen's University of Belfast: Unpublished report for the Department of Health and Social Sevices 1996 (Northern Ireland).

McAuley, C. (1996) *Children in Long Term Foster Care: Emotional and Social Development*. Aldershot: Avebury.

McAuley, C. and McColgan, M. (1995) *The Children (NI) Order: Challenges Ahead*. Belfast: Department of Social Work.

McCoy, K. (1994) *Promoting Social Welfare: First Annual Report of the Chief Social Services Inspector*. Belfast: DHSS (NI).

McCoy, K. (1995) *Promoting Social Welfare: Second Annual Report Of the Chief Social Services Inspector*. Belfast: DHSS (NI).

Rowe, J. Cain, H. Hundleby, M. and Keane, A.(1984) *Long-Term Foster Care*. London: Batsford/BAAF.

Thorpe, R. (1974) *The Social and Psychological Situation of the Long Term Foster Child with Regard to his Natural Parents*. University of Nottingham: Unpublished PhD thesis.

Weinstein, E. (1960) *The Self Image of the Foster Child*. London: Russell Sage Foundation.

CHAPTER 13

Residential Child Care
in England and Wales
The Inquiries and After

David Berridge and Isabelle Brodie

Introduction

The past decade has been very difficult for residential child care in England and Wales. 'Crisis' is a term that nowadays is used too indiscriminately. However, some observers would feel that the situation in the residential sector has reached a crisis; at the very least there has certainly been a crisis of confidence.

The reasons for this are varied. In the late 1980s and 1990s, several specific instances were uncovered of establishments and regimes in which young people were systematically maltreated, including physical and sexual abuse. These are discussed later. Local and national media also reported frequently about homes in which residents were allegedly out of control. Undoubtedly associated with this were unresolved obstacles in the management, role, status and skills base of residential child care.

This chapter discusses both the specific and structural problems in residential child care over the past decade. It introduces research findings in an effort to maintain an objective stance on the experience and effects of residence. We also look at the extensive measures that have been taken in the 1990s to try to redress the major shortcomings. Finally, some interim findings are outlined from a current national study of children's homes to try to ascertain the likely impact of these remedies, together with the nature and severity of current difficulties.

Background

The major problems in residential child care stem from a number of factors. Most significant is a negative perception of the service coupled with its low status. There has been a tendency for fieldworkers and managers to see children's homes as a last resort and thus to use them for negative rather than positive reasons (DoH 1991b; SSI Wales and Social Information Systems 1991). Hence, residential care and carers have been undervalued and this has influenced their self-esteem and morale (Berridge 1985). Managers have given the residential sector insufficient attention, while attracting and retaining high quality staff has been difficult. This low status has had a tangible and reciprocal impact on matters such as pay, where residential work – unlike some European approaches – has traditionally been much more poorly rewarded than field-work.

Linked to this lack of status has been the inadequate professional training for residential child care workers. Estimates vary of numbers of staff in children's homes who are professionally qualified: for heads of homes this has been put at between half and three-quarters, while barely one in 20 care staff hold social work qualifications (DoH 1992). A Department of Health report described this situation as 'deplorable' (DH 1991b, p.54), an epithet seldom used by the Civil Service. It is also a problem that has been acknowledged to exist for 50 years (*Report of the Care of Children Committee* 1946). The most damaged and problematic young people, therefore, have traditionally been dealt with by those social work staff who are among the most poorly trained, least well educated and worst paid. In other professions, such as law or medicine, the greater the problem posed the more enhanced are the skills of the individual employed, the opposite happens in this branch of child care. A recent furore emerged when a (senior) nurse was discovered to have assisted directly in the removal of a patient's appendix; the social and psychological equivalent occurs in children's homes every day.

In the light of the above, it is perhaps surprising to discover that research findings about the contribution of the residential sector have been rather more positive: one wonders what could have been achieved if the service had not been artificially constrained. Regarding use, the proportion of young people looked after by local authorities in England living in residential homes has virtually halved in the past decade from 29 per cent to 16 per cent (Berridge 1994). However, research has demonstrated that *adolescents* pass through children's homes in large numbers. One survey found three times as many residential as foster placements (the main alternative) for this age group (Rowe, Hundleby and Garnett 1989). And although the *proportion* of children who are living in foster placements at any one time has increased significantly, the *actual number* has remained remarkably constant over 30 years at around 32,000 (Berridge forthcoming, b). Cost differences between residential and foster care are also not as marked as is often assumed (Knapp and Robertson 1989) and the comparative cost with specialist foster care is probably quite similar.

However, a major concern is with the 'outcomes' of both residential and foster placements. A number of common deficiencies affect both services, for example in catering for children from minority ethnic groups, ensuring aftercare, and adequate concern for the health and education of residents

(Berridge 1994). In general, controlling for the nature of their populations, residential and foster care have been shown to be broadly equivalent in achieving their respective objectives (Colton 1988; Rowe *et al.* 1989). Furthermore one county in England – Warwickshire – which closed all of its own children's homes in the late 1980s, did not achieve significantly different results compared with localities which retained residential care (Cliffe with Berridge 1991). Ensuring an adequate supply of foster carers was a major problem. Young people's own views about residential care have also often been positive (Page and Clarke 1977; Kahan 1979; Triseliotis *et al.* 1995).

The major reports to have investigated the issue have concluded that residential care is a key element of a range of services for children and young people and continues to serve important functions (DoH 1991a and 1991b; Wagner 1988). It has been argued to be especially relevant for children who

> have decided that they do not wish to be fostered; have had bad experiences of foster care; have been so abused within the family that another family placement is inappropriate; are from the same family and otherwise cannot be kept together; or who require expert, multidisciplinary help with social and personal problems. (DoH 1991b, p.8)

The residential inquiries

The report by Sir William Utting in which the above summary appears was commissioned by the Secretary of State for Health following revelations in the media about what became known as the 'Pindown' regime, which was found to be operating in certain children's homes in Staffordshire. This emerged in England during the late 1980s and early 1990s alongside several other scandals in child care establishments. Three of these are analysed in detail below, namely events in Staffordshire (Levy and Kahan 1991), at Ty Mawr in Gwent (Williams and McCreadie 1992) and in Leicestershire (Kirkwood 1993). Other instances included the long-term systematic sexual abuse of residents from the Kincora boys' hostel in East Belfast, which has never been satisfactorily resolved (DHSS Northern Ireland 1986; see also Kelly and Pinkerton this volume); the appalling conditions discovered in 1988 by school inspectors at Crookham Court boarding-school in Berkshire (which was instrumental in Section 87 of the Children Act 1989 being introduced); and the presence of paedophiles associated with New Barns school in Gloucestershire, which led to its closure in 1992. Collectively these disclosures rocked public and professional confidence in residential child care and paved the way for the extensive measures set out later in the chapter.

Let us now look in detail at three of these inquiry reports, which were the most extensively publicised in England and Wales. (A useful account of this period is also provided by Kahan 1995a, 1995b.)

'Pindown' – Staffordshire

The existence of the regime which eventually became known as 'Pindown' first became known to the outside world in 1989, when an adolescent girl was discovered to have been confined to a barely furnished room for long periods; required to wear night clothes during the day; deprived of contact, education and sensory stimulus; and prevented from communicating with other children or going out. The architect of this distorted form of what was claimed to be 'behaviour modification' was Tony Latham, an Area Officer. It eventually emerged that 132 children aged from nine to 17 years had been subjected to Pindown between 1983 and 1989.

A detailed and insightful report (Levy and Kahan 1991), while not exonerating staff from this cruelty, took pains to set out the social services context in Staffordshire within which Pindown had flourished. The county had traditionally been a low spender on children's services and deep financial cuts had occurred throughout the 1970s. Management was judged to be remote, uninterested and incompetent. No secure provision existed in Staffordshire. Staffing levels were poor: it was reported that homes would sometimes be left under the sole control of a young unqualified (female) member of staff. Training was inadequate and there was said to be an introspective culture.

Ty Mawr – Gwent

Events in this Welsh former approved school were quite different from the above. They related essentially to concerns that young men were beyond control together with suicide attempts of a resident. Specific issues included allegations of staff brutality and boys barricading themselves in the building overnight and causing damage. Absconding by young people and staff absenteeism were frequent.

Staff perceived outside management to be aloof and unconcerned. Few staff were professionally qualified and recruitment was problematic: it could sometimes take place simply as a result of a visit to the job centre. The somewhat irregular practice also occurred of appointments being made by county council members. An inappropriate combination of boys attended the centre, which had no clear written objectives. The report concluded that

> Our assessment of the staff at Ty Mawr is that there has been a substantial loss of morale, that there is a feeling of isolation, and a degree of helplessness, that the perception is that 'County Hall' has little real interest in their problems or knowledge or understanding of them, and that they and the children at Ty Mawr are subject to an unstructured system which cannot possibly cope with the various demands made upon it. (p.13)

Leicestershire – Frank Beck

In November 1991 the late Frank Beck was sentenced to life imprisonment having been found guilty on 17 counts including attempted rape, buggery and other forms of sexual and physical assault involving children. He had been officer in charge of various Leicestershire children's homes between 1973 and 86. Numerous complaints had been made against him over the years, but these were inadequately dealt with by management. He also operated what was described as a form of 'regression therapy', in which children were brutally chastised in misguided attempts to 'break down their defences'.

Children and staff alike were reported to be afraid of Beck, a former Royal Marine. He discouraged training among his staff and cultivated small, tightly knit groups of young inexperienced workers. Management of the Care Branch in Leicestershire Social Services Department was described as ineffective. None of Beck's three line managers from 1974 onwards had backgrounds or expertise in child care.

Crises in residential child care: common themes?

Having briefly outlined the nature of three of the recent major crises in residential child care, the analysis will now go a stage further and see if there are any common themes which are highlighted in the inquiry reports. Table 13.1 attempts to present this diagramatically. First, however, a note of caution is required. Simply because certain shared factors were associated with abuse and mismanagement does not necessarily imply that these 'caused' them to occur. These common elements may be present too in situations where mal-practice did not take place, or may even be characteristic of residential child care in general. Interpretation is also subjective to a significant degree.

Table 13.1 reveals what are felt to be some of the most important common themes of the three inquiry reports. The interpretation here may not always be identical with the reports' own conclusions, depending on our analysis and interpretation of the texts. Initially, it is apparent that there are many areas of common ground. Deficiencies span management, policy and practice concerns; no doubt they are interrelated. It is also interesting to observe what are not common features. For example, with the exception of the Staffordshire report, a shortage of staff and financial resources within units did not appear to be major contributory factors. It seems more that problems stemmed from the calibre and preparation of staff, coupled with a sense of being overwhelmed with the task that confronted them.

In all three instances line management of facilities and heads of homes tended to be ineffective or non-existent. Line managers also had minimal, if any, direct contact with units and so were in no position to observe malpractice, assuming of course that they would have recognised it. Adequate complaints systems were not in place. Homes were often trying to achieve objectives that

Table 13.1 Themes from the Staffordshire, Ty Mawr and Leicestershire inquiry reports

	Staffordshire	Ty Mawr	Leicestershire
Management			
Inadequate line management	✓	✓	✓
Little direct management contact with children and staff	✓	✓	✓
Unsatisfactory or no complaints process	✓	✓	✓
Policy			
No clear objectives of homes	(objectives unacceptable)	✓	✓
Unsatisfactory placement policy and processes	✓	✓	✓
Recruitment process unsatisfactory	✓	✓	✓
Inadequate staff training	✓	✓	✓
Reluctance to use secure provision/ desire to contain own problems	✓	✓	✓
Social isolation of unit	?	✓	✓
Practice			
'Macho'/masculine charisma or culture	✓	✓	✓
Inappropriate practice/treatment methods	✓	x	✓
External adults unwilling to believe children	x	x	✓
Financial problems/physical shortcomings of units	✓	x	x
Insufficient staffing	✓	x	x
Inadequate or no specialist external professional advice	✓	✓	✓

Key

✓ felt to be a contributory element

x felt not to be a contributory element

? unclear whether or not a contributory element

were probably beyond them, so that unacceptable practices seemed attractive as a way of establishing order. This would appeal particularly to inexperienced and unskilled staff, encouraged by unsatisfactory recruitment policies and methods. The reluctance to use secure facilities and instead to be self-sufficient in tackling problems also added to difficulties. The Leicestershire and Ty Mawr units seem to have become socially isolated and problems may thus have been more likely to have remained undetected. However, it does not appear that this occurred in Staffordshire and it is hard to fathom how these abuses could have taken place over such a long period with so few professionals in other services as well as within the department objecting.

On practice criteria, unacceptable social work methods were clearly used in Staffordshire and Leicestershire, whereas Ty Mawr reads as more misguided and desperate than malevolent. Specialist external professional advice did not feature. Interestingly, the concept of masculinity appears significant to the three contexts: at risk of overlooking the obvious, the main protagonists were all men. In different ways, Beck and Latham in Leicestershire and Staffordshire embodied 'macho' forms of charismatic, authoritarian leadership – charisma misused can be a very dangerous quality. In contrast, in Wales there was reported to be a sub-culture of masculinity and low level violence that helped feed the unruliness and delinquency.

To reiterate, the combination of the above factors will not necessarily result in crisis. Acute problems and abuse can also arise in other ways. None the less, the existence of several factors in the list should alert councillors, managers, practitioners and parents to the fact that the potential is there for the residential care of children to go very seriously wrong.

Responses to the crises

The three cases had a major effect on professional and public attitudes to social work, child care and residential life specifically. They were widely reported in the media and also had the potential to develop into something of a political crisis. Indeed, events in Cleveland were not too distant in people's memories, in which over a six month period some 125 children were alleged to have been sexually abused by their parents, most of whom were removed from home (Butler-Sloss 1988). The Children Act 1989 was approved by Parliament the following year. It would have been unacceptable if it emerged that children and young people, whose own homes rendered them vulnerable, were at even greater risk when entering public care.

Following the Pindown revelations the Government acted swiftly and introduced a whole raft of new measures. The culture of the Children Act and the associated development programme made it possible for the Department of Health to continue with a range of initiatives from the centre specifically on residential care. This direction was needed. As a group, Directors of Social

Services had not shown particular interest in, or commitment to, residential child care. The voluntary sector, with its long-standing expertise in this area, had moved on to pastures new, partly as a result of uncertain local authority demand and arguably at a time when its contribution was most needed.

The developments occurring in the early 1990s to tackle problems in residential child care are set out in Table 13.2. Most but not all were initiated directly by the Department of Health. They constitute an impressive series of strategies, which at last address some of the longer-term structural problems of the residential sector identified at the beginning of this chapter, for example regarding status and pay.

Policy and practice

Several of the initiatives listed above relate to policy and practice in residential child care. For example Volume 4 of the Children Act Guidance and Regulations provided a comprehensive framework for the management and operation of residential homes within the context of the new legislation. A key feature of this was the requirement for responsible authorities to produce a statement of the purpose and functions of each home. The intention was to articulate what each home sets out to do and the methods by which this is to be achieved. It was intended that this would help tackle the unfocused approach of too much residential care and the 'dumping ground' mentality. Advantages would derive from making explicit what each home could and could not be expected to achieve. Incompatible groups of residents and inappropriate referrals might thus be avoided. In addition, the Guidance covered record keeping, staffing, training and supervision, the physical environment and aspects of daily care.

The two reviews in 1991 of residential child care in England and Wales were also significant documents. The first ('the Utting report') supplied a timely overview of the situation and identified some of the major areas of concern, including training as we have already seen. Several of the initiatives that commenced the following year flowed directly from 'Utting'. It was also important that the report emphasised the positive contribution of residential care, albeit not exactly in its present form.

The Welsh equivalent was more critical in tone. It concluded that the functions that homes are expected to achieve are too often ill-defined. Facilities in Wales were reported not to be particularly successful at controlling seriously challenging behaviour. Unplanned admissions were a major problem. It was recommended that there should be two types of children's home: one dealing exclusively with young people posing significant control problems and the other for a wider group of children in need. These ideas, while superficially attractive, did not find favour in England. However, more recent evidence that we provide later suggests that they may be worth reconsidering for specific groups of young people.

Table 13.2 Initiatives in the 1990s to address
problems in residential child care

1991   *Children Act 1989 Guidance and Regulations – Volume 4 Residential Care*
        (Department of Health 1991a). Detailed policy and practice guidance on
        residential child care in the context of the new legislation.

1991   National review of residential child care in England leading to the report
        Children in the Public Care (Department of Health 1991b).

1991   Similar exercise undertaken in Wales – *Accommodating Children: A Review of
        Children's Homes in Wales* (SSI Wales and Social Information Systems 1991).

1992   Committee chaired by Norman Warner, in response to events in
        Leicestershire, on selection and recruitment of staff in residential child care,
        Choosing with Care (Department of Health 1992).

1992   *The Quality of Care* (Local Government Management Board 1992): a
        wide-ranging review that had the specific effect of improving residential
        staff salaries.

1992   Efforts to enhance the inclusion of residential child care in social work
        qualifying training, resulting in setting *Quality Standards for Residential Care*
        (Central Council for Education and Training in Social Work [CCETSW] and
        Department of Health Expert Group 1992).

1992   *Residential Child Care Initiative*, aimed to increase the number of senior staff in
        children's homes who are professionally qualified.

1992   Setting up of *ARCC* (Advancement of Residential Child Care).

1993   *Guidance on Permissible Forms of Control in Children's Residential Care
        (Department of Health 1993).*

1993   Establishment of the *Department of Health Support Force for Children's Residential
        Care*, with a brief to offer advice to individual local authorities on issues
        associated with quality of care and management.

1993   Development of national project at the National Children's Bureau
        to identify, develop and disseminate good practice in residential child care.

1993   National Social Services Inspectorate inspection of children's homes (SSI,
        Department of Health 1993).

1993   Funding by the Department of Health of major research programme on
        residential child care.

1994   Publication of *Growing Up in Groups* (Kahan 1994), a multi-disciplinary
        project highlighting good practice in child care across education, health and
        social services boundaries.

On the practice front, initiatives have occurred more recently to try to assist agencies in implementing the policies identified by the Children Act 1989, 'Utting' and elsewhere. The Department of Health Support Force for Children's Residential Care (1994) has offered consultancy on a range of subjects including: staff selection and personnel practice; strategic planning; costing and contracting child care; the interface between residential care and education; management; the mix of residents in homes; and user involvement. However, the work of the Support Force has been limited to three years in total ceased during 1995. Practice development work has also been taking place at the Children's Residential Care Unit of the National Children's Bureau (1995). This national project has covered topics ranging from: secure provision; staff induction; preparation for adulthood; young people's rights; health and education; and peer group survey and evaluation of standards.

Finally in this section a necessary but controversial piece of work was the Department of Health's 1993 *Guidance on Permissible Forms of Control in Children's Residential Care*. This was required because the 'Pindown' report, in identifying unacceptable forms of control, led logically to the question of what measures could staff legitimately use to maintain orderly environments? The guidance was not popular among professionals. Political masters (or rather mistresses) also seem to have insisted on it being 'toughened-up' between drafts. Professional concern focused mainly on the specification that children's liberty could only be restricted in '...circumstances where immediate action is necessary to prevent injury to any person, or damage to property...' (p.7). It emphasised that control must be understood in the wider context of good practice and skilled, child-centred residential work. In response, it was claimed by some in the field that young people could misbehave with impunity. We return to this debate later, in the light of contemporary evidence. It is our view that the guidance judged the situation about right. However, residential staff are now having to deal with a range of situations and young people that probably were not envisaged when the Children Act and subsequent initiatives were developed. Consequently, an uneasy compromise seems to have emerged in many children's homes on the subject of control.

Staffing

Table 13.2 reveals that the four initiatives in 1992 addressed interrelated staffing issues. The *Quality of Care* group developed a broad remit but the increase in pay was a significant accomplishment. Fewer claims are now heard from the field about residential child care being underpaid. The work with CCETSW, deriving from a recommendation in the Utting report, attempted to enhance the profile of residential work in social work qualifying training and the effectiveness with which it was addressed. The training world sometimes appears an impenetrable one, with universities in particular sensitive as to their independence. There are also considerable difficulties in many regions in providing residential practice placements in sufficient volume and quality. Thus, it is not clear at the time of writing to what extent the Department of Health and CCETSW objectives have been achieved.

The activities of Frank Beck in Leicestershire led to questions being asked about ways in which individuals who set out to exploit and abuse children might be prevented from entering the profession. Even when his proclivities were known, a manager still wrote a positive reference for him for a post elsewhere. *Choosing with Care* ('the Warner report', Department of Health 1992) undertook an impressive body of work on these issues. The report contained a number of valuable suggestions on personnel and other matters including recruitment, selection procedures, appointment arrangements and staff development. Making progress on these fronts needs to go hand in hand with positive equal opportunities policies and non-infringement of individual liberties in a way that does not jeopardise children's safety.

Another important measure to tackle deficiencies in practice was the Residential Child Care Training Initiative (RCCI). This stemmed from the 'Utting' conclusion that all heads of homes and a proportion of care staff – about a third in all – should hold the Diploma in Social Work. A review of this initiative commented that, in itself, it will be valuable in aiding some 500 students to qualify (Lane 1994). However, it was criticised for 'short-termism': it has been argued that the programme was set up hastily; that it was already running down before the first group of students had qualified; and that the overall gain has been lower than intended. More fundamental issues in training, it was claimed, remain unresolved.

Regrettably, there is not the opportunity within the confines of this brief chapter to discuss the Department of Health research programme on residential child care. A very positive feature of child care law and policy over the past decade is the way in which it has been generally consistent with, and underpinned by, detailed research findings (DHSS 1985; DoH 1991c; Berridge forthcoming, a). In this respect it is virtually unique for social policy under the current government. It is encouraging that the same approach is being pursued for developments in residential care.

The current situation

We now bring the chapter up to date by introducing some interim findings from a current national research study of children's homes. This will be used to comment further on some of the issues brought out already in this chapter. The study in question is a follow-up of work undertaken ten years ago, in which 20 children's homes in three local authorities were investigated in detail (Berridge 1985). The same local authorities, and those original homes that are still open, are in the process of being revisited. Where possible, new ones have been substituted for those that have closed. Changes in residential child care over a decade can thus be systematically investigated. The particular focus of the study is the role and impact of homes. At the time of writing, participant observation in establishments is about half completed. We should obviously be cautious with the preliminary status of findings; none the less certain patterns are clearly beginning to emerge from the data. While these are early days in the implementation of the initiatives outlined in Table 13.2, to what extent are they succeeding in remedying problems in children's homes?

Initially, it may be useful to record what has happened to our group of homes overall in the intervening period. Sixteen of the original group of 20 have closed over the decade and, for different reasons, two of the remainder will probably do the same in the near future. The 20 homes included three private and three voluntary homes, all of which are now closed. As a result of the general downgrading of residential care, the current sample will comprise a total of 14 homes. In contrast to the original study, two of the facilities will cater specifically for younger children aged under 13. In line with the Children Act 1989 philosophy of seeking to bring services for children with disabilities more into the mainstream, another two units specifically offer respite care for this group and their families. Five of the 14 are privately run.

One of the main concerns of the Utting report and Children Act 1989 guidance was to sharpen the objectives of children's homes and to make them become more explicit about whom they could or could not help. Some control over intake would also be required. As we revealed earlier, this was an important feature of the inquiry reports. Our findings to date suggest that, with homes for adolescents, this has by no means always occurred. Even after almost four years, Statements of Purpose do not necessarily exist. An important factor in this is that managers sometimes seem unwilling for homes to define objectives in case they might be faced with specific young people they are unable to place. The 'dumping ground' mentality, therefore, persists in some locations.

No doubt related to this, another noticeable feature of homes for adolescents is that they are often found to experience major problems in controlling young people's behaviour. In comparison with the 1985 study, the resident group is older. They appear more delinquent, their social and personal problems are more acute and there is a greater sense of family rejection. One significant development is that community homes with education – CHEs – have virtually disappeared over the past decade. Although there was often dispute over their effectiveness (Millham, Bullock and Cherrett 1979), they did at least cater for a difficult group and filter these away from community facilities. The same applies to homes 'with observation and assessment' ('O & As'), which are also very scarce. Now there is usually no intermediate tier between small, local, open children's homes in the midst of communities and secure provision. These integrated facilities are often referred experienced delinquents, whose patterns of behaviour they find very difficult to withstand.

In something of a turn-around compared with its 1969 equivalent, the Children Act 1989 did not have a great deal to say about delinquents. Indeed, criminal activity was removed as one of the specific grounds for granting a care order. In contrast to public perception, juvenile justice policies in recent years, especially cautioning, have been very successful in restricting levels of crime among the young (Utting, Bright and Henricson 1993) and it seems preferable that this should continue rather than young offenders being diverted unnecessarily to social services. However, whether as a result of these 'down tariff' policies, insufficient intermediate treatment and other individual or group work or for different reasons, delinquents are being referred to children's homes in significant numbers. The emphasis in the Children Act on keeping young people local in their own communities, in touch with friends and in small open facilities, can pose problems in working with persistent offenders, sometimes including remands. From this point of view, the Welsh proposals for developing specific facilities for the most problematic youths may merit reconsideration (SSI Wales and Social Information Systems 1991).

For residential staff, difficulties in dealing with adolescents are compounded by the fact that a minority of school-age pupils in our study regularly attend school, barely a quarter so far. Similar proportions are permanently excluded, irregular attenders or not attending for other reasons. This evidence supports other recent research into the education of children looked after, in which high proportions of young people have been found to experience educational difficulties reflected in patterns of non-attendance and exclusion (Audit Commission 1994; DoH and Office for Standards in Education 1995). The effects of this are serious. The majority of those not attending school receive on average three hours of home tuition each week, a level of provision widely perceived as grossly inadequate. Young people also lack a basic structure to their day. Their peer group becomes restricted to the other residents within the home, making involvement in delinquent activity more likely, often out of sheer boredom. Young people leave care lacking both formal qualifications and basic academic skills, so their career prospects are extremely bleak.

It must be acknowledged that many young people entering the care of a local authority already have histories of educational difficulty, which cannot easily be solved. Increased numbers of exclusions among children looked after have also been linked to the changes which have occurred within the educational system, particularly Local Management of Schools (LMS) (Stirling 1991; Blyth and Milner 1993; Brodie 1995). However, as has been found in foster care (Heath, Aldgate and Colton 1994), it would seem that experience of residential care does not *enhance* educational prospects. Liaison between children's home and school is frequently inadequate. Where exclusion does take place, there is usually a lack of clearly defined policy and procedure regarding the response of social services. The allocation of responsibility for education between fieldworker and residential staff is also unclear. Given the importance of education to the social and academic development of these young people, a more effective and co-ordinated response from both education and social services departments is clearly necessary. Many residential staff interviewed comment that their greatest problems stem from young people not attending school.

Conclusion

In this chapter we have tried to highlight key issues in residential child care over the past decade, focusing specifically on certain inquiry reports and subsequent developments. Thus, a number of structural and specific problems in the service were identified. A wide range of responses emerged from government, some of which will be affected however by their time-limited nature.

Current research demonstrated that the major difficulties in residential care have certainly not disappeared. This is partly attributable to the fact that not all of the measures have been implemented. Local authority managers are not always willing to allow individual homes to define specific objectives and, thereby, cater for particular groups and circumstances. The fear of being presented with what are felt to be insoluble individual problems, namely a young person without a bed, overrides a wider strategic approach to residential care. Hence the needs of the many are sacrificed for those of the few.

This is exacerbated by what would appear to be other unanticipated problems. A number of referrals to children's homes, especially the persistent offenders, are not easily accommodated within a philosophy of providing care in small, open facilities within local communities. Those communities which are prepared to tolerate a children's home within their vicinity are themselves sometimes characterised by high levels of crime or unsafe. Given the current intake, the social and physical environment of children's homes can make the task particularly difficult and on occasions impossible. Staff also frequently misperceive the control and restraint guidance and can be insufficiently proactive in exercising control or lacking in confidence. All of this is intensified by the major educational problems that have arisen.

The responses to the major crises were laudable, albeit long overdue. They resulted in probably the most comprehensive package of reforms ever to bear on the children's residential sector. However, commitment at all levels of the service is required and certain other problems need urgently to be addressed, otherwise they will be ineffective.

Acknowledgements

We are grateful for comments on an earlier draft of this chapter by Barbara Kahan and John Rowlands and colleagues from the Department of Health Social Services Inspectorate.

References

Audit Commission (1994) *Seen But Not Heard: Co-ordinating Community Child Health and Social Services for Children in Need.* London: HMSO.

Berridge, D. (forthcoming, a) Families in need: crisis and responsibility. In H. Dean (ed) *Parents' Duties, Children's Debts: The Limits of Policy Intervention.* Aldershot: Ashgate Publishing.

Berridge, D. (forthcoming, b) *Foster Care: A Research Review.* London: HMSO.

Berridge, D. (1994) Foster and residential care reassessed: a research perspective. *Children and Society 18,* 2, 132–150.

Berridge, D. (1985) *Children's Homes.* Oxford: Blackwell.

Blyth, E. and Milner, J. (1993) Exclusion from school: a first step in exclusion from society? *Children and Society 7,* 3, 255–268.

Brodie, I. (1995) *Exclusion from School. Highlight Series.* London: National Children's Bureau.

Butler-Sloss, Lord Justice E. (1988) *Report of the Inquiry into Child Abuse in Cleveland 1987 Cm 412.* London: Department of Health and Social Security.

Central Council for Education and Training in Social Work and Department of Health Expert Group (1992) *Quality Standards for Residential Care.* London: Central Council for Education and Training in Social Work.

Cliffe, D. with Berridge, D. (1991) *Closing Children's Homes: An End to Residential Child Care?* London: National Children's Bureau.

Colton, M. (1988) *Dimensions of Substitute Care.* Aldershot: Gower.

Department of Health (1991a) *Children Act 1989 Guidance and Regulations: Volume 4 Residential Care.* London: HMSO.

Department of Health (1991b) *Children in the Public Care: A Review of Residential Care.* London: HMSO.

Department of Health (1991c) *Patterns and Outcomes in Child Care: Messages from Current Research and their Implications.* London: HMSO.

Department of Health (1992) *Choosing with Care: The Report of the Committee of Inquiry into the Selection, Development and Management of Staff in Children's Homes.* London: HMSO.

Department of Health (1993) *Guidance on Permissible Forms of Control in Children's Residential Care.* London: Department of Health.

Department of Health and Office for Standards in Education (1995) *The Education of Children Who Are Looked After by Local Authorities.* London: Department of Health and Office for Standards in Education.

Department of Health and Social Security (1985) *Social Work Decisions in Child Care: Recent Research Findings and their Implications.* London: HMSO.

Department of Health and Social Services Northern Ireland (1986) *Committee of Inquiry into Children's Homes and Hostels.* Belfast: DHSS.

Department of Health Support Force for Children's Residential Care (1994) *Newsletter No 4.* London: Department of Health.

Heath, A., Colton, M. and Aldgate, J. (1994) Failure to escape: a longitudinal study of foster children's educational attainment. *British Journal of Social Work* 24, 241–260.

Kahan, B. (1979) *Growing Up in Care.* Oxford: Blackwell.

Kahan, B (1994) *Growing Up in Groups.* London: HMSO.

Kahan, B. (1995a) Residential care of children and young people: Children Act 1948 to Children Act 1989. *Highlight Series No. 133.* London: National Children's Bureau.

Kahan, B. (1995b) Residential child care in the 1990s and beyond. *Highlight Series No.134.* London: National Children's Bureau.

Kirkwood, A. (1993) *The Leicestershire Inquiry 1992.* Leicester: Leicestershire County Council.

Knapp, M. and Robertson, E. (1989) The cost of services. In B. Kahan (ed) *Child Care Research, Policy and Practice.* London: Hodder and Stoughton.

Lane, D. (1994) *An Independent Review of the Residential Child Care Initiative.* London: Central Council for Education and Training in Social Work.

Local Government Management Board (1992) *The Quality of Care: Report of the Residential Staffs Inquiry (Chair Lady Howe).* London: Local Government Management Board.

Levy, A. and Kahan, B. (1991) *The Pindown Experience and the Protection of Children.* Stafford: Staffordshire County Council.

Millham, S., Bullock, R. and Cherrett, P. (1979) *After Grace – Teeth: A Comparative Study of the Residential Experience of Boys in Approved Schools.* Brighton: Chaucer.

National Children's Bureau Children's Residential Care Unit (1995) *Newsletter No 1.* London: National Children's Bureau.

Page, R. and Clarke, G. (1977) *Who Cares? Young People in Care Speak Out.* London: National Children's Bureau.

Report of the Care of Children Committee (1946) Interim Report on Training in Child Care. Cmd 6760.

Rowe, J., Hundleby, M. and Garnett, L. (1989) *Child Care Now.* London: British Agencies for Adoption and Fostering

Social Services Inspectorate Wales and Social Information Systems (1991) *Accommodating Children: A Review of Children's Homes in Wales.* Cardiff: Welsh Office.

Stirling, M. (1991) Absent without leave. *Special Children 52,* 10–13.

Triseliotis, J., Borland, M., Hill, M. and Lambert, L. (1995) *Teenagers and the Social Work Services.* London: HMSO.

Utting, D., Bright, J. and Henricson, C. (1993) *Crime and the Family: Improving Child-Rearing and Preventing Delinquency.* London: Family Policy Studies Centre.

Wagner, G. (1988) *Residential Care: A Positive Choice.* London: HMSO

Williams, G. and McCreadie, J. (1992) *Ty Mawr Community Home Inquiry.* Cwmbran: Gwent County Council.

CHAPTER 14

Adoption in England and Wales
Current Issues and Future Trends

Murray Ryburn

Introduction

Despite the relatively low number of orders, adoption is still accorded a key place in debates about the provision of child welfare services. There are several reasons for this. Adoption, as a permanent and irrevocable order, raises much wider and more fundamental issues than its status as just one of a range of court orders might suggest. Thus it challenges us to consider both whether nurture and environment can supplant nature, and whether it is desirable that they seek to do so. It calls into question the extent to which the State should act as an arbiter and regulator of family life, and in seeking to build permanent new families, adoption raises vital questions about the status to be accorded to original families. The fact that adoption orders stretch backwards as well as forwards in time in the ways that they affect relationships has been equally important in widening its focus of interest beyond the immediate issues. More than anything, perhaps, adoption has reflected in microcosmic form key social issues of the times and it continues today to operate as a barometer of public attitudes to families, child care and parenting.

The Government White Paper *Adoption: The Future* (1993) can leave us in little doubt that adoption is still regarded as an essential part of a comprehensive State child welfare provision, even if it seems equally clear that the 'cost neutrality' (p.18 para. 7.14) basis of the White Paper's proposals for reform will compound existing shortfalls in resources. However, if the White Paper's answer to the question 'does adoption have a future?' is clearly 'yes', on the more challenging moral question 'should adoption have a future?' the White Paper is silent. Some consideration of both these questions is necessary in order to set the context for any discussion of possible future trends and developments in adoption policy and practice.

Is there a future for adoption?

Both adoption societies and informal adoptions were common long before the introduction of adoption legislation. Thus it was estimated that from 1890 to 1926 one adoption society alone arranged some 20,500 *de facto* adoptions in England and Wales (Ryburn 1995). It was an awareness of this demand, more than anything else, which propelled the reluctant Tomlin Committee to recommend that legislation for adoption be introduced. The number of adoptions in England and Wales reached a peak of 24,831 in 1968, and declined thereafter until 1990. However, by 1992, the latest year for which figures are available, there were 7342 adoptions, representing a 6 per cent increase over the 1990 figure (House of Lords 38 17 January 1995). It is too soon to say if this represents a definite trend. It is, though, an indication that adoption, which seemed likely to wither and die during the 1970s and early 1980s as a consequence of the availability of a greater range of choices for young pregnant women, is instead being transformed into a different sort of institution.

Should adoption continue?

Adoption is a legal order which bestows all of the rights, duties and responsibilities of parenthood for a child on to a new parent or parents. In law it extinguishes absolutely all of the rights, duties and responsibilities of original parents and other relatives, so that the birth parents become in law 'former parents' as far as their adopted children are concerned. The 1993 White Paper makes it clear that no modification to the legal effects of an adoption order are now contemplated. The only obvious moral justification for an order as irrevocable in its legal effects as adoption is that it offers significant advantages over any less far-reaching alternatives, but the evidence for this is not clear-cut.

Birth parents and other relatives

Historically adoption law has never grasped the paramountcy principle that the best interests of the child should be the determining factor in any court decisions in the same unequivocal way that other children's legislation has since the implementation of the Guardianship Act of 1925. This reluctance has stemmed from an historical emphasis in public law on the inalienability of parental rights (Pettit 1957) and a recognition of the severe consequences for birth relatives, where they are opposed to adoption, of an order whose legal effects will be irreversible.

There is indeed considerable evidence that for birth relatives the long-term consequences of an adoption may be very harmful, especially when there is no continuing contact with the children who have been adopted. Thus an Australian study by Winkler and van Keppel (1984), which surveyed 213 mothers who had relinquished children for adoption, found that 48 per cent reported an intensified feeling of loss over the period from relinquishment to the time of the research study. For almost three-quarters of the sample it had been ten years or more since the relinquishment. Only 10 per cent of women reported that they no longer experienced any loss in relation to the adoption. Sachdev (1991) found of a sample of 78 birth mothers that: 'a huge majority (77 per cent) of the sample…admitted to having very frequently or somewhat frequently thought of the child they relinquished some fourteen years previously with considerable mixed guilt, pain, and loss' (p.259). The prevalence of a sense of loss following adoption has been identified by many others (Bouchier, Lambert and Triseliotis 1991; Howe, Sawbridge and Hinings 1992; Wells 1994). Only one study to date has considered birth fathers (Deykin, Patti and Ryan, 1988) but here too the findings were similar. Other birth relatives such as grandparents (Tingle 1994) also report severe loss reactions to adoption.

Adoptees

It is difficult to assess the success of adoption from the perspectives of those who are adopted. Generally adoption is regarded as a successful institution. As with birth families, the majority of adoptees grow up to adulthood within their adoptive families satisfied and well integrated (Triseliotis 1991). However, there have been only a few studies which have considered the views of adoptees in adulthood (McWhinnie 1967; Triseliotis 1973; Raynor 1980; Sachdev 1991). Nor, with the exception of the Swedish Adoption Twin Study of Ageing (Pedersen et al. 1991), which is focused especially in genetics research, have there been any studies which have exclusively studied adoptees in later life.

We should note there is evidence to indicate that adoptees are over-represented as regards behaviour or mental health problems in clinical populations and in random population samples (Bohman 1970; Brodzinsky et al. 1987; Goldberg and Wolkind 1992; Lipman et al. 1993). We know too that appreciable numbers of adoptees, unhappy with the legal consequences of adoptions which have separated them from their first families and backgrounds, wish to search their origins (Picton and Bieske-Vos 1982; Haimes and Timms 1985; Hodgkins 1987; Sachdev 1991). To give some indication of the possible prevalence of this wish to search, in New Zealand it has been estimated that half of all adults adopted by strangers have now used the provisions of 1985 legislation to seek identifying information (Griffiths 1994).

There have been an enormous number of research studies in the adoption field, yet there is a great deal we do not know. Available evidence seems to indicate that adoption offers a secure family life to the majority of adoptees, but it is also likely that for a substantial minority this may not hold true. It would be unwise to regard adoption as inherently the best option for children and young people needing permanent alternative care.

Other forms of permanence

Adoption is unique among child care orders in that it creates legal relationships for life. However, though adoption orders can create lifelong legal relationships they afford, obviously, no guarantee that these will prove happy and successful. An adoption order may symbolise a degree of commitment from parents at the time it is granted, but whether this commitment is able to stand the test of time depends on other aspects of the relationship. Thus we know from a variety of research studies (Rutter 1980; Rutter and Rutter 1993) that the depth of attachment between parents and children derives in particular from qualitative aspects of their relationship and that positive interactions between parents and children are more important in building attachment than the amount of time each spends in the other's company (Fox 1977).

Lahti (1982) found in a range of placements planned as permanent that children's sense of security seemed to derive from the quality of care they received rather than the legal status of the placement. There is also evidence that legally permanent placements other than adoption can offer extremely viable and effective placement options (Rowe et al. 1984; Thoburn 1989; Bullard, Mallos and Parker 1990). These alternatives placements have been shown to be no less stable than adoptions (Fratter et al. 1991)

Sense of entitlement

It might, however, be argued that the absolute legal permanence of an adoption order adds something qualitative to the approach that adopters will take in their parenting so that it is the order of preference where children need alternative permanent placements. The word that has been to used describe this qualitative difference is a sense of 'entitlement' (Raynor 1981). In this line of reasoning adopters, and indeed their children and other relatives, attach symbolic importance to an adoption order as a guarantee of the placement and the tangible evidence of a child's full and complete inclusion in the family network. As a consequence more confident parenting, a greater sense of commitment and a child's fuller integration in the family can, it is argued, be expected. For some parents this is likely to be true; equally, perhaps, there are potential dangers in seeking to use adoption as a visible symbol of what can never be.

Though in law adoption would treat any adopted child as a child born to the adopters, the social reality is very different. Research suggests that adopted children have a birth heritage which should always be acknowledged by adopters if children are to be parented most effectively (Kirk 1964, 1981; Haimes and Timms 1985; Kaye and Warren 1988; Sachdev 1991). It could be claimed that the acknowledgement of this birth heritage will more readily be achieved through alternative forms of permanent order such as residence or the new *inter vivos* guardianship that is proposed in the White Paper, rather than by an order which in law treats children, their birth parents, siblings and other relatives as if they were strangers to each other.

Poverty and consent

The moral argument for adoption to continue into the twenty-first century as a final and irrevocable order would be stronger were there not substantial evidence pointing to a close association between poverty and all forms of substitute care for children, including adoption (Pinderhughes 1991; Williams 1991; Ryburn 1994b). Historically most adoption orders have been granted following the giving of consent by birth parents. If we examine the record however we discover that 'consent' has all too often been a misnomer for a decision of last resort when there seemed to be no other viable alternatives (Rockel and Ryburn 1988; Najman *et al.* 1990; Howe, Sawbridge and Hinings, 1992; Wells 1994; O'Shaughnessy 1994; Ryburn 1995). With the beginnings of the permanency movement from the end of the 1970s, adoption entered a new phase where an increasing proportion of orders began to be granted without the consent of parents. In these circumstances not even the argument that a consent was signed is available to offer moral sanction for adoption. Its case must instead rest solely on the grounds that it would better serve the welfare of the child than any alternative – an argument, as I have indicated above, that is not necessarily sustainable.

In circumstances where children are thought to be in need of care and protection, in accordance with the principles of the Children Act 1989, the preferred plan should normally lie in supplementing their own families' capacities and resources to care for them. However, the amounts of money spent on supporting the families of children seen to be at risk are woefully inadequate (Audit Commission 1994). When the record of preventive services is examined, we are drawn inescapably to the conclusion that children may be adopted against the wishes of their parents when with reasonable levels of help and support they could have remained in their families of origin (Trent 1989; Williams 1991; Walton *et al.* 1993). Indeed, as I shall later elaborate, the very existence of an order like adoption which offers a relatively cheap and, from the professional's point of view, uncomplicated solution to the problems of families and children in need, may be seen as a major disincentive to the concentration of efforts on preventive measures aimed to retain children in their original family networks.

As we enter the next century there seems little reason to expect, in a social order where the poor are increasingly marginalised (Rowntree 1995; WHA 1995) that adoption services will be averted from their historical course as a medium for the transfer of children across wealth and class divides. The current review of adoption law has failed to grapple effectively with the question of whether adoption would better be replaced.

Future directions envisaged by the White Paper

More of the same

In November 1993 the Government published a long-awaited White Paper on the future of adoption. In her preface to the White Paper the Minister of Health declared that 'Our adoption service is established on a solid base', and the document itself states that the 'Government considers the basic structure [of adoption] to be sound' (p.1 para. 1.6). As a vision for the future, which is what its title purports it to be, the White Paper offers little other than more of the same.

New orders

Although the intention is clear to retain adoption as an irrevocable order with all of its current legal effects, the White Paper does propose two new forms of order. *Inter vivos* guardianship would differ from a residence order only in that it would invariably last to age 18 (a residence order may be extended to 18) and it would give such a guardian the power to appoint a testamentary guardian. It could only be revoked by leave of the court, but the power to limit applications in respect of residence orders also potentially exist in Section 91(14) of the Children Act.

The White Paper also proposes a new form of parental responsibility agreement where step-parents wish to formalise a relationship with a child. The current requirement that birth parents adopt their own child in the case of step-parent adoptions would be abandoned. The new parental responsibility order for step-parents is presumably an attempt to reduce the number of step-parent adoptions, though this is not spelled out.

Step-parent adoption

Step-parent adoptions constituted rather less than a quarter of all adoptions in 1962 (Houghton Report 1972 table 3 p.125) but are now one half of all adoptions (White Paper p.5 para. 3.9). However, at a time when as the result of higher remarriage rates (Halsey 1993) we might have expected a much sharper increase in step-parent adoptions we have, since 1971, witnessed their numerical decline broadly in parallel with the diminishing popularity of adoption itself. The White Paper's proposals may well lead to some decline in their number but it would be surprising if this were marked, since they continued largely unabated despite attempts to discourage them under Section 14(3) of the Adoption Act 1976, which provided that a step-parent adoption application should be dismissed if the court considered the matter would be better dealt with by making an order under Sections 42–44 of the Matrimonial Causes Act now repealed by the Children Act 1989 (Dodds 1989).

Complaints procedures

The White Paper promises some procedural changes which will include a requirement that agencies introduce a complaints procedure modelled on that required under the Children Act. This proposal is largely redundant (except where voluntary agencies are concerned) since adoption matters are not, in any case, excluded from existing local authority complaints procedures. There are proposals to create adoption panels with a more independent membership than at present, but at the heart of this, one suspects, is a populist, anti-professional appeal rather than any attempt to ensure that the interests of adoption consumers are better represented in decision-making forums. Certainly there are no suggestions that would ensure the representation on panels of those who have had direct service user experience of adoption services.

Contact and information

Despite substantial support in research for the importance of contact between children who are adopted and their birth families (Ryburn 1994a), the White Paper is essentially concerned with the exchange of information. It tends to the position espoused in some recent writing (White 1991; McWhinnie and Smith 1994) that direct contact potentially undermines placements, even though this is unsupported in research (Fratter *et al.* 1991; Ryburn 1996 forthcoming).

Even on the issue of access to information few changes are in prospect. There are suggestions for a procedural change so that a copy of background information is retained with court records. This would help ensure that at the age of 18 adopted people can gain access to information about the circumstances of their lives before adoption, provided they seek access to court records. A provision is recommended to permit birth parents and relatives and adopted people to register a veto against the disclosure of information. This latter proposal has brought great distress elsewhere, and it can generate great hostility on the part of those who feel that they are being denied the right of access to fundamental information about their own lives. In some instances a veto appears to make people more determined to gain information by alternative means (Rockel and Ryburn 1988).

There are, disappointingly, no proposals to extend rights of access to information to those aged below 18, even though the current failure to do so would seem to be a denial of rights to children within the terms of the United Nations Convention on the Rights of the Child to which the United Kingdom is a signatory. Article 13(1) for example states that children have the right 'to seek, receive and impart information and ideas of all kinds, regardless of frontiers, either orally, in writing or in print...' The only permitted restrictions are in order to respect the rights and reputations of others, or in order to protect national security, public order or the public health and morals (13(2)).

It is difficult to imagine how the latter grounds could be relevant. Some might argue that the restriction permitted in order to protect the rights or reputations of others applies to adopters, but even were this so such a right is already disregarded in law when adoptees reach 18 years of age and are permitted access to identifying information. Furthermore it is clearly established in case law and in legislation that children are entitled to make informed requests and decisions well below the age of 18. Nor can an argument be sustained that it is desirable that parents be entitled to control and restrict the access of any child to information, since the only means by which this could absolutely be ensured would be as the consequence of a child's complete isolation. Children have rights that are independent of those of their parents, and one of the rights in the Convention on the Rights of the Child is for children 'to preserve [their] identit[ies], including name, nationality and family relations' (Article 8).

Only changes in current adoption legislation which entitled children below 18 years access to information about their birth families and backgrounds would permit children the exercise of these rights. It is a matter of great regret that this is not considered in the White Paper's proposals. It is a failure that, together with the omission of any suggestions to improve the rights of access to information for all birth relatives of adopted people, will ensure these issues retain a central place in future debates about adoption policy and practice.

Other rights

The White Paper does, paradoxically, propose to strengthen the duty to seek children's wishes and, where older children are concerned, to be guided by their views about adoption. Given the failure to suggest the extension of children's rights to the area of access to information, however, this is not a recipe for a thorough overhaul of the law. Ultimately professionals and the courts will remain entitled to put their own gloss on what children 'really want'.

The White Paper argues that 'commonsense' judgements must be taken when considering such matters as the suitability of adoptive applicants. Ethnicity and culture rate a mention as 'factors alongside others' (p.9 para. 4.31) to be considered in the placement of children, but it would be foolish to regard this as any sort of prescription for same-race placement policies.

The White Paper proposes the abandonment of freeing for adoption, where a child becomes legally adoptable before prospective adopters may have been found, though its reasons for doing so appear to be based much more on the procedural problems that freeing creates than the injustice that it has created for birth parents since its introduction in 1984 (Ryburn 1994a). The White Paper's detailed proposals for its replacement seem to entail just as many problems (Ryan 1994).

Inter-country adoption

In contrast with some countries where there is virtually no domestic adoption (e.g. Sweden, Denmark, Holland) intercountry adoptions constitute a very small minority (perhaps 4 per cent) of all adoption orders, and this is the one significant 'growth area' envisaged by the White Paper.

The White Paper refuses to acknowledge that the debate about inter-country adoption is a moral debate which centres on many crucial issues. These include the sale of children and the other sorts of abuses referred to in Article 21 of the UN Convention on the Rights of the Child, as well as the likely loss for children of both their genealogical and their national heritage, and the fact that intercountry adoption is a market only for those able to pay. This unwillingness to recognise the moral dimensions of intercountry adoptions is underscored by the statement that adoption policies should be 'free from any prejudice against the principle of intercountry adoption' (p.17 para. 6.34). The White Paper then proceeds to lend active support to intercountry adoption, concluding that in 'all suitable cases' they should be 'supported and facilitated' (p.15 para. 6.10) and that a voluntary agency committed to doing so would be 'a valuable addition' (p.16 para. 6.22).

Intercountry adoption can never offer an effective solution to the global inequalities that are at the heart of the massive and escalating problems of child poverty, homelessness and abandonment in less developed countries (WHO 1995). The desperate need of less developed countries is for aid programmes to support and enhance existing traditional kinship care systems for children, and to foster new indigenous initiatives (Rutayuga 1992), not to attempt to 'transplant' children from one country to another. However the active encouragement the White Paper lends to intercountry adoption marks it out as a future adoption growth area in England and Wales.

Adoptions without consent

Yet if a single current trend were to be identified as the central force that will shape adoption policy and practice as we enter the new century it would be unlikely to be any of the issues that I have considered above. The rising tide of adversarialism in adoption proceedings and the resultant increase in compulsory orders prefigure, more than anything else, the future shape of domestic adoption services.

From the beginning of the 1970s adoption began to change and to diversify so that it became the linchpin of the permanency movement (Fox Harding 1991). Its position at the pinnacle of the various placement options for children was supported by a coherent, if misguided, philosophy which sought, where initial (and often limited) attempts to restore children to original families had failed, to place them permanently in new adoptive families. Past links were severed in the belief that this would aid the formation of new attachments.

Often these placements were made compulsorily against a background of protest and despair on the part of birth relatives.

Increasingly the permanency movement has been discredited because it has insufficiently attempted to mobilise and supplement the resources of children's own families, both as a result of its serious underestimation of the importance of kinship and its misunderstanding of the nature of human attachment (Ryburn 1994a). Despite the movement's decline, however, and the antidote it is afforded by the Children Act 1989, with its emphasis, for example, on the maintenance of contact, the number of compulsory adoptions has risen significantly in the past eight years.

Evidence for adversarialism

There are no national statistics concerning the number of adoption or freeing applications that are contested by birth parents. We do however have court records data from the *Pathways to Adoption* survey (Murch *et al.* 1993). These researchers found (p.28) that of 393 agency adoption applications concerning non relative placements 26 per cent (101) were contested, while of 102 freeing applications 75 per cent (77) were contested. We cannot assume that all the remainder were not contested, however, since here the figures include situations where it was not known if an adoption order or freeing application was contested. Nor do these figures give any indication of how many birth parents were deeply unhappy with an agency's plan for adoption but lacked the will, ability or resources to contest it.

In the *Pathways* study (p.55) 48 per cent of children compulsorily adopted and 72 per cent of those freed for adoption were previously in compulsory care. Given the association between being in care and contested adoption, any rise in the number of children adopted from care would be likely to constitute evidence of increasing adversarialism in adoption. The number of children in England committed to care who were subsequently adopted shows a 35 per cent increase from a figure of 1029 in 1988 to 1386 in 1991 (the latest year for which figures are available). This increase in adoptions from care cannot be explained by higher overall numbers of adoption orders, since there were 219 fewer adoptions in 1991 than 1988 (Hansard W/A 38 17 January 1995). It also occurred during a period when there was an overall reduction in the number of children committed to care. These figures are significant evidence for a greater tendency to compulsion in adoption than in other areas of child care. The likely trend to compulsion and adversarialism is also supported by the evidence of the numbers of children adopted following [voluntary] reception into care. Here there was a reduction of 17 per cent from 1272 in 1988 to 1053 in 1991 (DoH 1988, 1991).

Compulsion and the market

If compulsory adoptions are increasing proportionately yet their impetus derives less than before from the application of permanency movement principles, it is important to look elsewhere for the source of this trend.

The survival of adoption in its legal form is guaranteed, I have suggested, by the capacity it has historically demonstrated to adapt to meet new purposes and demands. The social, political and economic climate has changed enormously since the mid 1970s when adoption numbers first began to decline significantly and adoption services began to gear themselves to meet the requirements of the permanency movement. Most notably, the market policies which have been the principal hallmark of the present Government in the years since 1979 have continued to drive a larger wedge between the beneficiaries of the market place and an underclass that depends entirely on state welfare as a means to survival (Rowntree 1995). It is those in this latter group who are almost exclusively the recipients of state social work services and child care services in particular (Becker and MacPherson 1989; Becker and Silburn 1990). It is the former who offer them services.

As the poor become relatively more poor, many of the problems they encounter become commensurably more intractable, and the social services required to alleviate them are more likely to be long-term and materially focused. However child welfare services, in response no doubt to contracting or at best static budgets, are developing more than ever as services only for those families and children deemed most to be at risk (Audit Commission 1994; Gibbons, Conroy and Bell 1995). This concentration of child welfare resources in the 'risk assessment' area, in combination with the lack of any growth in social service budgets, has resulted in the scaling down of or failure to initiate the preventive services once intended to be at the heart of Part Three of the Children Act 1989 (Audit Commission 1994).

In the absence of any intervention to ensure an adequate income and the improved life chances that would flow from this, many families will remain in a state of chronic need where only long-term palliative services offer them any realistic chance of survival as family units. Increasingly, though, there is now unlikely to be the infrastructure of preventive services, including respite care, available on a long-term basis to assist these families. Nor, in the shift to brief and risk-focused services, is there the philosophical orientation that would favour a long-term partnership between these families and the local authority in order to help children to remain within their own family networks. Permanent substitute care comes to have an almost inescapable appeal in this climate. It is here, more than anywhere else, that we are likely to find the explanation for the continuing rise in compulsory adoptions. No longer are compulsory adoptions philosophically motivated as they were at the height of the permanency movement, rather they have become resource led.

Conclusion

If we take this argument to its logical conclusion, notwithstanding the apparent decline in support in law and principle for compulsion as a necessary instrument of policy, mandatory adoptions are likely to increase unless there is a fundamental shift in resource allocation and philosophy of service delivery. There seems no realistic likelihood that either will occur.

Just to maintain current levels of access to, and availability of, social services is now likely to be beyond the means of any Central Government or local authority, whatever its political complexion, as relative poverty grows and an ageing population leads to greater demand (Halsey 1993). Nor is a change of Government likely to turn back the clock on the fiscal management of social need which has become the key tool for rationing the social services in the 1990s (Gray 1992).

Adoption by strangers has always been a cheap alternative to other forms of care, including the support of children's own kin networks, since in essence it involves the transfer of the cost of care from the public to the private purse (Kirk and McDaniel 1984). The very clear intention to keep adoption as a low cost service is reflected in the White Paper's statement that the Government will 'have regard to the need for cost-neutrality' so far as any changes to adoption are concerned, since it 'does not intend that they will create extra costs' (p.18 para. 7.4). Money, in other words, will be available for a basic adoption service but not for the implementation or development of the post-adoption programmes that most local authorities can still not afford to provide.

Yet the 'cost neutrality' rubric is applied not only to adoption, but across the total child welfare provision. The pressure this creates to find fiscally sound alternatives to long-term partnerships with the families of children in need has become irresistible. In comparison with all other alternatives adoption is remarkably cheap. On this basis alone adoption, without a post-placement service, and even if birth relatives do not agree, has a very secure future.

References

Audit Commission (1994) *Seen but not Heard, Co-ordinating Community Child Health and Social Services for Children in Need, Detailed Evidence and Guidelines for Managers and Practitioners.* London: HMSO.

Bohman, M. (1970) *Adopted Children and their Families.* Stockholm: Proprios.

Bouchier, P., Lambert, L. and Triseliotis, J. (1991) *Parting with a Child for Adoption.* London: BAAF.

Brodzinsky, D., Radice, C., Huffman, L. and Merkler, K. (1987) Prevalence of clinically significant symptomatology in a nonclinical sample of adopted and non adopted children. *Journal of Clinical Child Psychology 16,* 350–356.

Bullard, E., Mallos, E. and Parker, R. (1990) *Custodianship Research Project: A Report to the Department of Health*. Bristol: Socio-Legal Centre for Family Studies, University of Bristol, 1990.

Department of Health (1988) *Children in Care 1988*. England. A/F 88/1, London: HMSO.

Department of Health, (1991) *Children in Care 1991*. England. A/F 91/1, London: HMSO.

Department of Health, Welsh Office, Home Office, Lord Chancellor's Department (1993) *Adoption: The Future*. London: HMSO, Cm 2288.

Deykin, E. Patti, P. and Ryan, J. (1988) Fathers of adopted children: a study of the impact of child surrender on birthfathers. *American Journal of Orthopsychiatry 58*, 2, 240–48.

Dodds, M. (1989) Step-parent adoptions in the domestic court. *Justice of the Peace 153*, 731–2.

Field, J. (1990) Long-term outcomes for birth mothers before and after reunion. *Adoption and Fostering 14*, 3, 14–17.

Field, J. (1991) Views of New Zealand birth mothers on search and reunion. In A. Mullender (ed) *Open Adoption: The Philosophy and the Practice*. London: BAAF.

Fox Harding, L. (1991) *Perspectives in Child Care Policy*. London: Longman.

Fratter, J., Rowe, J., Sapsford, D. and Thoburn, J. (1991) *Permanent Family Placement: A Decade of Experience*. London: BAAF.

Gibbons, J. Conroy, S. and Bell, C. (1995) *Operating the Child Protection System, a Study of Child Protection Practices in English Local Authorities*. London: HMSO.

Goldberg, D. and Wolkind, S. (1992) Patterns of psychiatric disorder in adopted girls: a research note. *Journal of Psychology and Psychiatry and Allied Disciplines 33*, 5, 935–40.

Gray, J. (1992) *The Moral Foundations of Market Institutions*. London: IEA Health and Welfare Unit.

Griffiths, K. (1994) The realities of adoption for the adopted person. In J. Morris (ed) *Adoption: Past, Present and Future*. Auckland: Uniprint.

Haimes, E. and Timms, N. (1985) *Adoption, Identity and Social Policy*. Aldershot: Gower.

Halsey, A. (1993) Changes in the family. *Children and Society 7*, 2, 125–136.

Hodgkins, P. (1987) *Adopted Adults: An Evaluation of their Relationships with their Families*. Oxford: NORCAP.

House of Lords (1995) *Weekly Hansard 16 January 1995 to 19th January 1995*. London: HMSO No 1619 W/A 38.

Houghton Report (1972) *Report of the Departmental Committee on the Adoption of Children*. London: HMSO, Cm 5107.

Howe, D., Sawbridge, P. and Hinings, D. (1992) *Half a Million Women: Mothers who Lose their Children by Adoption.* London: Penguin.

Kaye, K. and Warren, S. (1988) Discourse about adoption in adoptive families. *Journal of Family Psychology 4,* 406–33.

Kirk, D. (1964) *Shared Fate: A Theory of Adoption and Mental Health.* New York: Free Press.

Kirk, D. (1981) *Adoptive Kinship; A Modern Institution in Need of Reform.* Toronto: Butterworths.

Kirk, D. and McDaniel, S. (1984) Adoption policy in great Britain and North America. *Journal of Social Policy 13,* 1, 75–84.

Lahti, J. (1982) A follow-up study of foster children in permanent placements. *Social Service Review.* Chicago: University of Chicago.

Lipman, E., Offord, D., Boyle, M. and Racine, Y. (1993) Follow-up of psychiatric and educational morbidity among adopted children. *Journal of the American Academy of Child and Adolescent Psychiatry 32,* 5, 1007–12.

McWhinnie, A. (1967) *Adopted Children: How They Grew Up.* London: Routledge and Kegan Paul.

McWhinnie, A. and Smith, J. (eds) (1994) *Current Dilemmas in Adoption: The Challenge for Parents, Practitioners and Policy-makers* University of Dundee. Dundee.

Murch, M., Lowe, N., Borkowski, M., Copner, R. and Griew, K. (1993) *Pathways to Adoption Research Project.* Bristol: Socio-Legal Centre for Family Studies, University of Bristol/DOH.

Najman, J., Morrison, J., Keeping, J., Andersen, M. and Williams, G. (1990) Social factors associated with the decision to relinquish a baby for adoption. *Community Health Studies 14,* 2, 180–90.

O'Shaughnessy, T. (1994) *Adoption, Social Work and Social Theory.* Aldershot: Avebury/Gower.

Pedersen, N., McClearn, G., Plomin, R., Nesselroade, J., Berg, S. and DeFaire, U. (1991) 'The Swedish adoption twin study of ageing: an update.' *Acta Geneticae 40,* 1, 7–20.

Pettit, P. (1957) Parental control and guardianship. In R. Graveson and F. Crane (eds) *A Century of Family Law.* London: Sweet and Maxwell.

Picton, C. and Bieske-Vos, M. (1982) *Persons in Question: Adoptees in Search of Origins.* Melbourne: Published by the author.

Pinderhughes, E. (1991) The delivery of welfare services to African American clients. *American Journal of Orthopsychiatry 61,* 4, 599–605.

Raynor, L. (1980) *The Adopted Child Comes of Age.* London: Allen and Unwin.

Rockel, J. and Ryburn, M. (1988) *Adoption Today: Change and Choice in New Zealand.* Auckland: Heinemann/Reed.

Rowe, J., Cain, H., Hundleby, M. and Keane, A. (1984) *Long Term Foster Care.* London: Batsford/BAAF.

Rowntree Foundation (1995) *Enquiry into Income and Wealth, vols. I and II.* York: Joseph Rowntree Foundation.

Rutayuga, J. (1992) Assistance to AIDS orphans within the family/kinship system and local institutions: a program for East Africa. *AIDS Information and Prevention Fall,* 1992, 57–68.

Rutter, M. (1980) *Maternal Deprivation Reassessed.* Harmondsworth: Penguin.

Rutter, M. and Rutter, M. (1993) *Developing Minds: Challenge and Continuity Across the Life Span.* London: Penguin.

Ryan, M. (1994) Contested proceedings: justice and the law. In M. Ryburn (ed) *Contested Adoptions: Research, Law, Policy and Practice.* Aldershot: Gower/Arena.

Ryburn, M. (1994a) *Open Adoption: Theory, Research and Practice.* Aldershot: Gower.

Ryburn, M. (1994b) The use of an adversarial process in contested adoptions. In M. Ryburn (ed) *Contested Adoptions: Research, Law, Policy and Practice.* Aldershot: Gower/Arena.

Ryburn, M. (1995) Secrecy and openness in adoption: an historical perspective. *Journal of Social Policy and Administration 29,* 2, 150–168.

Ryburn, M. (1996, forthcoming) A study of post adoption contact in compulsory adoptions. *British Journal of Social Work.*

Sachdev, P. (1991) The triangle of fears: fallacies and facts. In E. Hibbs (ed) *Adoption: International Perspectives.* Maddison CT: International Universities Press.

Thoburn, J. (1989) *Success and Failure in Permanent Placement.* Aldershot: Avebury/Gower.

Tingle, N. (1994) A view of wider family perspectives in contested adoptions. In M. Ryburn (ed) *Contested Adoptions: Research, Law, Policy and Practice.* Aldershot: Gower/Arena.

Tomlin Report (1925) *First Report of the Child Adoption Committee.* London: British Parliamentary Papers, Cm 2401.

Trent, J. (1989) *Homeward Bound.* Ilford: Barnardos.

Triseliotis, J. (1973) *In Search of Origins.* London: Routledge and Kegan Paul.

Triseliotis, J. (1991) Adoption outcomes: a review. In E. Hibbs (ed) *Adoption: International Perspectives.* Madison CT: International Universities Press.

Walton, E., Fraser, M., Lewis, R., Pecora, P. and Walton, W. (1993) In-home focused reunification: An experimental study. *Child Welfare 72,* 5, 473–87.

Wells, S. (1994) *Within me, Without me: Adoption: An open and shut case?* London: Scarlet Press.

White, R. (1991) Adoption in a framework of child welfare legislation. In E. Hibbs (ed) *Adoption: International Perspectives*. Madison CT: International Universities Press.

Williams, C. (1991) Expanding the options in the quest for permanence. In J Everett, S. Chipungu and B Leashore (eds) *Child Welfare: An Africentric Perspective*. New Brunswick: Rutgers University Press.

Winkler, R. and van Keppel, M. (1984) *Relinquishing Mothers in Adoption*. Melbourne: Institute for Family Studies.

World Health Authority (1995) *Bridging the Gap*. Geneva: WHO.

CHAPTER 15

Adolescents Leaving Care or Leaving Home and Child Care Provision in Ireland and the UK
A Critical View

Eoin O'Sullivan

Introduction

Homeless children appear to have been neglected in practice, in legislation and in the literature on child care, yet are increasingly becoming a feature of urban landscapes across Western Europe (Daly 1994). The needs of these children who have left or been forced from the care of their home have yet to materialise into a coherent body of work and an object of concern that can be translated into a legitimation of their needs within a child care discourse. The majority of studies that have examined the issue of children leaving care have tended to focus almost exclusively on children leaving substitute care, primarily in the form of residential or foster care. The focus of the literature in this area is embedded within a child care discourse and it stresses the need to view their after-care, not as a discrete entity in the care career of the child, but as an integral aspect of the successful graduation of children from substitute care (Aldgate 1994). The literature (and indeed increasingly child care legislation), views care leavers as requiring adequate preparation for leaving care, advice and support, financial assistance and accommodation. The needs of substitute care leavers have been highlighted by a range of factors such as the formation of campaigning groups to represent the needs of children in care and the general disadvantaged position of care leavers, but more particularly by a series of studies that have highlighted disproportionate over-representation of care leavers amongst the young homeless (Young Homeless Group 1991).

As a result of this concern, legislation has been passed, or is in the process of being passed, in England and Wales, Northern Ireland and the Republic of Ireland, outlining a degree of statutory responsibility for care leavers. Thus,

Section 45 of the Irish Child Care Act 1991 states that a health board may assist a care leaver under this section by causing him to be visited or assisted; by arranging for the completion of his education and by contributing towards his maintenance while he is completing his education; by placing him in a suitable trade, calling or business and paying such fee or sum as may be requisite for that purpose; by arranging hostel or other forms of accommodation for him and by co-operating with housing authorities in planning accommodation for children leaving care on reaching 18 years of age (Ferguson and Kenny 1990; O'Sullivan 1993). Likewise the English and Welsh Children Act states that 'Where a child is being looked after by a local authority, it shall be the duty of the authority to advise, assist and befriend him with a view to promoting his welfare when he ceases to be looked after by them' (Article 24 (1), while the Northern Ireland Children Order provides similar provisions for care leavers. Although these legislative provisions are minimalist in terms of the support being made available to children leaving care, it nevertheless represents an admission on the part of the state that children leaving substitute care may require a degree of support to ensure they make a successful transition to the post-care environment and a legitimation of their needs within a political, legislative, administrative and professional context.

This chapter attempts to conceptualise children leaving care within a broader framework of children who leave both substitute care *and* care within their family of origin, with the point of interconnection between them being the high probability of homelessness amongst those who have left without adequate preparation or support. While a plethora of studies have consistently highlighted the disproportionate number of substitute care leavers who become homeless within a short period after leaving substitute care, there has been little attention within the child care/social work discourse given to the pathways and needs of those homeless children who have come from their families of origin. Partly as a result of the imbalance within child care research on this issue, the causes of youth homelessness are located in the changing nature of the housing market, lack of access to adequate social security, demographic changes, alcohol and drug abuse and physical and sexual abuse. As a result, responses to youth homelessness are conceptualised primarily in terms of accommodation and financial support only. On the other hand, the needs of children leaving substitute care are embedded within a child care discourse and more importantly within child care legislation which views the promotion of the welfare of children as entailing a more multi-dimensional and integrated approach than merely arranging basic accommodation.

Nevertheless, it is clear from research into post-substitute care careers that the aspirations of after-care programmes and projects are largely unmet. Research has highlighted that those admitted to substitute care in the first instance are significantly more disadvantaged than their peers (Bebbington and Miles 1989; O'Higgins 1993). For those who have graduated from substitute care, there is an impressive body of pessimistic evidence to suggest that substitute care leavers are highly susceptible to homelessness, unemployment, involvement in delinquent activity and low levels of attachment to both their family and other social institutions (Biehal *et al.* 1994). Yet within these studies on post-substitute care careers, which have suggested that between 30 and 40 per cent of the young homeless had previously been in some form of substitute care, rarely has there been any discussion within a child care framework as to where the remaining 60 to 70 per cent of the young homeless population have emerged from and how best to respond to their needs within a child care framework.

Conceptualising homeless children

Part of the difficulty of encapsulating homeless children within a leaving care framework is the variety of labels we attach to children who are homeless. In addition, there are substantial definitional problems surrounding what we mean by homelessness itself. In my view we need to define homelessness in its broadest sense, comprising three central dimensions: 1) the absolute or relative lack of an adequate place of habitation, 2) in which materially and psychologically one can be and feel 'at home', and 3) detachment from meaningful social networks. Such a concept of homelessness should be embedded in the broader social structure in that youth homelessness does not occur in a vacuum, nor is it voluntary. North American literature refers to homeless children predominantly as 'runaways', suggesting a degree of choice about the process of removing oneself from adversarial situations. As outlined by Gustavsson and Segal (1992):

> A homeless youth is defined as a person under 18 years of age who is without a place of shelter where he or she receives adult supervision or care. A runaway youth is defined as a person under 18 years who absents himself or herself from home or a place of legal residence without permission of parents or legal guardians. (p.123)

While there may be legal reasons for attaching such labels, in my view the term runaway simply describes the act of removing oneself from an adversarial situation or being forced from home, be it substitute or primary, whereas the term homelessness refers to the situation in which those who leave or run from adversarial situations predominantly find themselves. The very act of removing oneself from a risk situation may be a rational one and should not be interpreted by those agents and agencies charged by the state to provide care and protection for children as absolving them of their responsibility for these children. As Doogan (1988) has argued:

> We distance ourselves from any patronising attitudes to young people that one might find, for example, in the United States where the young

homeless are often referred to as 'runaways' implying a fickle youth, over mischievous and stubbornly refusing the bosom of the American family. (p.88)

We should be mindful that there are real political and professional pressures to deny that children who remove themselves from adversarial or abusive situations are deserving of care and protection. As Carlen (1994) stated:

> Some social workers inappropriately invoke real or imagined counselling skills in the service of accommodation-scarcity management, and attempt to convert young single homeless forced out of the 'family' home into unruly teenagers who have merely had a 'tiff' with their parents and now need advice as to how to 'make up and be friends. (p.27)

From the limited research available on the characteristics of the young homeless, they would seem to share many common traits with children who have been provided with substitute care, yet for a variety of rationales have not been provided with the services required to ensure a successful graduation to adulthood. For example in a recent Canadian study of 'runaway' adolescents, it was argued that

> This population of late-aged adolescent runaways have been the victims of chronic, extreme abuse, experienced at home at a younger age, and perpetrated by a biological parent, often the mother, with the abuse unknown to anyone outside the home. This abuse was experienced prior to running away to the street. For this sample at least, running away from home was not a benign experience, nor an indication of conduct-disordered behaviour. (Janus *et al.* 1995, p.44)

The needs of the young homeless are mentioned both in the Irish Child Care Act 1991 and the English and Welsh Children Act 1989. Yet in neither Act are the young homeless viewed as an integral concern of the child care systems envisaged by the passing of this legislation. Yet children who are homeless have either left substitute care or, in the majority of cases, their primary family care. In other words, the homeless are perhaps better understood as children who have left or have been forced from a variety of family or care situations. It is clear that such young people need more than mere accommodation. For example, the Council of Europe has argued that in addition to accommodation, young people who are homeless also require 'appropriate reception and counselling services and social and material support' (1993, p.47). Rather than viewing their needs primarily through the prism of accommodation and basic income support, the needs of homeless children should be addressed within the broader philosophy of the child care legislation that recognises the multi-faceted nature of promoting the welfare of children rather than the reductionist approach taken to date.

An analysis of current practices towards homeless children in the Republic of Ireland aims to support the hypothesis offered above. The increasing differentiation and segregation of categories of children within child care and social work practice highlights the complexity of providing services for children out-of-care within a discursive practice that focuses narrowly on child protection (Ferguson 1995). Yet as Ferguson has argued, there is scope within the Irish child care system to expand the disciplinary frameworks of child care within an inter-agency context: 'It is a question of building institutions and policies and developing a mind-set which can take the child care system in that direction while at the same time improving the technology of practice around child protection' (p.31).

Research on leaving substitute care in the Republic of Ireland

To date, there has been no specific research conducted on leaving substitute care in the Republic of Ireland. This is despite a substantial reorientation of substitute care over the past decade. There has been a developing trend, starting in the early 1980s, towards a reduction in the placement of children in residential care and an increase in the usage of foster care. This decline in residential places has been particularly marked in voluntary sector provision and is still continuing with plans for further reductions. The proportions of children in residential care and foster care remained virtually static at around 57 per cent for a number of years after 1970. However by 1991 (latest figures available) of the 2944 children in substitute care only one-quarter of children were in residential care, highlighting a steep rise in the percentage of children in care placed in foster care to three-quarters of all placements. A further trend which has been emerging within substitute care is the increasing use of court orders rather than voluntary admission to care. By 1991 almost half of the children were in care on a voluntary basis and half were in care under court orders, compared to nearly 90 per cent placed in care on a voluntary basis in 1980.

The Irish Department of Health in their annual Survey of Children in the Care of Health Boards only produce data on the reason why children have been discharged from care in that year, not where the children are one year or two years later after leaving substitute care. In addition we do not know at what age these children left substitute care, what form of care they left, how long they were in care or even their gender. Thus the concept of children leaving care in the Republic is somewhat ambiguous. Some children enter care at a young age and return to their families of origin after a relatively short period of time in care and thus do not need after-care in the sense that we talk about the need for after-care for adolescents leaving care after a comparatively long period of time in care. In the most recent DoH survey, that of 1991, it was stated that of the 955 children discharged from substitute care in that year 80 per cent were reunited with their family or relatives; 1.3 per cent were in after-care; 6.6 per cent were deemed self-sufficient; 7.1 per cent had been adopted and 3.5 percent had absconded. In her survey of one Health Board region in the Republic of Ireland, O'Higgins found that only one-fifth of children discharged from care in the area had reached the legal age limit of 16 (1993, p.106). Thus it can be assumed that the other four-fifths were returned home, although these children may resurface again with further unmet needs. Nevertheless, it is clear from research on youth homelessness that substantial numbers of children leaving substitute care do not graduate from care as successfully as the rudimentary data produced by the Department of Health would suggest.

The only quasi-longitudinal information we have on the leaving-substitute-care population is indirect, garnered from research on youth homelessness. Specific pieces of research on the general issue of homelessness amongst young people have been published over the past decade in the Republic of Ireland (Dillon et al. 1990; Harvey and Menton 1989; Kennedy 1987; McCarthy and Conlon 1988). The bulk of this research is primarily descriptive in its orientation, attempting in the main to quantify the extent of youth homelessness. One of the key findings from this research has been the significant numbers of young homeless who had previously been in substitute care. An unpublished study of youth homelessness found 22.2 per cent of those they came in contact with had previously been in *residential* care (Eastern Health Board 1987). A further study of youth homelessness in selected areas of the Eastern Health Board found that of those they contacted, 38 per cent had previously been in *long-term* care (Focus Point/Eastern Health Board 1989). A study of youth homelessness in Limerick gave further evidence of the connection between young people leaving care and their vulnerability to becoming homeless, with 29 per cent of those out-of-home in Limerick having previously being in care (Keane and Crowley 1990). A research project on youth homelessness carried out by the Eastern Health Board in conjunction with voluntary organisations showed that 40 per cent of the 427 homeless children encountered in the Eastern Health Board region in 1993 had previously been in residential care (Eastern Health Board 1994).

The high numbers of homeless children who had previously been in substitute care, particularly residential care, was not particularly surprising in the light of research conducted in 1991 on the organisation of residential care in the Republic of Ireland. The research showed that over 16 per cent of homes surveyed had no formal after-care system. There also appears to be a degree of confusion over who should be responsible for the administration of an after-care service. (McCarthy et al. 1991). This situation was in spite of a call in 1970 that 'Aftercare, which is now practically non-existent, should form an integral part of the child care system' (Kennedy Report 1970, p.60).

Strikingly, almost all of those children who left substitute care and end up as homeless had been in residential rather than foster care. This is despite the fact that nearly two-thirds of children in substitute care in Ireland are placed in foster care. For instance in the above-mentioned confidential Eastern Health Board survey of homeless children in 1993, less that 3 per cent of those encountered as homeless had previously been in foster care compared to 40 per cent who had been in residential care. This situation may in part be explained by the changing function of residential child care in Ireland. It can be argued that residential care is currently taking in some of the most damaged and difficult children who are in need of substitute care (cf. Berridge and Brodie this volume). Residential care is effectively becoming a place of last resort, rather than an equal partner in the continuum of care. This trend is in all probability likely to continue for the foreseeable future (O'Sullivan and Pinkerton 1994). This development is not unique to Ireland. In a recent comparative study of trends in residential and foster care in Europe, it was found that 'although the number of children in residential care is falling, there is a widely held view that youngsters in residential care are more challenging than was traditionally the case' (Colton and Hellinckx 1994). Thus, it could be plausibly argued that it is the nature of the process by which children are selected for residential care and the increasingly residual nature of residential care, rather than residential care *per se* that is contributing to the substantial numbers of residential care leavers who become homeless. Nevertheless, the lack of structured after-care projects for the majority of residential homes does not inspire confidence in the fact that those children leaving residential care are fully equipped to make a successful transition to post-care careers.

Homelessness as a child care issue

With the passing of Section 5 of the Child Care Act 1991 in the Republic of Ireland and Section 20 (3) of the Children Act 1989 in England and Wales, there has been an opportunity to evaluate to what degree child care legislation has improved the position of the young homeless and to what degree the young homeless are formally incorporated within the child care system. Part II, Section 5 of the Child Care Act 1991, which came into effect from 1 October 1992, reads as follows:

> Where it appears to a health board that a child in its area is homeless, the board shall enquire into the child's circumstances, and if the board is satisfied that there is no accommodation available to him which he can reasonably occupy, then, unless the child is received into the care of the board under the provisions of this Act, the board shall take such steps as are reasonable to make available suitable accommodation for him.

Prior to the implementation of Section 5, Gilligan argued that this measure could only be effective if adequate funding was provided and if coherent directions were given to the Health Boards by the Minister for Health. Gilligan also posed a crucial question, wondering:

> will Section 5 allow homeless children to be blamed for their own plight? In other words, will the authorities be tempted to convey the impression that there is no reason for a particular young person to be homeless, if only they were reasonable and accepted the hostel place offered or returned to their family. (1992, p.14)

Gilligan's paper was followed by a critique by O'Sullivan (1995) of the operationalisation of Section 5 by the health boards since its implementation in November 1992. O'Sullivan argued that the implementation of this section excluded homeless children from mainstream child care services and effectively positioned them within a secondary child care system that provided minimal levels of support and accommodation rather than care and protection. O'Sullivan concluded that 'It is as though Section 5 has no relationship with the remainder of the Child Care Act, and its operationalisation was a cynical manoeuvre on the part of some health boards to divest themselves of the responsibility for adequately promoting the welfare of homeless children' (p.98). In England and Wales Section 20 (3) of the Children Act, 1989 states: 'Every local authority shall provide accommodation for any child in need in their area who has reached the age of 16 and whose welfare that authority considers is likely to be seriously prejudiced if they do not provide him with accommodation.'

An evaluation of this provision concluded that 'In most areas the Act has not led to improved or increased access to services for young homeless people' (McCluskey 1994, p.89). Section 5 of the Child Care Act 1991 allows health boards to provide accommodation only in theory to children of any age. In practice it has not been used for children under 12 years of age. Thus a comparison with the Children Act 1989 in the English and Welsh system is not strictly comparable.

Marginalising homeless children: legislation and practice in the Republic of Ireland

The background to the introduction of Section 5 of the Child Care Act 1991 is detailed elsewhere (O'Sullivan 1995). An analysis of this section allows us to tease out some of the problems of providing child care services to a population whose status within the disciplinary framework of child care and social work is ambiguous and threatening.

Initially, the main of focus of the debate regarding Section 5 was on the second element of the section, namely by what criteria could 'take such steps as are reasonable' be evaluated and what constituted 'suitable accommodation'. Due to lack of sufficient emergency residential beds and with health boards now forced to provide a service to an age category for whom they hitherto had no statutory responsibility (16- to 18-year-old children), homeless children were increasingly being placed in bed and breakfast accommodation. Voluntary and professional organisations grew increasingly concerned about this development and were critical of the practice. The first substantial challenge to the use of bed and breakfast accommodation as reasonable accommodation for homeless children came in 1994 when the Children and Young Persons' Legal Centre initiated High Court action to test the legality of placing children in bed and breakfast accommodation under the terms of Section 5 of the Act. In the case of P.S. v. The Eastern Health Board it was argued that the Eastern Health Board had failed to provide for the welfare of the applicant under Section 3 of the Act and that they had failed to provide suitable accommodation for the applicant under Section 5 of the Act. The applicant, who was 14 years of age at the time, had a history of different care placements since he was very young. He had been discharged from a residential home and had spent 35 consecutive nights sleeping rough before the Eastern Health Board agreed to intervene and provide him with accommodation. By the time the case had reached the High Court, the applicant had been placed in Health Board premises along with another child and a number of security staff. The Board made the point that under current legislation they had no powers of civil detention and if the applicant would not co-operate, they were limited in what service they could provide.

The ruling in this case argued that Section 5 of the Act dealt only with accommodation and not with other aspects of care. Furthermore, although the health board had taken undue time before they responded to the accommodation needs of the applicant, the accommodation he was currently residing was adequate under the terms of the Act on an emergency basis. Nevertheless, the ruling did suggest that prolonged temporary emergency accommodation could not be construed as reasonable and more appropriate accommodation should be sought for the applicant. Thus, the minimal provision of basic emergency accommodation for homeless children was confirmed by the ruling of the High Court.

The second visible trend in the changing conceptualisation of homeless children came early in 1995 when the Eastern Health Board (the largest board in the Republic of Ireland) issued their annual *Report on the Adequacy of their Child Care and Family Support Services*. The Report in its section on youth homelessness made a distinction between what it termed children who are unable to return to home/care and children who in the view of health board child care professionals are unwilling to return to home/care. Such a distinction has parallels to Carlen's analysis of agencies' perceptions of youth homelessness in England. Carlen argued that those who are deemed intentionally homeless or unwilling to return to home or care are those who have not attained victim status, have refused to claim victim status or who have not had victim status conferred upon them. This line of demarcation is for Carlen a fluid index of social change which distinguishes 'between those who wish to manage social change by maintaining the fiction that the benefits of the nuclear-heterosexual familiness always outweigh the costs; and those who, knowing the family-mongers are wrong, refuse to adopt, or, for financial reasons cannot adopt, the nuclear-heterosexual family lifestyle' (Carlen 1994, p.30).

The Eastern Health Board report raised the question as to whether children who are in their opinion unwilling to return to home/care are no longer the responsibility of the Board which thus has no statutory obligation to provide these children with accommodation under Section 5 of the Child Care Act 1991. Interestingly, those children deemed to be unwilling as opposed to being unable to return home were now to be classified as 'Out of home' rather than homeless. As Carlen (1994) has argued:

> In conditions of severe shortage of affordable housing and hostel places, local authorities, in combination with a variety of professionals involved with homelessness, have developed a very fine interdisciplinary mesh for the deterrence and denial of homelessness and the disciplining of the homeless. Such creative and coercive interdisciplinary accounting has resulted in the manufacture of an agency-maintained homelessness which, at its moment of birth, is either rendered invisible or translated into something other than it is. (p.21)

The Section 8 report further stated that the Board may have a moral, rather than a statutory, obligation to provide a service for these children and that this moral obligation may be discharged by providing some funding for voluntary organisations who may wish to provide a service for these children. The basis for this decision was argued in financial rather than child care terms, yet it is clear that this financial argument conceals a deep-rooted professional unease towards homeless people who do not conform to predetermined agency perceptions of 'homeless children'. The report stated that 'the Board operates with limited resources. These resources, if allocated without discrimination to all young people who are out of home, and in cases where the board has not a clear statutory responsibility, would divert these resources from areas where the board must meet other pressing obligations' (1995, p.106–107).

While the report makes some mention of the need for a professional assessment to be conducted before it is determined whether a child can return home or not it is unclear what this assessment entails and its covert function is to operate as a gatekeeping mechanism to monitor and control the young homeless. Such a process ensures that children are rendered into docile bodies and either return home or satisfy the gatekeepers that they are amenable to social work expertise and intervention. In other words those young people who leave care or home need to be converted into objects of knowledge by child care and social work experts if they are to be accepted as homeless. Those who are viewed as unconvertible or unnameable to a narrow professional intervention are reclassified as children 'out of home', 'runaways' or 'intentionally homeless' and excluded from the care and protection envisaged in the Child Care Act 1991 and relegated to the secondary child care system of minimalist intervention. Thus, the secondary position of children within child services, who leave home to escape from adversarial situations, was legitimised as a result first of the interpretation of the High Court of Section 5 of the Child Care Act 1991 and then of the distinction between intentional and unintentional homelessness by the Eastern Health Board.

Conclusion

It can be argued that the needs of substitute care leavers have been legitimised and popularised within child care legislation, discourse and practice. While the impact of this legitimisation may fall short of its desired objective, such is the case in many spheres of child care interventions. Nevertheless, there exists a professional commitment within a legislative and administrative framework to strive towards the realisation of the needs of substitute care leavers. It has been argued that for those children who reject their family of origin due to the adversity faced in the familial situation and leave home without achieving a 'victim' status, no such legitimisation of needs exists within current legislative, professional and administrative frameworks. Such children raise awkward questions regarding the relationship of the state, the family, professional intervention and children that few are prepared to address. They have to 'prove' their need to the relevant professionals, who in turn are constrained by the narrow disciplinary frameworks in which they are allowed to operate and by the limits of financial resourcing of this area. Unless the child who has left his or her family of origin can prove successfully to the gatekeepers that he or she is amenable to character moulding by professional intervention, the child leaving primary care may risk being rediagnosed as undeserving of professional input unless in the context of conflict resolution within his family with the aim of successfully returning the errant child home. In conclusion, it can be argued that unless the needs of children who leave home as opposed to leaving substitute care are integrated and legitimised with a political, legislative, administrative and professional framework, the position of these children will remain marginal in terms of child care practice and policy.

References

Aldgate, J. (1994) Graduating from care – a missed opportunity for encouraging successful citizenship. *Children and Youth Services Review 16*, 3/4, 255–272.

Bebbington, A. and Miles, J. (1989) The background of children who enter local authority care. *British Journal of Social Work 19*, 5.

Biechal, N., Clayden, J., Stein, M. and Wade, J. (1994) Leaving care in England: a research perspective. *Children and Youth Services Review 16*, 3/4, 231–254.

Carlen, P. (1994) The governance of homelessness: legality, lore and lexicon in the agency-maintenance of youth homelessness. *Critical Social Policy 41*, 14, 2, 18–35.

Colton, M. and Hellinckx, W. (1994) Residential and foster care in the European Community: current trends in policy and practice. *British Journal of Social Work 24*.

Council of Europe (1993) *Homelessness.* Strasbourg: Council of Europe Press.

Daly, M. (1994) *The Right to a Home, The Right to a Future.* The Third Report of the European Observatory on Homelessness. FEANTSA.

Department of Health *Survey of Children in Care of Health Boards.* Various Years. Dublin: Child Care Division, Department of Health.

Dillon, B., Murphy-Lawless, J. and Redmond, D. (1990) *Homelessness in Co. Louth.* A Research Report. SUS Research for Dundalk Simon Community and Drogheda Homeless Aid.

Doogan, K. (1988) Falling off the treadmill – the causes of youth homelessness. In G. Bramely (ed) *Homelessness and the London Housing Market.* Bristol: School of Advanced Urban Studies. Occasional Paper 32.

Eastern Health Board (1994) *Report on the Adequacy of Child Care and Family Support Services.* Dublin: Eastern Health Board.

Eastern Health Board. (1987) *Homeless Young People.* Unpublished Report.

Ferguson, H. (1995) Child welfare, child protection and the Child Care Act 1991: key issues for policy and practice. In H. Ferguson and P. Kenny (eds) *On Behalf of the Child: Child Welfare, Child Protection and the Child Care Act 1991.* Dublin: A&A Farmer.

Ferguson, H. and Kenny, P. (eds) (1990) *On Behalf of the Child: Child Welfare, Child Protection and the Child Care Act 1991.* Dublin: A&A Farmar

Focus Point and the Eastern Health Board (1989) *Forgotten Children – Research on Young People who are Homeless in Dublin.* Dublin.

Gilligan, R. (1992) Can the Child Care Act, 1991 be effective in Addressing the Problem of Youth Homelessness? In *The Child Care Act, 1991 and Youth Homelessness. An Opportunity for Progress.* Papers from a conference jointly organised by the National Campaign for the Homeless and Barnardos.

Gustavsson, N.S. and Segal, E.A. (1992) *Critical Issues in Child Welfare.* London: Sage.

Harvey, B. and Menton, M. (1989) Ireland's Young Homeless. *Children and Youth Service Review,* 11 31–43.

Ireland's Young Homeless (1985) *Report of the First Survey on Homelessness among Young People in Ireland, with Analysis and Recommendations.* Young Homeless Group.

Janus, M.D., Archsmbault, F.X., Brown, S.W. and Welsh, L.A. (1995) Physical Abuse in Canadian Runaway Adolescents. *Child Abuse and Neglect 19*, 4, 433–447.

Keane, C. and Crowley, G.(1990) *On My Own. Report on Youth Homelessness in Limerick City.* Mid-Western Health Board and Limerick Social Service Centre.

Kennedy, S. (ed) (1987) *Streetwise. Homelessness Among the Young in Ireland and Abroad.* Dublin: The Glendale Press.

McCarthy, P., Butler, C., O'Sullivan, E., O'Brien, J., Kennedy, S. and McVerry, P. (1991) *At What Cost? A Research study on Residential Care for Children and Adolescents in Ireland.* Streetwise National Coalition in collaboration with the Resident Managers Association. Dublin: Focus Point.

McCarthy, P. and Conlon, E. (1988) *A National Survey On Young People Out of Home In Ireland.* Dublin: Streetwise National Coalition.

McCluskey, J. (1994) *Acting in Isolation: An Evaluation of the Effectiveness of the Children Act for Young Homeless People.* London: CHAR.

National Campaign for the Homeless (1985) *Ireland's Young Homeless 1985.* Dublin.

O'Higgins, K. (1993) *Family Problems – Substitute Care: Children in Care and their Families.* Dublin: The Economic and Social Research Institute. Broadsheet No 28.

O'Higgins, K. and Boyle, M. (1988) *State Care – Some Children's Alternative.* An Analysis of the Data from the Returns to the Department of Health, Child Care Division, 1982. The Economic and Social Research Institute. Broadsheet No 24, May.

O'Sullivan, E. (1993) Irish child care law – the origins, aims and development of the 1991 Child Care Act. *Childright.* June, No.97.

O'Sullivan, E. (1995) Section 5 of the Child Care Act, 1991 and Youth Homelessness. In H. Ferguson. and P. Kenny. (eds) *On Behalf of the Child: Child Welfare, Child Protection and the Child Care Act 1991.* Dublin: A&A Farmer.

O'Sullivan, E. and Pinkerton, J. (1994) (eds) *Focus on Children – Blueprint for Action.* Dublin: Focus on Children.

Report on the Reformatory and Industrial Schools System (The Kennedy Report) (1970) Dublin: The Stationery Office.

Stein, M., Rees, G. And Frost, N. (1994) *Running the Risk: Young People on the Streets of Britain Today.* London: The Children's Society.

Young Homeless Group (1991) *Carefree and Homeless. Why so many Careleavers are Homeless and Will the Children Act make a Difference?* London.

PART 4

Evaluation and Outcomes

CHAPTER 16

Consulting Service Users
The Views of Young People

Isobel Freeman, Alex Morrison,
Fiona Lockhart and Moira Swanson

This chapter looks at developments in consulting young people about the services they receive. In particular, it describes work carried out in one authority (Strathclyde) to try and ensure that consultation with young people was undertaken as part of producing a child care plan. Although discussion of the process of consultation is important, especially when methods of consultation are still being developed, this should not be allowed to overshadow the views of young people themselves. Therefore in addition to discussing these, the chapter also looks at what the young people said during the exercise.

Background

The United Nations Convention on the Rights of the Child included in Article 12 the right of children to express an opinion and to have that opinion taken into account, and in Article 13 the right to information and freedom of expression. Although the duty to consult children has existed since the Children Act 1975, much more attention has been paid to the need for consultation in recent years (Triseliotis et al. 1995). The 1989 Children Act in England and Wales stressed the importance of consultation and joint planning, as does the Children (Scotland) Act 1995.

Policies developed in Social Work and Social Services Departments have generally stressed the need to listen to children. In Strathclyde, for example, the core values and principles which inform the Department's delivery of services seek to ensure that children's rights as enshrined in the UN Convention are applied. This includes a recognition of the need to give children and young people the opportunity and support required for effective involvement in decision-making which affects their lives.

In practice consultation takes place at different levels. Three important levels include consultation with:

- individual young people about their needs and wishes

- co-resident groups of young people about specific services

- young people who have experienced being in care about the care system and the care they receive in general.

This chapter focuses on the consultation at the third level, i.e. it concerns populations of young people from a range of care services.

Consultation and research

Before presenting details of the Strathclyde consultation, it is helpful to note that this forms part of a clear trend to take more account of consumer/user feedback when formulating policy. Social work research has increasingly recognised the need to include clients' views, as well as information from case records and staff interviews (see Hill *et al.* this volume). Clients' views provide one set of information which alongside information from other sources can help researchers gain an understanding of social work processes (Hodgeson 1988). Two important studies of this type, relevant to the Strathclyde consultation, are *Not Just a Name*, a survey carried out by the Who Cares? Trust and the National Consumer Council (Fletcher 1993), and a consultation exercise undertaken by staff at Southampton University known as the Dolphin Project (Buchanan, Wheal and Coker 1993). The National Consumer Council and the Who Cares? Trust sought views of young people in care by asking them to return a questionnaire contained in the Who Cares? magazine which is circulated to over 20,000 young people. Over 600 young people responded. The study did not claim representativeness but raised useful issues and identified collective concerns whilst also reflecting the diversity of experiences (Fletcher 1993). The Dolphin project sought to assist children in learning about the 1989 Children Act in England and Wales and to elicit their views about the changes it involved. One of the central principles of the Act was to hear the voice of the child and yet the researchers argued that little account had been taken of young people's views. Forty-five young people were consulted in total, i.e. two groups of young people in each of three authorities. Each group ran for three sessions of two hours and carers were also consulted. The young people and carers were further consulted during the analysis stage. The approach of the Dolphin Project was very similar to that used by Strathclyde.

The aim of the two projects discussed above was to obtain young people's views on key issues and present them in a clear concise way. By appropriate dissemination of their findings both projects hoped to influence policy (Fletcher 1993; Buchanan 1993). The projects themselves, however, were not commissioned by those responsible for developing law, policy and practice guidance. One was initiated by a group representing users views and one arose from a research interest.

These were examples of external research, but in addition consultation exercises initiated by policy makers and those responsible for drawing up practice guidance are becoming increasingly common. The NHS and Community Care Act 1990 places statutory responsibilities on local authorities to consult with users and carers when preparing their community care plans. This experience has contributed to a recognition of the need to give a similar emphasis to consultation with users when developing child care plans.

Consultation exercises initiated by policy makers often require the use of research methods, but involve more than simply seeking the client's perspective on the social work process. These exercises must provide users with the opportunity to influence policy and planning and to raise issues which are important to them. Reviews of attempts at consulting with users and carers about community care plans show some authorities to be more committed to the process, and more skilled at it, than others. Research surveys are a standard method of seeking users' views but they may not always be the most effective approach. As Barnes and Wistow (1994) stress, it is important that consultation is not just seen as an end in itself but as leading to action. Connor and Black (1994) identify three key applications for user feedback obtained as part of a consultation process:

- informing resource allocation decisions
- setting standards
- providing overall performance review information.

The rest of this chapter describes how a consultation exercise undertaken in Strathclyde sought to obtain and make use of the views of young people using child care services, and reports on what these views were. User feedback was sought in Strathclyde by the Social Work Department to assist in the preparation of a plan for the development of child care services in Strathclyde. The purpose of the plan was to inform resource allocation decisions, promote practice standards and review the extent to which these standards were achieved. Thus its purpose was in line with the three key applications identified by Connor and Black (1994).

The preparation of the plan was seen as part of a dynamic process which should allow for discussion and feedback (Strathclyde Regional Council 1994). Although some research methods were used, this was a consultation not a research exercise.

Methodology

The consultation with users began before the first draft of the plan was produced because it was intended that users' views should inform the content of the plan and the issues it covered. The approach followed the principle advocated by Barnes and Wistow (1994), that people who use services should not be viewed solely as respondents as in satisfaction surveys; rather they are participants who have a role in defining the questions to be asked. The Dolphin project report (Buchanan *et al.* 1993) suggested targets should be developed 'bottom up' rather than 'inspection down'.

As a first step a consultation exercise was carried out with around 150 young people 'in care' aged 11 or over, from two of Strathclyde's twelve social work districts. Over two-thirds of the young people consulted were physically in the care of the social work department in local authority children's homes. There were, however, also a substantial number on supervision, and involved in several types of supervision.

The consultation focused on the standards framework which it was proposed that the child care plan would adopt. These standards were concerned with ensuring that:

- children were protected and their rights promoted
- the department's intervention was appropriately planned and implemented
- services provided were of good quality.

Discussion of these broad standards was used as a starting-point in the dialogue with young people because it was important to check out whether these were legitimate standards to be pursuing in the views of the young people, and to find out to what extent the young people felt the standards were being met. Both research and groupwork staff were involved in the exercise and a consultant was provided by Who Cares? (Scotland). The need for consultation to be meaningful rather than superficial was recognised from the outset. It was felt that the consultation should not be a one-off event but that time should be taken to get to know the young people involved and build up a degree of trust. The Dolphin project team had found it was important that teachers, who had experience of working with groups of children, act as facilitators rather than as field social workers, because the young people felt more able to criticise social work care (Buchanan *et al.* 1993). In Strathclyde, the value of using non-social workers to elicit the views of young people was also recognised. Groupwork and research skills were particularly relevant to the exercise.

There were two stages in the consultation. Firstly, a set of meetings took place in all of the children's units and intermediate treatment (I.T.) groups in the two districts covered. The intention was to elicit young people's views on the child care services in general, not just their own children's home or intermediate treatment unit. It was perhaps inevitable that in these sessions some young people responded almost exclusively about their own personal living situations. The young people were committed to the discussion and participated fully. They were given the opportunity to opt out of the exercise but only a small number did so at this stage, so the vast majority of residents in each unit and members of the I.T. groups attended the discussion.

All of these sessions were handled as group discussions and lasted between an hour and an hour and a half. The general experience was of 'opening the floodgates', and many of the respondents indicated that having an opportunity to put forward their views on the care system was a new experience to them. There is an obvious danger in such sessions that young people will be inclined to say negative things and be discouraged by their peers from offering positive comments, especially if they have the ear of an apparently uncritical adult. It was found, however, that young people spoke positively within the groups and also that there was considerable self-regulation imposed when exaggerated horror stories were presented.

The second stage involved a three day residential event. Barnes and Wistow (1994) suggest that consultation, unlike a research survey, does not require a representative sample although they recognise that it is important to understand who does and does not respond to invitations to be consulted. They suggest it may be more appropriate to seek a range of mechanisms to secure involvement rather than seeking representativeness. The Dolphin project (Buchanan *et al.* 1993) had attempted to obtain a representative sample but in the end, when many of those selected did not turn up and others brought friends, they accepted the sample they had. By having initial meetings in the young people's units and groups almost all the young people the Strathclyde exercise sought to make contact with had an opportunity to make their views heard. Those who were willing to invest further time discussing their views more fully were encouraged to do so and were offered the opportunity of attending the residential event which would involve leisure activities as well as activities designed to elicit their views on social work services. A three day mid-week programme was planned to take place at the National Sports Centre, Largs. Arrangements were made for all the young people (40) who put their names forward to attend.

Consultation sessions were interspersed with football and gymnastic sessions, and with other group activities designed to help the group communicate, as well as for fun. The methods used in the residential consultation sessions included group discussions, workshops where groups worked on presentation of sketches and role plays on selected themes, and the use of questionnaires. Group leaders wrote reports on the activities of their groups, group discussions were recorded and the group presentations videotaped. Issues raised in this way were written up by the research staff involved in the exercise and checked back with the young people involved to ensure they truly reflected their feelings. Throughout the consultation process basic groupwork techniques were used which encouraged young people to have fun, get to know each other, build trust, test out adults, raise issues and resolve conflicts. The adults strove to show that they regarded the issues raised by the young people as important and worth listening to.

It is difficult to do justice to the discussions which took place. Those involved often expressed very strong emotions, sometimes positive but often negative. The young people in the main said the consultation exercise was valuable and the staff involved found it stimulating and moving.

We believe the consultation would have produced little if young people:

- had not felt genuinely listened to

- had not had the opportunity to communicate in a variety of ways (besides just talking or filling in forms)

- had not had the opportunity to get to know the adults over period of time.

Questionnaires were used in some of the sessions. For example, young people were asked to fill in a similar questionnaire to that used by the Who Cares Trust (Fletcher 1993), but many of the young people found it difficult to complete. The Dolphin project also referred to the difficulties of using questionnaires:

> Many of the findings would not have been elicited by a simple questionnaire or interview method. Looked after young people are well trained in 'saying the right thing'. It is not until they feel relaxed with their peers that they share what they really think. The natural setting for young people is really the group setting. The dilemma not only for researchers but for anyone involved in such a process, is what value do you place on to what might be a passing opinion of one young person in a group. (Buchanan *et al.* 1993)

This dilemma can be resolved to a large extent by ensuring that consultation with the young people continues through the analysis and report-writing stage. This was done in both the Strathclyde and the Dolphin projects.

The young people's views

From the initial discussions a number of general themes were identified as the focus for the intensive consultation stage. These were: their experience of being consulted, their knowledge of rights, their experience of reception into care and family support, the quality of services they received, the support they received from key individuals, their experience of care planning reviews and children's hearings and their views about leaving care.

Experience of being consulted and knowledge of rights

The young people did not feel they had been consulted much before and few were involved with Who Cares?. They accepted, willingly, the opportunity this exercise gave them to influence policy. They had some knowledge of their rights but gaps in their knowledge were identified. For example, although most knew their rights when stopped by the police, many were unsure about their rights in relation to the children's hearings system.

Reception into care and family support

Much of the discussion involved the young people remembering and describing their own experience of being received into care. Most described feelings of powerlessness and they appeared to find it difficult to understand the process of being taken into care especially when the decision was made by a children's panel. In Scotland when compulsory measures of care are being considered, cases are referred to the Reporter to the children's panel who will arrange for a children's hearing to take place if he agrees compulsory measures of care may be appropriate. The panel will then decide whether the child should be placed under a compulsory order. Many young people said they were unsure of the reasons why they had been taken into care.

Often the actual reception into care seemed to have happened very quickly. This was the experience not only of those children admitted in an emergency on a voluntary basis but also of several children who had been made the subject of a compulsory order. One young girl whose hearing lasted less than half an hour felt the decision had been made before the hearing started and that her views and her parents' views had been ignored. Some of the young people became quite emotional when remembering their first reception into care which had, in many cases, been an extremely traumatic experience.

Many worried how they would manage to maintain links with family and friends after reception into care. Triseliotis et al. (1995) found from their interviews with teenagers coming into care that because of family tensions, most felt they had to tackle rebuilding their relationships at their own pace (cf. Buchanan 1993). In the Strathclyde study, younger children often relied on social workers to keep them in contact with their families. Some were very critical of social workers who failed to realise how important it was for them to know what was happening in their family while they were in care. It was also important to the young people that their families were given the support they required while they were in care. Describing his view of a good social worker one boy said:

> You come into care, you're worried about your Ma, maybe your Da's had a drink and is hitting her. You ask to phone your social worker. A good social worker would say: It's OK. I've already been in touch with your family and I'm bringing them to see you tomorrow.

Quality of services

The young people were generally very positive about their experiences of Intermediate Treatment and groupwork; for example, one said: 'It helps keep you off the street and out of care'. Some were concerned that their access to I.T. resources ended when they were received into care. Comments on supervision focused on their desire to see their social workers more frequently and this is discussed in more detail below.

Most were relatively positive about foster care, especially for younger children, although one or two had bad experiences and stressed the need for thorough assessment of foster parents to take place. Almost all young people thought that siblings should be kept together (cf. Buchanan 1993). Some said they had never really felt part of the foster family they were placed with (cf. Fletcher 1993). When placements were successful it was felt they should be maintained until age 21 if the young person so wished. There was some fear about the feelings and attachments that may grow in short-term foster placements and how to cope with them when such placements end (cf. McAuley this volume). As would be expected, they found frequent changes of placement disruptive.

The criticisms of children's homes mainly focused on the restrictions this type of living arrangement placed on freedom of choice (cf. Fletcher 1993, Triseliotis *et al.* 1995). Smaller homes were generally preferred (cf. Buchanan *et al.* 1993). Residential care was not seen as appropriate for younger children although it was felt to be important that siblings were kept together even if this resulted in young children being placed in children's homes. The young people disliked homes in inaccessible places. Living in residential care would be better, it was felt, if there was more privacy, a place where you could make private phone calls and no 'Germolene motors' (social work transport was painted in standard colours and felt to be stigmatising). They wanted the staff in their units to be more consistent in their treatment of them so that they always knew what was and was not acceptable. Some felt the rules were constantly changing. They wanted more freedom to go out with friends, to keep pets, to eat better food and to have more choice about what food they ate, what toiletries they used and how their rooms were decorated. They were also concerned about the disruption being in care caused to their education. Many had suffered from a disrupted education and had been poor attenders at school prior to entering care (cf. Kendrick 1995). While they understood the need for staff at the unit to share some information about them with the school, they disliked being identified as being in care and being different.

The young people involved in the consultation did not have experience of residential schools or secure care although in discussing children's rights many felt very strongly children should not be locked up.

Support from key individuals

The young people appreciated the support provided by key individuals, both field social workers and staff in residential and I.T. units. Some were critical of the infrequent contact they had with their field social worker (cf. Buchanan 1993). Most said they wanted to see their social worker once or twice a week. Many complained that they saw them much less frequently, for example 'only when it suits them', 'only when there are problems', 'once in a blue moon'. They had clear ideas about what kind of support they required – someone to talk to, someone who listened, someone who was there when they needed them and 'not off sick'. They also wanted someone who was 'allergic to the telephone' (telephone calls often hampered or interrupted attempts to talk). A social worker, it was suggested, should be someone who was consistent, who would act as their advocate, who did not make promises they could not keep; and finally someone who did not talk down to them, but talked their language.

Most of the young people had experiences of good and bad workers and certainly valued workers they felt had been good. The right to be able to change residential key workers and field social workers if they were not getting on well with them was seen as essential. Changes of worker imposed on them because workers got new jobs were found to be very disruptive. One young person described how upsetting it was to have to explain all about their background to each new worker allocated to them. Young people felt let down when their case was not allocated quickly and when vacancies were left unfilled. There was resentment that planned meetings with a young person were seen as unimportant and cancelled when an emergency came up. Although residential workers were important to the young people it was field social workers to whom they looked to progress their care plans. They believed that without their social worker's input nothing moved. As Triseliotis et al. (1993) pointed out, it was the field social workers who were the source of information about choices and available options.

Care planning

All the young people involved in the exercise had some experience of attending reviews and being consulted about their care plans. The young people felt that it was very important that they were consulted about any decision made which would affect their lives. They thought they should always be allowed to attend reviews and planning meetings and they should be able to choose who they wanted to accompany them to reviews (cf. Buchanan et al. 1993). Earlier research in Scotland however found three-quarters of young people satisfied with the review process (Kendrick and Mapstone 1991).

Whenever reviews and care planning were discussed, most of the young people also mentioned the children's panel system, of which they were very critical (cf. Triseliotis et al. 1993). The young people saw the children's panel system as a crucial influence on their lives and yet many found the experience of attending panels very difficult (cf. Triseliotis *et al.* 1993). Panel members, they felt, were 'not people like them' and too ready to judge them negatively and look down on them. Social workers were described as 'posh' while panel members were seen as 'snobby'. Most felt alienated by the panel process and clearly felt more could be done to improve the way hearings were handled. Two of the role plays the young people presented demonstrated this. Both role plays began with the young people and their parents entering the room where the panel was to be held and sitting down. The chair of the panel then suggested that the family had 'sat in the wrong place' and asked them to move, thus the meeting began with an awkward rearrangement of the seating and the families felt uncomfortable and in the way before the panel had begun. Each group had devised these scenes independently.

Young people thought care plans were not progressed speedily enough and found this difficult to cope with. Social workers who did not take action within reasonable timescales and who broke promises were criticised. Once a plan was underway, however, some felt it was difficult to get it changed if they had second thoughts.

Leaving care

The young people frequently raised their concerns about leaving care. They were worried about the consequences for their employment prospects of their disrupted education and were often critical about mainstream education provision. Some had been excluded from mainstream education (see Sinclair this volume). They were concerned about their ability to obtain housing and employment when leaving care and recognised a need for ongoing social work support. One of the greatest fears was that support would be withdrawn. In spite of the development of throughcare and after-care programmes, some still believed that support would automatically be withdrawn when they reached the age of 16 (Triseliotis *et al.* (1995) found this fear to be justified). The children who attended I.T. groups were especially worried about not being able to go to the I.T. group any more. Many were concerned about drug use and wanted help to avoid the harm drug use could cause. They also wanted advice about contraception. One of the groups worked on a presentation about life choices. The group leaders found the young people had limited knowledge about AIDS and HIV and still cited friends as their main source of information about sex, alcohol and drugs.

The impact of the consultation exercise on the production of the Child Care Plan

In Strathclyde, although the main purpose of the consultation had been to inform the child care plan, it was felt that some of the young people involved in the exercise should also be given the opportunity to present the findings of the exercise to the Social Work Committee. Four of them took a report to the committee and spent an hour discussing it with Regional Councillors who endorsed specific recommendations.

The views of the young people were also used as intended to inform the child care plan. Many of the issues raised in the child care plan might well have been included whether or not the consultation exercise had taken place, but there was no doubt that the views of the young people did affect the priority given to the issues raised.

In the policy and service objectives section of the plan there was a recognition of the need for:

- consultation work to continue
- better use to be made of resources to help prevent family breakdown
- a review of the level of provision and distribution of social workers, home support and I.T. resources
- further improvements in residential care including more smaller units
- better assessment and support of foster parents
- improved liaison with education and the children's hearings system
- the development of more throughcare support.

Specific actions were identified in line with the above objectives and money was allocated (within the current budget restraints) to increase the number of social workers, I.T. and throughcare staff, develop foster care support and improve the quality of residential care. For example, steps were taken to increase the privacy afforded to young people in residential units. Practice standards relating to the above issues, particularly in relation to care planning and reviews, were also set and methods of monitoring their achievement identified.

Future developments

As was said earlier, the consultation exercise was seen as a first step only, and the Department was aware that further work was required. A shortened version of the Child Care Plan has been drawn up for young people and a brief questionnaire has been attached for them to respond, if they wish. Our experience is, however, that while the opportunity to respond should always be given to young people, the response is likely to be poor or non-existent when it relies on impersonal contact. Greater, more personal efforts have to be made if young people are to be convinced that their opinions are really wanted and valued.

The Department was aware that the consultation exercise had not adequately sought the views of young people attending residential schools, young people currently in foster placements and the parents of young people in care. Work is currently underway to set up consultation with these groups. Methods of consulting younger children also require to be developed and piloted. Interviews with young people resident in a number of small residential units set up to promote high quality residential care are being undertaken as part of a specific evaluation of the implementation of the Department's Residential Action Plan. The views of children who have left care are also being sought through monitoring exercises undertaken by throughcare staff (McDonald and Watson 1995). Local government reorganisation means that further developments cannot, at present, be planned (see Tisdall this volume). It is hoped that work on consultation, building on current experience, will be progressed further in the new authorities.

Conclusion

The importance of seeking young people's views about the care provided to them has been recognised. Research projects generally incorporate users' perspectives by means of traditional research tools such as interviews or questionnaires. More innovative methods of consulting users' views are being developed and both the Strathclyde and the Dolphin project have tried to develop methods appropriate to interviewing young people. The experience gained suggests:

- informal group discussions are a useful way of eliciting the views of young people
- the staff facilitating the exercise should have appropriate research and groupwork skills
- the young people should be enabled to identify their own agenda as far as possible, rather than respond to an imposed one.

The issues highlighted by the young people consulted in both the Dolphin project and the Strathclyde project were very similar. Both projects found for example that the young people wanted:

- greater efforts to be made to keep families together and to maintain family contact once received into care
- staff they could respect and who were available when needed
- smaller children's homes
- assistance with educational issues
- throughcare support.

Although the young people were critical of particular aspects of the service provided by the social work department, the key criticism was that there was not enough support. Social workers were needed to sort things out with families, to act as their advocates at panels and to help them get things sorted out when they left care. Social work support was clearly valued (cf. Thoburn this volume). Ensuring that young people feel secure, and know that support will always be there when required, has to be a priority and those consulted identified room for improvement.

References

Barnes, M. and Wistow, G. (1994) Involving carers in planning and review. In A. Connor and S. Black (eds) *Performance Review and Quality In Social Care. Research Highlights in Social Work 20*. London: Jessica Kingsley Publishers.

Buchanan, A. (1993) *Evaluating the Views of Young People Answering Back*. Social Services Research, University of Birmingham.

Buchanan, A., Wheal, A. and Coker, R. (1993) *Answering Back, Report by Young People Being Looked After on the Children Act 1989*. CEDR, Department of Social Work Studies, University of Southampton.

Connor, A. and Black, S. (1994) Getting and using user views in performance reviews. In A. Connor and S. Black (eds) *Performance Review and Quality In Social Care. Research Highlights in Social Work 20*. London: Jessica Kingsley Publishers.

Fletcher, B. (1993) *Not Just a Name – The Views of Young People in Foster and Residential Care*. London. National Consumer Council/Who Cares? Trust.

Hodgeson, D. (1988) Participation not principles. *Insight 2* August.

Kendrick, A. and Mapstone, E. (1991) Who decides? Child care reviews in two Scottish social work departments. *Children and Society 5*, 2, 165–181.

Kendrick, A. (1995) *Residential Care in the Integration of Child Care Services*. Edinburgh: Social Work Services Group.

McDonald, F. and Watson, N. (1995) *Thirty Care Leavers, Their Experiences and Thoughts*. Strathclyde Regional Council.

Strathclyde Regional Council (1994) *Child Care Plan*. Glasgow: SRC.

Triseliotis, J., Borland, M., Hill, M. and Lambert, L. (1993) The rights and responsibilities of adolescents in need or trouble. *International Journal of Children's Rights 1*, 315–330.

Triseliotis, J., Borland, M., Hill, M. and Lambert, L. (1995) *Teenagers and the Social Work Services*. London: HMSO.

CHAPTER 17

Constructing and Implementing Measures to Assess the Outcomes of Looking after Children Away from Home

Harriet Ward

Introduction

The part played by tradition in social work practice has been extremely influential, though rarely recognised. Until the beginning of this decade children were still being taken into care under legislation which owed its basic structure to the reforming zeal of the nineteenth-century philanthropists; they were still frequently placed in homes that had been built over a hundred years ago to house the 'orphans' the philanthropists rescued; once separated, it was also common for children to be kept apart from their families on the traditional assumption, again held since the nineteenth century, that the care provided by birth parents could easily be replicated and, in many circumstances, improved upon (Ward 1990).

However, the last few years have seen a considerable erosion of these traditions. The Children Act 1989 swept aside many of the legislative structures through which children could be separated from their families. Indeed, birth parents can no longer lose parental rights and responsibilities except through adoption, although they may on occasion be required to share them with the local authority. Straitened resources, combined with the belief that foster care is better able to meet the needs of the majority of children looked after away from home, have resulted in the sale or reallocation of many of the large residential units inherited from the past. Perhaps the greatest change has been the increasing tendency to question the assumption that local authorities and other child care agencies can benefit deprived children by separating them from their families and placing them in substitute care.

These changes can best be understood if they are seen within the context of other developments, among which has been a loss of faith in the expertise and authority of professionals: faced with an increasing demand for evidence of their efficacy, social workers can no longer assume that interventions which appear to have been satisfactorily accomplished will necessarily prove beneficial to the families concerned (Bullock 1995). Moreover, partly as a backlash to the rigid severance policies adopted in the 1980s, a number of consumer groups have arisen which represent the rights of children and young people in care or accommodation and their relatives. Pressure from these groups has done much to introduce the concept of partnership to the relationship between social worker and birth parent. Increased demands for social workers to be more answerable to their clients are also part of a wider movement towards greater accountability in public services. The introduction of customers' charters, complaints procedures and assessment exercises all represent an appreciation of the need to gain value for money and to prove that public funds have been wisely spent.

The prominence of such issues has produced a climate in which the need to develop a means of assessing the outcomes of social work interventions with children has become a pressing concern. It is no longer acceptable to ignore questions such as: what happens to children looked after away from home? Do they or their families benefit from the experience? Do the advantages of substitute care outweigh the disadvantages of separation?

Moreover, the results from a growing body of research undertaken from the 1970s onwards have emphasised the need to ask such questions, for there is evidence that the care service does not always succeed in meeting the needs of the children and young people for whom it is designed. Research on foster care has demonstrated the fragility of many placements, leading to uncertainty as to how far substitute carers can be expected to replace the unconditional commitment of parents and other relatives (Parker 1966, 1980; Berridge and Cleaver 1987). Other studies have shown how children in local authority care or accommodation are often poorly educated (Jackson 1987, 1994; Heath, Colton and Aldgate 1989, 1994; Fletcher-Campbell and Hall 1990) and socially isolated (Millham et al. 1986; Bullock, Little and Milham 1993). There is also evidence to suggest that children in care or accommodation are rarely given specialist help with emotional and behavioural difficulties, although these may have been a major factor in the decision to look after them; indeed, such disorders may become more prominent after admission (Cornish and Clarke 1975; Millham, Bullock and Hosie 1978; Millham et al. 1988, 1989; Department of Health 1995a).

An issue of particular concern has been the discovery that children and young people are not always protected from abuse while in the care of public agencies (Hughes 1985; Levy and Kahan 1991; Williams and MacReadie 1992; Department of Health 1995a). The failure of many child care agencies to provide adequate protection is also demonstrated by their willingness to withdraw support from young people several years before their peers in the community are expected to leave their families. Indeed, teenagers who have left local authority care or accommodation to cope on their own have often been ill-equipped to do so (Stein and Carey 1986; Stein 1990; Biehal et al. 1992; West 1995).

Although research studies such as those cited above have increasingly asked questions about outcome, child care agencies have rarely gathered the information which might provide the answers. When local authorities have looked at the outcomes of their interventions they have tended to confine their enquiries to single issues such as the stability of placements or the proportion of children in foster or residential care. There has been little attempt to find out how the experience of being looked after has affected children's subsequent development. Moreover, many local authorities gather only haphazard information about both the characteristics and the progress of children for whom they accept and share responsibilities, making it difficult to undertake comprehensive assessments. Some authorities, for instance, do not systematically collect information about the ethnic origin of the children for whom they accept responsibility, thereby obstructing the planned recruitment of appropriate foster carers. Only a very few record the immunisation histories or the examination results of the young people in their care (Ward 1995).

Developing a means of assessing outcomes in child care

It has been in response to concerns such as those described above that, over the last eight years, the Department of Health has funded a major project designed to develop, and now implement, assessment measures in the child care service. The materials produced by this project are not the only method by which outcomes in child care can be measured (Huxley 1994); however, they appear to be the most comprehensive means of regular assessment for all children looked after available at present and the intense interest they have attracted both in Britain and abroad warrants their position as the main focus of this chapter.

Perhaps the greatest strength of the Department of Health project has been the recognition given to the need to construct a theoretical framework before any attempt could be made to produce a practical means of assessment. The project began with the establishment of a working party of academics and practitioners who spent 18 months defining the elusive concept of outcome in child care and identifying criteria by which it might be measured. The deliberations of the working party have been described in other publications (Parker et al. 1991; Ward 1993) and only the conclusions will be given here. Two important early decisions were that outcome measures should adopt the perspective of the children concerned rather than that of their parents, the agency or the wider society and that, since the purpose of a social work intervention should be to safeguard and enhance children's welfare, the outcomes of care or accommodation should be evaluated by asking what effect the experience had had on each child's subsequent development.

This presupposed the construction of developmental measures which would ask how far the specific objective of each particular intervention had been achieved within the context of assessing how far children's overall life-chances had been improved. The overall objective of the social work intervention was perceived as enabling the child to achieve 'long-term well-being in adulthood', a global concept that was defined as meaning successful development across a spectrum of seven key developmental dimensions: health, education, identity, family and social relationships, social presentation, emotional and behavioural development and self-care skills. Because the measures would focus on children's long-term development, they could be applicable to all children and not restricted to those looked after away from home, thus making it possible to track outcomes through a series of moves both within and outside care or accommodation. Universally applicable measures would also create the impetus to raise expectations for children in care or accommodation from the disappointingly low level at which they are often set.

A significant feature of the system produced by the working party would be the extent to which it linked long-term outcomes to the quality of children's experiences, thereby introducing the question of accountability into the assessment process. It was argued that since local authorities accept parental responsibilities for the children they look after, they should be held accountable, in the same way as are ordinary parents, for the manner in which they fulfil their parental duties. Children will not develop satisfactorily unless they receive a high standard of parental care. Outcome measures should therefore not only assess how far children are progressing across the spectrum of development, but also examine the extent to which they are given the opportunity to succeed. The measures, therefore, would identify how far local authorities were providing, or failing to provide, children with the type of experiences they need in order to make satisfactory progress.

Finally, the type of outcomes to be measured were conceptualised not as discrete incidents with clearly defined beginnings and endings, but as continuous chains of events. It was therefore thought most appropriate to devise an ongoing system of assessment which would have the potential to unpick a link in the chain and identify not only how far the child had progressed, but where improvements might be made. Subsequent assessments would continue to monitor the child's progress and check that appropriate action was being taken to remedy any deficits in the quality of care received.

The theoretical framework constructed by the working party was used as a basis for developing a series of practical outcome measures: the Assessment and Action Records. The Records were designed to be used by carers and field social workers in consultation with parents and the children and young people concerned. Within each of the seven areas of development they ask whether children are receiving a range of experiences identified by research as being necessary to successful development. After completing these questions, respondents are invited to assess how far the child is progressing towards a series of age-specific objectives. Respondents are encouraged to note how omissions will be rectified and to give explanations for any decisions not to take actions that would appear to be warranted. To make the task of measurement more manageable, the group of children for assessment are divided into six age-groups, chosen to cover key stages of psychosocial development rather than equal chronological periods.

Further research

The Assessment and Action Records were briefly piloted and then published in 1991 together with a package of complementary forms designed to encourage local authorities to integrate them into a comprehensive system for planning and reviewing children's cases. The complete series of practical measures produced by the Working Party on Assessing Outcomes in Child Care are known as the Looking After Children materials. Although the materials were immediately incorporated into the official series on the Children Act 1989 and were widely disseminated throughout England and Wales, they were seen as experimental measures and a number of questions still needed to be answered.

An extensive programme of evaluation was carried out in the three years following publication of the first edition in order to test out some of the assumptions upon which the Assessment and Action Records were based (see Ward 1995). As part of this programme, staff in five local authorities completed Assessment and Action Records with a looked after study group of 204 children and young people who were expected to spend at least a year in care or accommodation. Researchers also completed Records with a community group of 379 children and parents living in ordinary families in two of the areas from which the looked after group had been drawn. This part of the research was designed to test one of the key hypotheses: that, despite a diversity of lifestyles, there is widespread agreement about the fundamental aims and objectives of the parental task and considerable consensus as to how these might be achieved. Early suspicions that the content of the Records might simply reflect the white, middle-class prejudices of the original working party made this work particularly necessary.

Responses from parents and children in the community group proved that these concerns were unfounded. No parents disagreed with the age-related objectives identified within each of the seven developmental dimensions and almost all parents, from all walks of life, thought it important to provide their children with the opportunities recommended by the Records as being most likely to lead to successful outcomes. The questions on the Records are based on research evidence about effective parenting, but the responses from the community group suggest that many of these messages are now widely understood. Almost all parents of four-year-olds knew, for instance, that if they wanted their children to do well at school they needed to read to them and give them access to books; parents were also aware of children's need to acquire social skills, of the relationship between diet and health and of the damage caused by cigarettes, drugs and alcohol. This is not to say that all were able to make use of this knowledge: some were too poor to offer their children a healthy diet, some too isolated to help them make friends and develop a sense of self-esteem, while others lacked the confidence or the academic skills to support their education. A number of parents felt that they lacked the authority to insist that their children avoided particular temptations, especially if they themselves had been unable to exercise restraint over issues such as smoking or alcohol consumption. Nevertheless, wherever it was possible to separate intention from action, there was evidence of a clear consensus of the desirability of providing children with the experiences recommended by the Records.

The two study groups were selected in order to test the applicability of the Assessment and Action Records and not to provide a means of comparing how the experiences of children looked after by public agencies differ from those of their peers. While direct comparisons could not be made between the original groups because of the criteria on which they were chosen, it is clear that, if assessment measures such as these come into common use, it will eventually be possible to identify where the differences lie. The data from the samples suggested that two issues which might merit closer scrutiny are the attention given by social services departments to the education of children they look after and the extent to which carers are encouraged to seek specialist help for young people with challenging behaviour.

The data also demonstrated that agencies, in common with parents, are not always able to provide children with all the experiences that would be conducive to their long-term well-being. Priorities need to be identified and articulated. There was evidence from the assessments of the looked after study group that use of the Records would enable local authorities and other child care organisations to engage in a debate about the standard of care it would be most appropriate for them to provide within the resources available.

Social workers, carers, parents and children who completed Records for the two study groups were asked to provide formal feedback on the content of the materials. Similar information was also solicited from practitioners who began using the Assessment and Action Records and other Looking After Children materials as an integral part of their practice before the research had been completed. Responses from these groups identified a number of matters that needed further consideration: the concerns of children with disabilities were not adequately addressed by the original Records; nor were the materials always applicable to children from minority ethnic groups. It was also evident that further work needed to be undertaken to ensure that outcome measures used by social services departments aligned with procedures already in place in health authorities and education departments. Anomalies such as these were dealt with in the revised version, published in 1995 (Department of Health 1995b). Despite these difficulties, responses demonstrated that the issues covered by the Assessment and Action Records were generally both acceptable and important to carers, social workers and children and young people in care or accommodation.

Setting an agenda for discussion

The research on the looked after study group was designed to discover how, or indeed whether, carers, social workers and children would use the Records and the circumstances under which the work might best be undertaken. The findings showed that the Records can be implemented on three different levels: as discussion documents, as planning tools and as data-gathering instruments.

At the simplest level, carers and others found that the Records were a useful means of setting an agenda for work with children and young people, who often welcomed the opportunity to open up discussion of difficult areas of their lives. Early fears that foster carers, in particular, might object to being asked to participate in formal assessments of the care they provided proved to be unfounded: in fact they generally found that the experience increased their sense of professionalism. Residential workers also thought the experience was useful, although they did not always find it easy to organise their time in such a way as to allow for the concentrated one-to-one discussions with children that the Records require. This is an interesting training issue, which says much about the low priority given to the need to undertake direct, structured work with children and young people – a point that has been noted in another study (Sinclair, Garnett and Berridge 1995). Where residential workers were able to allocate time to use the Records they were appreciated as a valuable means of enabling a key worker to build up a relationship with a young person that went beyond 'the two of us sitting on either side of the fire and wondering what to say to one another'.

It was important to make sure that the exercise was undertaken as a partnership between the key people involved and that the forms were not filled in by social workers without further consultation or given to young people to complete on their own. When the Records were used appropriately they enabled those people who were responsible for children's care to identify important issues that could easily be addressed. For instance, one pilot revealed that 25 per cent of 16-year-olds had received no information about contraception or sexually transmitted diseases. Use of the Records also identified several short-sighted children who had lost or broken their glasses in earlier placements but whose new carers were not aware that they needed to have them replaced. The research also showed that many children and young people did not know why they were being looked after away from home, while others wanted help in deciding how to respond to probing questions from their peers. Small discoveries such as these can direct the attention of carers towards simple actions which can be undertaken to improve the situation of any child even when he or she labours under other difficulties which may seem intractable.

When used as a focus for discussion, the Records ensured that all aspects of development were monitored and assessed. Because the Records are based on research evidence about effective parental practices, their regular use will convey important information to carers in an easily digestible form. New information will also be passed on as the Records are updated to take account of the growing body of knowledge about effective parenting.

Plans and reviews

Although few participants experienced difficulties in completing the Records as a single exercise, it was not so easy to repeat it a year later. The main problem was not, as we originally suspected, that practitioners lost their initial enthusiasm, but that a high proportion of the children were no longer in their original placements when the time came to assess them a second time. Sixty-nine per cent of the children and young people selected for the looked after study group in one authority changed address in the period between assessments. Social workers rarely felt a commitment to organise repeated assessments for children who were no longer part of their caseload and new carers were often unaware of the research. Since the research study, the Records have been implemented throughout a number of local authorities as an everyday part of social work practice for all children looked after for six months or more. Widespread implementation should overcome the difficulties encountered by the research team and indeed establish a greater degree of continuity in the care that children receive.

A key feature of the Assessment and Action Records is that they are completed by those people who are most likely to be responsible for taking remedial action to improve the quality of care identified in the course of the exercise. The research showed that the Records do make it easier to plan improvements and monitor how far these are carried out and that implementation throughout an authority makes it easier to translate plans into action when children change address. However, some participants did not appreciate this function: there were several instances of carers carefully putting away completed Records between assessments although areas where care could immediately be improved had been clearly identified.

These difficulties demonstrate a need for better training of carers and for careful supervision of the work. It should be the role of the supervisor to make sure that assessments are properly completed at the recommended intervals and to check that plans are being made and translated into action. The research showed that this task is likely to be made much easier if the Assessment and Action Records can be introduced into existing structures for planning and reviewing children's cases. In view of this finding, further work was undertaken to develop the Records and the accompanying materials into a streamlined system for information-gathering, planning and review that meets the detailed requirements of the Children Act 1989.

The principle employed in reconstructing the planning and review forms was that they should replicate on paper the processes which parents go through informally in making plans and monitoring their children's progress. In developing these materials further, we took the opportunity to link them not only with the Assessment and Action Records, but also with other, potentially overlapping, procedures currently employed by other agencies. Thus the planning forms demonstrate how the responses to certain questions can be used to meet the requirements laid down by the Children Act Guidance for care plans produced in court proceedings and the review forms remind respondents of the need to link social services procedures with reviews of statements of special educational needs (Department of Health 1991).

Of particular interest in this context is the work undertaken on the information-gathering form: the Basic Facts Sheet. This document was originally conceived as a means of gathering together all the information about a child that would not change from year to year and thus reducing the repetition on the Assessment and Action Records. The original form resembled the front sheet of many social work files; but the revised version (the Essential Information Record) was designed as a means of collecting all the information that needs to be preserved, but is often lost, when children stay long in care or accommodation. Part One of this form now provides the essential information needed immediately by carers who are asked to look after a child in an unplanned placement; Part Two asks for more comprehensive details about the child or young person's background, including the legal and placement history. This form has now been linked with the Personal Child Health Record used by a large number of health authorities. Not only does the Essential Information Record address the need for authorities to gather adequate information about the children for whom they share responsibilities and to be aware of that stored by other agencies, it has also been designed in such a way that the data collected can be used to complete the statistical returns required annually by the Department of Health. The computerised version of this form can aggregate the data and produce returns and reports automatically. The Essential Information Record is now in widespread use, and its development has facilitated further debate between researchers, policymakers in central government and managers in local authorities about standardising the information that organisations hold about their clients. Such a debate should be welcomed as having the potential to improve the quality of information upon which policy decisions are made at a national level.

Gathering data

The introduction of Looking After Children throughout an authority will produce a pool of information about children's experiences and progress. Data on individual children, collected over time through the Assessment and Action Records, will provide a historical record of progress across the range of developmental dimensions and will show where additional help is needed. These data are collected in a format which can be aggregated. If this is done systematically, evidence about group outcomes can demonstrate the strengths and weaknesses of the service as a whole, so the information can be used to direct policy and decide where scarce resources can best be deployed. It is only when the Records are employed for this purpose that they will be properly integrated into the structure of an organisation and their full potential exploited. Developing a means of collecting, analysing and aggregating such information was the main objective of the work on assessing outcomes.

It seems clear that Looking After Children can be used for this purpose, but a number of issues will need to be addressed before the system runs smoothly. The Assessment and Action Records are likely to be used to improve the quality of care that children receive because they can be completed by fieldworkers and frontline carers who are directly responsible for acting on the findings; in contrast, procedures which can only be administered by staff who have had specialist training in psychometric assessment may be seen as somewhat divorced from practice. However, the evidence from the evaluation study showed that a disadvantage in gathering information from frontline workers was that some of them did not give a high priority to meticulous recording. For instance, second assessments showed some children whose height had apparently diminished a year after the first Record was completed. We also found that social workers almost invariably underestimated the numbers of different carers children had experienced when we compared their responses to questions on the Records with centrally recorded data on placement changes.

Those social workers who had little regard for accuracy tended to view the exercise as descriptive: they often objected to the questions which asked for information about children's challenging or disturbed behaviour on the grounds that responses might produce a negative picture. Although they valued the opportunity to open up discussions with the children concerned and to strengthen their relationships, they tended to overlook the purpose of the assessment, which was not to provide a picture of the children's circumstances but to analyse how they might be further helped. Effective strategies which make it possible to improve children's life-chances must be based on accurate and objective information: this needs to be properly understood if respondents are to give greater attention to careful recording. This message will be easier to appreciate if fieldworkers and frontline carers can understand how the information which they collect about individual children can be used to benefit the group as a whole; this will mean making explicit the process by which the data are aggregated and analysed and then used to direct future policy.

Processes of implementation

As the above discussion demonstrates, completed assessments in the two sample groups indicated many of the issues which would need to be addressed by an organisation attempting to assess outcomes in the manner we propose for all the children for whom it shares parental responsibilities. Successful implementation will require social workers and carers to use the Assessment and Action Records to set an agenda for work with children and young people and to gather accurate evidence about their experiences in order to plan strategies to improve their progress. Managers and supervisors will need to monitor this work and ensure that appropriate plans are carried out and followed through to new placements. This can best be done by ensuring that the Records are set within a comprehensive structure for information-gathering, planning and review, such as that provided by the Looking After Children Planning and Review Forms. Policymakers will need to ensure that the data collected are aggregated and analysed and then used to inform future decisions.

An in-depth study of implementation in one of the local authorities participating in the evaluation study also revealed a number of broader issues that need to be addressed by any organisation contemplating the introduction of materials such as these, which require extensive changes to the way in which practitioners think about and undertake their work (Jones 1995; Corrick, Jones and Ward 1995). This study showed that successful implementation requires a climate in which staff are receptive to new ideas and managers are aware of possible sources of dissatisfaction. The implementation of the Children Act 1989, which coincided with the publication of the original materials, prepared the ground for the introduction of assessment procedures. The researchers noted a marked change in practitioners' receptiveness to the ideas embodied in Looking After Children as they followed the training which accompanied the Act. Although the ground has been well prepared, managers need to be aware of the danger that disenchanted staff might disregard the purpose of the exercise and insist that the paperwork simply adds to the bureaucratic burden.

The evidence from the study also suggested that once a decision to implement has been made, it is important to identify all those people whose commitment to the introduction of the system needs to be secured and invite them to sit on an implementation group. The group needs to be led by someone who has sufficient authority to ensure that the materials are accepted at all levels of the organisation and sufficient time set aside to undertake the considerable work involved. The first task of the group should be to review the authority's current assessment, planning and review structure and consider how Looking After Children might fit within it. The group then needs to decide which existing forms will be replaced or adapted and draw up departmental procedures explaining the new system. It is important to ensure that these are properly circulated and that redundant forms are destroyed: the research uncovered several instances where practitioners were struggling to use two overlapping systems and were complaining at the unnecessary duplication. The implementation group also needs to ensure that the new procedures mesh with other systems such as those employed in child protection or youth justice and those used by related organisations including health authorities and education departments. Within the written procedures it is important to demonstrate how the information gathered by individual practitioners will be used to shape policy.

The next task is to identify those people who will need additional training in both the philosophy and the practice of the system. As has already been demonstrated, the research uncovered a number of issues that staff need to be aware of if the system is to function properly. A video and other training materials have been produced and distributed nationally in order to facilitate this process (Department of Health 1995c).

Finally, the group needs to draw up plans for both implementation and training and set clear timetables for their achievement. It is also necessary to make arrangements for monitoring the smooth running of the system once it is in place.

Future directions

At the time of writing, the complete range of Looking After Children materials is being used for gathering information, making and reviewing plans and assessing the experience and progress of all children looked after in about a third of local authorities in England and Wales; there are indications that, in a year's time, this number will have doubled. The more widespread the system becomes, the greater will be the advantages of using it. As we have shown, several practitioners who participated in the evaluation found it difficult to make follow-up assessments because children moved away from the areas in which the research was taking place: if the materials are implemented throughout an authority it is easier to maintain continuity in planning and to monitor children's progress wherever they are placed. National implementation will improve the chances of continuity as paperwork can then follow children from one authority to another. It would also mean that practitioners and others would not need to be retrained to use a new system when they moved to work in a different organisation. The extensive data generated from the current level of implementation already make it possible to compare children's experiences and progress in different settings and there are plans to establish a national database. Moves to introduce the system in Belgium, Norway, Sweden, Canada, Australia and Hungary open up exciting possibilities for making cross-national comparisons.

Assessment procedures such as those described have the potential to produce considerable benefits. However, it is all too easy to overlook their purpose in the excitement of watching their widespread adoption. The ultimate test of Looking After Children, or indeed of any system of assessment, is not the number of authorities which decide to use the materials, but whether, when implemented, they can genuinely improve outcomes for the children concerned – and that is a question we have yet to answer.

References

Berridge, D. and Cleaver, H. (1987) *Foster Home Breakdown.* Oxford: Basil Blackwell.

Biehal,N., Clayden, J., Stein, M. and Wade, J. (1992) *Prepared for Living? A Survey of Young People Leaving the Care of Three Local Authorities.* London: National Children's Bureau.

Bullock, R., Little, M. and Millham, S. (1993) *Going Home: The Return of Children Separated from their Families.* Aldershot: Dartmouth.

Bullock, R. (1995) Change in organisations: likely problems in implementing looking after children. In H. Ward (ed) *Looking After Children: Research into Practice.* London: HMSO.

Cornish, D. and Clarke, R. (1975) *Residential Treatment and its Effects on Juvenile Delinquency.* London: HMSO.

Corrick, H., Jones, D. and Ward, H. (1995) *Looking After Children: Management and Implementation Guide.* London: HMSO.

Department of Health (1991) *The Children Act 1989 Guidance and Regulations: Volume 3, Family Placements.* London: HMSO.

Department of Health (1995a) *Child Protection: Messages from Research.* London: HMSO.

Department of Health (1995b) *Looking After Children: Trial Pack of Planning and Review Forms and Assessment and Action Records (Revised).* London: HMSO.

Department of Health (1995c) *Looking After Children: Good Parenting, Good Outcomes Training Resources Pack.* London: HMSO.

Fletcher-Campbell, F. and Hall, C. (1990) *Changing Schools? Changing People? The Education of Children in Care.* London: National Foundation for Educational Research.

Heath, A., Colton, M. and Aldgate, J. (1989) Educational progress of children in and out of care. *British Journal of Social Work 19*, 6, 447–460.

Heath, A., Colton, M. and Aldgate, J. (1994) Failure to escape: a longitudinal study of foster children's educational attainment. *British Journal of Social Work 24*, 3, 241–260.

Hughes, W.H. (1985) *Report of the Committee of Inquiry into Children's Homes and Hostels.* Belfast: HMSO.

Huxley, P. (1994) Outcome measurement in work with children: comparing plans in the UK with experience in the US. *Child Abuse Review 3*, 120–133.

Jackson, S. (1987) *The Education of Children in Care. Bristol Papers No.1*, University of Bristol School of Applied Social Studies.

Jackson, S. (1994) Educating children in residential and foster care. *Oxford Review of Education 20*, 267–279.

Jones, D. (1995) Implementation in Authority C. In H. Ward (ed) *Looking After Children: Research into Practice.* London: HMSO.

Levy, A. and Kahan, B. (1991) *The Pindown Experience and the Protection of Children: Report of the Staffordshire Child Care Inquiry.* Staffordshire County Council.

Millham, S., Bullock, R. and Hosie,K. (1978) *Locking Up Children.* Aldershot: Saxon House.

Millham, S., Bullock, R., Hosie, K. and Haak, M. (1986) *Lost in Care: The Problem of Maintaining Links between Children in Care and their Families* Aldershot: Gower.

Millham, S., Bullock, R., Hosie, K. and Little, M. (1988) *The Characteristics of Young People in Youth Treatment Centres: A study based on leavers from St Charles and Glenthorne between 1982 and 1985.* Totnes: Dartington Social Research Unit.

Millham, S., Bullock, R., Hosie, K. and Little, M. (1989) *The Experiences and Careers of Young People Leaving Youth Treatment Centres: A Retrospective Study of 102 Leavers from St Charles and Glenthorne between 1982 and 1985.* Totnes: Dartington Social Research Unit.

Parker, R. (1966) *Decision in Child Care: A Study of Prediction in Fostering.* London: Allen and Unwin.

Parker, R. (ed) (1980) *Caring for Separated Children: Plans, Procedures and Priorities.* London: Macmillan.

Parker, R., Ward, H., Jackson, S., Aldgate, J. and Wedge, P. (1991) *Looking After Children: Assessing Outcomes in Child Care.* London: HMSO.

Sinclair, R., Garnett, L. and Berridge, D. (1995) *Social Work and Assessment with Adolescents.* London: National Children's Bureau.

Stein, M. (1990) *Living out of Care.* Ilford: Barnardo's.

Stein, M. and Carey, K. (1986) *Leaving Care.* Oxford: Blackwell.

Ward, H. (1990) The Charitable Relationship: Parents, Children and the Waifs and Strays Society. University of Bristol, PhD Thesis (unpublished).

Ward, H. (1993) The Looking After Children Project: current perspectives. In B. McKenzie (ed) *Foster Family Care for Children and Youth*. Toronto: Wall and Emmerson.

Ward, H. (ed) (1995) *Looking After Children: Research into Practice*. London: HMSO.

West, A. (1995) *You're on Your Own: Young People's Research on Leaving Care*. London: Save the Children.

Williams, G. and MacReadie, J. (1992) *Ty Mawr Community Home Inquiry*. Gwent County Council.

CHAPTER 18

Outcomes of Social Work Intervention with Young People

Malcolm Hill, John Triseliotis, Moira Borland and Lydia Lambert

Introduction

Judging the success of social work interventions aimed to help children and young people is a complex but vital process. This chapter examines different ways of judging 'success' and in particular explores the concept of outcome. We then present evidence about the impact of social work intervention on a sample of young people who received services at home or away from home in local authorities in England and Scotland. Details of other aspects of the study including qualitative findings on the young people's experiences are presented elsewhere (Triseliotis *et al.* 1995).

The issue of success is addressed primarily from a research point of view, but we would argue that many of the considerations are similar for practitioners, managers and policy makers in deciding how effective their services are – for individuals or for populations of children. It will be seen that it is valuable to take account of several criteria and perspectives in order to build up a picture of what works well and what does not work so well. Moreover it is not enough to identify successful interventions unless there are indications of how and why they were helpful. Hence it is also important to examine the results of services in the light of the contexts and processes involved. Using a variety of measures in this way, our study showed that interventions with young people who had serious difficulties were mostly positive, though the impact was often limited.

Outcomes, success and progress

Ideas about how to assess success in relation to child care have two main sources. First, there are general approaches to the evaluation of any intervention, treatment or service. These have been dominated by quantitative and quasi-experimental designs (Rossi 1992), but there is a growing body of support for qualitative evaluation (Patton 1990). Both types of evaluation may either concentrate on the *effects* of the intervention under consideration or on the *processes* by which those effects are achieved, though quantitative measures have mostly been used to evaluate results. For example, early research on adolescents in residential care mainly focused on custodial settings and assessed effects by means of reconviction rates, which were sometimes related to carefully documented categorisations of regimes (the treatment process). These studies concentrated on long-term placements, mostly in custodial settings, and hardly any attention was given to the measurable consequences of residential care for young people in care who were not offenders (Kendrick and Fraser 1992; Bullock, Little and Milham 1993a).

Second, there is a specific tradition of judging child care placements going back to the 1950s when writers like Trasler (1960) and Parker (1966) first drew attention to the high breakdown rates of long-term foster placements. For many years, placements were usually classified into one of two simple categories – breakdowns and non-breakdowns, with the latter presumed to have been successful. Subsequently, the term 'disruption' became popular instead of 'breakdown', with the intention of conveying the view that all was not lost when placements ended prematurely and that children could be successfully 're-placed'. Little systematic evidence is available about how well children do following such re-placement.

It has become clear that there is no straightforward relationship between the nature of placement ending and the effects of the placement. Also those effects are often quite mixed. Thoburn (1990) showed how different criteria can result in quite diverse pictures of the apparent success of permanent placements. Besides, since social services deal with many children and young people who are never placed away from home and others who move back home, so indicators other than placement factors need to be used to assess the impact of services on them. As a result a wider view has been taken in recent years of the concept of 'outcome' as involving multiple measures. This has been considered in relation to individual placements, longer care careers or global interventions (Rowe, Hundleby and Garnett 1989; Parker *et al.* 1991). Our own study drew on this approach, but we also wished to take account of the processes involved and of information which could shed light from other directions, especially as our sample was not confined to young people living away from home. Before describing our own measures, we outline the four main ways in which social work interventions for children have been assessed.

Progress of the child or young person
This involves assessing various aspects of a child's development or behaviour. The Assessing Outcomes Project identified seven core dimensions and went on to develop detailed measures covering each dimension in relation to different age groups (Parker *et al.* 1991; Ward this volume). These are based largely on

evidence about generally desirable achievements at particular ages and formed an important part of our own investigation. The Dartington researchers offer a similar set of criteria (with respect to adolescents) which are more rooted in local social circumstances and aspirations (Bullock *et al.* 1993b):

- Conformity to general social norms of behaviour

- Adjustment to the young person's actual or aspirational subculture

- Progress from a baseline in relation to a matter of concern (e.g. school attainment, absconding)

- Self-perception, aspirations and satisfactions with lifestyles and opportunities.

Since children can be at very different stages or have widely differing degrees of difficulty at the start of any intervention, it is not fair to make judgements based only on the end position. For instance, it is important not only to know how serious are a child's behavioural or emotional difficulties at the end of an intervention, but also how much change occurred.

Even when good progress is apparent it cannot be assumed that this is simply the 'outcome' of the intervention. Other factors may have contributed to the change, including maturation, subsiding of a family crisis ('natural recuperation'), other life events or environmental changes. Interestingly, the helpful analysis by Parker *et al.* (1991) tends to side-step the issue of causality. Without controlled, randomised experiments it is strictly not possible to judge what contribution intervention made to the later situation, except perhaps in a negative sense. If things turn out badly, then it can be stated that the action taken failed to remedy the effects of adverse circumstances.

Another issue concerns the length of time over which progress is determined. Initial consequences can be misleading, as they may differ from intermediate and long-term impact, as the Head-Start evaluations showed. There can be wash-out effects (early gains fade away) or sleeper effects (long-term benefits are not easily detectable at first). It is well known that improvements may not be sustained once there is a change of environment (e.g. move from residential care back to the community or alteration in family circumstances). Sequences or chains of outcomes may occur (Quinton and Rutter 1988). The progress of children and families who have major difficulties is usually complex, with improvements and reverses, different patterns of change depending on which aspects of development are considered.

Features of service or placement endings

The production of welfare approach developed at the University of Kent analyses inputs (of services and clients) in relation to the quantity and quality of outputs. For example the approach has been applied to assessments of foster placements. This type of analysis identified prior factors which affect chances of success and failure, with a combination of serious school and offending problems being particularly hard to overcome (Fenyo, Knapp and Baines 1989).

In relation to children away from home, placement factors have often been used as indicators of outcome, although strictly these describe a living arrangement and do not necessarily correlate with particular consequences for the child or family. The unplanned ending of a placement (breakdown) remains a prime measure used in studies of residential care, foster placements and adoption (Berridge and Cleaver 1987; Kadushin and Martin 1988). The analysis of placement patterns by Rowe *et al.* (1989) sought to differentiate more sensitively the nature of placement endings and judged outcomes within the wider context of aims, needs, planned duration and helpfulness. In their summary of 'outcomes', they regarded a placement as a success if it lasted as long as planned *and* had its aims met in most respects. In other studies, frequency of contact with birth parents has been used both to signify a consequence of placement away from home and as a predictor of the likelihood of return home (Millham *et al.* 1986; Fanshel, Finch and Grundy 1990).

It can also be helpful to consider where a child moves on to after an individual placement or at the culmination of a care career. In North America many evaluations judge outcomes according to the 'restrictiveness' of the post-placement living environment. A standardised 'Restrictiveness Scale' has become popular there which comprises a list of placement types whose degree of restrictiveness or freedom with respect to space, movement and involvement in 'normal' community activities have been agreed by experts (Hawkins *et al.* 1992). Thus there is a progression from the least restrictive setting (parental home or living with relatives) via foster care then residential home to secure unit. However the list ignores the wide variations within placement types. As our own study was to reveal, some young people see foster care as more limiting than residential care, whilst for others the reverse is true. Return home from care is not always a satisfactory or liberating outcome and not uncommonly proves to be an unstable or unhappy experience (Farmer and Parker 1991; Bullock *et al.* 1993b). Young people leaving care at the upper age limit who live alone or with peers, supported or unsupported, have freedom in the community but often face poverty, loneliness and depression (Stein and Carey 1986; Garnett 1992). Supporters of the restrictiveness scale tend to equate restrictive with undesirable, yet some children are happier or progress well in a less free setting. Sometimes society insists that a child's freedom should be restricted and some make good progress in secure accommodation (Harris and Timms 1993). Thus it is important to examine the *particular qualities* of each particular living situation in a placement sequence rather than make global generalisations.

Professional and expert evaluations

Many studies have relied largely on information and evaluations from (field) social workers. Often they are in a good position to provide an overview and give details of events and decisions. They also have access to official records from their own and other agencies, which can act as a check on personal recall. Crucial though such information is, it is important to bear in mind that social workers' involvement as key actors and decision-makers may colour their views of outcomes and they may be less well informed than parents, carers or teachers about a child's day to day activities.

It is also possible to use 'experts' who do not already know the children to provide specialised assessments. For example, psychiatrists may diagnose the presence of disorders or health visitors identify developmental delay and health difficulties. Occasionally researchers have themselves produced global assessments of each case based on their summative view of all the evidence (Farmer and Parker 1991). This can usefully integrate and classify an array of disparate information, though there are dangers of bias unless there is some kind of external check. An alternative though more expensive approach is to ask an expert panel to give opinions about success, taking account of difficulties and achievements in each case (Fuller 1988).

Consumer evaluations

By law social workers are obliged to take account of parents' and children's own wishes. Growing attention to children's rights and partnership with parents means that the degree of involvement of children and parents in decisions and planning can itself be an outcome measure. However good the plan in terms of a child's interests and progress, it is not satisfactory if key parties feel excluded or resentful.

From a research point of view, too, it is important to identify whether the felt and expressed needs of consumers have been met and to ascertain their satisfaction levels. Only a few researchers have spoken directly with children and parents (e.g. Buchanan, Wheal and Coker 1993, McAuley this volume). Their studies have been very valuable, both in giving expression to user perspectives and in identifying matters which can be more salient for children than adults realised, such as: peer relationships, privacy, stigma and bullying.

The desirability of multiple measures

Each of these ways of measuring success has its advantages and disadvantages. Evaluations by consumers, professionals and others may be subjective and impressionistic, but they are often firsthand, holistic and individualised. Assessments of developmental progress can be precise indicators of change, permitting standardised comparisons between children, but they may not be closely related to the service or may miss important considerations for particular cases. Service characteristics are important to take account of, though their significance for the children concerned needs to be established rather than taken for granted. It is important to consider the living situation where children or young people end up after intervention, and then to make individualised rather than global judgements about whether a particular kind of home is good or bad. A combination of measures and perspectives ('triangulation') is likely to yield a more full picture than any of these alone, which is why we used elements of all four approaches in our study of young people. As we found out, such a multiple approach can reveal inconsistencies and even contradictions, but that reflects reality more accurately than a single measure.

Measures of success and progress used in the study of young people

The study was conducted during the period 1991–3 to assess the impact of arrangements for supervision and care of young people provided in five local authorities, three in England and two in Scotland. Funded by the Department of Health, the research was planned on a longitudinal basis over one year in order to compare initial expectations with later achievements and to trace progress following intervention. As outlined above, the intention was to tap the perspectives of professionals and consumers concerning both individual development and the characteristics of services and living situations.

A sample was identified of 116 teenagers aged 13–17 who were experiencing the start of a new form of social services intervention or a significant change in care or supervision arrangements. (In this chapter, 'care' is taken to include 'accommodation'.) Three-fifths of the sample were male and two-fifths female. Nearly all were white. The presenting problems were of three main kinds:

- family conflict
- schooling issues
- offending or addictions.

In each case, interviews were held with the young person, field social worker and parental figures at the start of intervention and again one year later (except for a small number where individuals were not available or refused to take part). Additional information was gathered at the outset from case records and carers in residential establishments and foster homes.

Some young people only experienced one kind of service (in addition to direct help from their field social worker), but many experienced more than one at the same time or in succession (e.g. group work and residential care). Therefore we obtained information about (1) individual services and placements, (2) the overall intervention.

In relation to specific services, respondents were asked about both the nature and the effects, though it is the latter with which we are mainly concerned here. For example:

- What were their initial expectations and were these met?
- How satisfied were participants?

- Did the young person benefit?
- What were the effects on the initial problems?
- Were there improvements in areas such as offending and school non-attendance?

To facilitate comparisons, several questions devised by Rowe *et al.* (1989) for their large survey were used when young people were in residential and foster placements:

- Did the placement last as long as planned?
- Did the placement last as long as needed?
- Was the placement helpful?
- Were aims met?
- What was the subsequent living arrangement?

To assess broader end-of-year results we used a variety of indicators concerning the young person's functioning at the end of the year and progress since the start of the year. The main ones were:

1. Measures concerning the young person's performance according to the seven dimensions of the Assessing Outcomes project, i.e. health, education, network relationships, emotional and behavioural development, self-care and competence, self-esteem and identity, self-presentation. Two standardised scales were used – the Rutter behaviour scale and the Coopersmith Self-Esteem Inventory (Rutter, Tizard and Whitmore 1970; Coopersmith 1990).

2. Participants' judgements on the young person's past, current and future functioning and on the overall impact of intervention.

To sum up, we sought to assess the 'success' of social work intervention by means of five main types of assessment, whilst acknowledging that other factors in young people's lives would have impinged on these:

1. **end-position measures** – positive or negative results at the follow-up stage according to developmental indicators

2. **change measures** – presence or absence of significant improvements shown by the developmental indicators

3. **goal measures** – initial expectations or plans for the year were fulfilled or not

4. **satisfaction measures** – participants were (dis)satisfied or believed the situation had improved or not

5. **prognosis measures** – participants' views about the young person's future prospects.

We now present our findings on outcomes or, strictly, the provisional position one year after intervention. Firstly we consider the evidence concerning progress over the year for the sample as a whole. Then we briefly summarise the differential impact of particular services.

Progress following intervention

In the majority of cases, respondents observed improvements in the young person's well-being or behaviour and expressed at least moderate satisfaction with what had happened over the year.

Behaviour and development

The Rutter scale indicated that services were being targeted at a particularly difficult population. Although there were considerable discrepancies between social workers', parents' and young people's ratings, they all showed that a high percentage of the sample were of 'clinical concern' (85 per cent according to social workers, 95 per cent according to parents and young people). Over the course of the year, there were substantial improvements with the proportion with very high scores being nearly halved from 63 per cent to 36 per cent. Nevertheless four-fifths of those who were rated both times still showed levels of disturbance which would merit further investigation if they had been tested at random. This emphasises the continuing difficulties faced by many participants, even when there had been gains.

Although they did not agree in every case, both parents and young people indicated that the relationship between them had improved over the year in about half the cases. Some others had started with a good relationship in any case. Relationships with step-parents were more often described as poor at the start and were less likely to have improved.

Information on schooling was complicated by the age range, with many of the sample having left school by the end of the study year. Half the sample had experienced special educational measures before or during the year of the study. Only one in three had acquired any qualifications or expected to do so. Social workers reported that about two-fifths of those with initial educational problems were still said to be making 'poor' progress at follow-up, but more than half were said to have improved.

The picture was less positive with regard to self-esteem. On the standard Coopersmith Inventory which young people completed themselves, most showed little change and as many deteriorated as improved. However, social workers judged that nearly half had improved in self-esteem and thought nearly all the others had had no overall change, so they appeared often to be overestimating changes in this respect. Both at the outset and after one year, females were more likely to have low self-esteem than males. One-third had 'low' self-esteem at both referral and follow-up compared with one in ten of the boys.

The majority of teenagers were reported to be in good health, but almost half the young people said they had had particular health problems during the year. Most said their general health was little changed, but a higher proportion of girls than boys reported a deterioration.

Subjective views of the year following intervention

Two in three young people said at the end of the year that their situation had improved and only 12 per cent thought they were worse off. Usually, social workers and parents confirmed the general pattern of improvements. Similarly about one-quarter of the young people were very satisfied with how things had turned out and most of the rest were quite content, although again one in eight were not at all satisfied. The proportion of those who were very satisfied ranged from over one-third in one agency to only one-eighth in another.

Although the majority of young people who saw their lives as better at the end of the year than at the start also believed they had been helped a lot by the social worker, nearly one-third stated that they had not been helped at all. Even more strikingly, half of the young people who said their situation had deteriorated over the year nevertheless stated that the social worker had helped them a lot. Clearly the direct action of the social worker can sometimes appear marginal in its impact compared with other influences on young people's lives. Over half the parents and about 80 per cent of young people reported that the overall intervention (including placement, group work etc.) had been helpful, although sometimes only a little.

Were expectations met?

When the situation was thought to have got better, this need not bear any relation to the changes hoped for at the beginning of the year, so we assessed how far initial expectations had been met. This had to be done separately for each of the three parties in the study, since in many instances there had been little congruence in expectations at the outset. In fact, under half of the initial hopes for the year were fulfilled, even partially. Social workers tended to express larger numbers of aims and also more intangible ones like improving self-image. They had fewer than one-third of their expectations fulfilled.

Expectations were more frequently met in relation to certain key areas of concern than others. For example, when parents or young people had wanted change in relation to offending or drugs, this was forthcoming in 60 per cent of the cases according to both parents and teenagers, whereas hopes for a young adult to be successfully managing on their own came to fruition in fewer than one-quarter. The wished-for changes which occurred mainly took the form of improved behaviour or attitudes, especially in the eyes of parents. However, there were also references to such things as increased maturity or reduced family conflict. Here is an example where everyone was in broad agreement about the nature and extent of improvement:

YOUNG PERSON: 'I have ironed out the difficulties with my mother. I feel more mature and more responsible, more grown-up.'

SOCIAL WORKER: 'He broke up the pattern of bad behaviour with his mother. He manages to control his temper better.'

MOTHER: 'He has improved in his behaviour though he's still a bit disobedient.'

The most common explanation of improvements by both parents and young people was in terms of the young person's own efforts. Next most frequent influences were the placements (for those away from home), the social worker's input and changed attitudes within the family.

Perceptions of the future

Most young people reported feeling moderately confident about their future. At either extreme, about one in five admitted to lacking confidence that things would work out well for them or said they were very confident about the future. Two-fifths of young people thought their prospects had been improved by the intervention, a small number thought they had been made worse and nearly half stated it had made little difference. For the most part, worries about the future related to general practical difficulties typical of young people from disadvantaged backgrounds (like employment and money), rather than their personal troubles which had prompted social work intervention.

Half of the social workers said they felt fairly or very optimistic about the teenagers' future prospects, but the rest had significant doubts or concerns, with about one in nine confessing to being very pessimistic. Deepest concern was expressed for those few individuals seemingly entrenched in crime or addiction. In contrast, amongst the factors which led to optimism were:

- good co-operation over the previous year
- satisfactory or high academic achievement
- personal determination
- a supportive environment (in the parental or substitute home).

More social workers than young people believed that the intervention had enhanced the young person's capacity to cope as an adult, with half noting significant gains in this respect.

Overall success?

We sought to establish an integrated measure which could identify the young people who had the best outcomes at the end of the year. We were mindful that this need not result from the intervention alone or indeed at all, but might reflect more favourable initial prospects or external influences. We used several of the standardised measures (concerning individual progress and placement/service features) and subjective evaluations (professional and consumer evaluations). These were combined to form two indices – one indicating good progress and the other indicating success in terms of both progress and final position (for details see Triseliotis *et al.* 1995).

Using these indices, nine cases were identified as having been particularly successful. Three had required a single service (besides social work support) – either a foster home or residential school which had suited them and lasted. The others had received two or more services at the same time and/or in succession. For instance, two young people had experienced home supervision with group work, but also brief periods of care as 'respite' from the difficulties at home. A larger number (19) had made extensive progress.

Extensive progress had occurred in similar proportions for individuals with low, medium and high scores on the Rutter scale at the start of the year, showing that good results had been obtained with some of the teenagers with the greatest difficulties as well as relatively easier cases. However, it appeared that high self-esteem was a good predictor of success. Three-quarters of cases who made extensive progress had begun with high self-esteem compared with only one-third of low-progress cases. Young people who admitted to involvement with drugs, solvents or alcohol in their first interviews had as good a record of success as others. However, the teenagers who had major involvement during the year in any anti-social behaviour, self-harm or abuse had low rates of even moderate success.

Differences according to service and placement

Given the diversity of circumstances and services offered, together with the fact that many young people experienced several different forms of intervention during the course of the year, it was impossible to separate out all the influences which contributed to the eventual pattern of progress. However, we can indicate some associations between our measures and different forms of intervention, as well as report the direct appraisals of participants about particular services (see also Hill, Triseliotis and Borland 1995).

By the end of the year, our sample could be divided into three main categories:

- those who had been supervised at home all the time
- those who were placed away from home (sometimes in addition to supervision at home)
- those living on their own or with friends (sometimes after a period in care).

The combined indices and indeed most of our other evidence showed that *on average* the second group (in care) did best and the third group (living 'independently') did worst. Of course the three groups also had different starting-points which will have affected the pattern. Even so, this does indicate that placement away from home can be a positive action – in contrast to the gloom and sense of failure which tended to be expressed by social workers in our study and in earlier research (Packman, Randall and Jacques 1986). It is not surprising that young people who stay at home will be less affected by intervention, since that generally impinges much less on their lives, usually involving at most seeing a social worker every one to two weeks and perhaps attending a group once a week. The poor outcomes for young adults of 16–18 seeking to manage on their own after a period of care or supervision repeats the findings of earlier research and sadly showed that little had changed despite the attention given to leaving care in the last ten years.

The key findings from our different measures in relation to particular services or placements are set out below. For the most part there were not major differences on our measures of behaviour, self-esteem and schooling (or else numbers were too small to establish links) so these are only reported where relevant.

Social workers' direct input

Social workers were generally well liked for being understanding, reliable and active on behalf of the young person. However both young people and parents were less inclined to credit the worker with effectiveness in achieving what they had wanted them to do. A quarter each felt that the social worker had helped a lot, only a little, not much or not at all. Some parents thought the social workers sided too much with the young person. Unsuccessful cases included more of those where there was infrequent contact with the social worker and a poor relationship.

Supervision at home

Two-thirds of young people said they liked supervision, but most young people and parents reported that it only helped a little or not at all. Social workers too indicated only moderate impact and meeting of expectations. More of the teenagers on formal panel or court orders found the service helpful than those receiving informal supervision (which tended to involve less clear aims, *ad hoc* planning and less monitoring). Some young people with offending and other behaviour problems reported that they had been encouraged to desist by warnings and advice within a relationship of trust, but others resented being nagged or told what to do.

Group work and befriending

Group workers were nearly always perceived by young people as friendly and easy to talk to. Most groups were activity based and this was enjoyed. However, very few young people thought there had been much influence on the problems that led to intervention. Social workers thought that groups had helped a lot in only a quarter of cases and in as many as a third they were thought not to have helped at all. Befriending and outreach services produced very similar feedback to groups – mostly well liked, but thought to have assisted with problems in only a minority of cases.

Psychiatric/psychological services

Often the contact was brief, because the purpose was assessment or because the young person refused to continue attending. Although some psychologists and psychiatrists were experienced as very understanding, the majority were regarded quite negatively. Many young people were alienated or puzzled by the style of communication, so that any potential benefit from their specialist expertise was neutralised by the failure to engage. Social workers reported that the referral was unhelpful in half the cases and very helpful in only a few.

Residential units

The majority of placements were considered by social workers to have been beneficial and by parents to have met expectations. Young people mostly began placements by feeling wary or negative, but later became more positive. Most residential staff and key workers were well liked by young people, although both social workers and teenagers expressed concerns about staff turnover. A high proportion of those in residential units at the end of the year had low scores on the indices of success, but this may reflect the fact that admission to residential care sometimes followed failure of a previous placement.

Residential schools

On every measure these came out well, even though they were dealing with a population with particularly high levels of 'disturbance' according to the Rutter scale. For example, residential schools were seen as very helpful by young people in 59 per cent of cases (compared with 29 per cent for residential units) and in nearly every case social workers reported being satisfied with the placement – quite often contrary to their initial expectations. Parents, too, were generally well pleased. The features which were valued included – small classes and individually tailored teaching; low turnover of staff and residents; planned entry and programmes; flexible links with families.

Foster homes

These provided some of both the most successful placements and the least successful. Relatively more foster than residential placements ended prematurely in terms of both plans and needs. However, when the placement persisted this was usually seen by the social worker as having helped a lot, whilst 80 per cent of the young people regarded their situation as improved and satisfactory. A crucial factor in success appeared to be the match in expectations as regards intimacy, family involvement and autonomy.

Conclusions

In this chapter we first examined ideas about 'outcomes' in relation to care and supervision of children and young people. Outcomes can refer to progress during the course of intervention or achievements at the end of intervention, though other influences should be ruled out before it can be claimed that any positive outcomes resulted from the intervention itself. Four main methods were identified for assessing successful outcomes:

- progress in the child's or young person's behaviour and development
- features of service or placement endings
- professional or outside 'expert' evaluations
- consumer evaluations.

All four methods were used to assess the results of social work intervention in five local authorities with a total of 116 young people aged 13–17 who nearly all had serious difficulties. Information was gathered from young people, social workers and parents at the beginning of intervention and again one year later. The resulting picture was broadly a positive one. There were significant improvements in the behaviour and adjustment of many young people; the majority of interventions were regarded positively and seen to be of appropriate duration by the three parties; all but a few young people were satisfied with developments over the year. On the other hand, changes and benefits were often seen as small, whilst commonly the initial expectations of those involved were not fulfilled, even partly.

The most successful provision in this sample was, surprisingly, the residential school. However, the qualities which participants referred to in explaining improvements and satisfaction could be provided elsewhere and not necessarily away from home. These include: planned admission; consistent programmes; individualised education; stable staff and flexible family involvement.

References

Berridge, D. and Cleaver, H. (1987) *Foster Home Breakdown*. Oxford: Basil Blackwell.

Buchanan, A., Wheal, A. and Coker, R. (1993) *Answering Back* (Dolphin Project). Department of Social Work Studies: University of Southampton.

Bullock, R., Little, M. and Millham, S. (1993a) *Residential Care: A Review of the Research*. London: HMSO.

Bullock, R., Little, M. and Millham, S. (1993b) *Going Home*. Aldershot: Dartmouth.

Coopersmith, S. (1990) *Self Esteem Inventories*. Palo Alto: Consulting Psychologists Press Inc.

Fanshel, D., Finch, S.J. and Grundy, J.F. (1990) *Foster Children in a Life Course Perspective*. New York: Columbia University Press.

Farmer, E. and Parker, R. (1991) *Trials and Tribulations*. London: HMSO.

Fenyo, A., Knapp, M. and Baines, B. (1989) *Foster Care Breakdown: A Study of a Special Teenager Fostering Scheme*. University of Kent: PSSRU.

Fuller, R. (1988) *The MARS Project: A Study of Preventive Work*. University of Stirling.

Garnett, L. (1992) *Leaving Care and After*. London: National Children's Bureau.

Harris, R. and Timms, N. (1993) *Secure Accommodation in Child Care*. London: Routledge.

Hawkins, R.P., Almeida, M.C., Fabry, B. and Reitz, A.L. (1992) A scale to measure restrictiveness of living environments for troubled children and youths. *Hospital and Community Psychiatry 43*, 1, 54–59.

Hill, M., Triseliotis, J. and Borland, M. (1993) Social work services for young people. In M. Hill, R. Kirk and D. Part (eds) *Supporting Families*. Edinburgh: HMSO.

Kadushin, A. and Martin, C. (1988) *Child Welfare Services*. New York: Columbia University Press.

Kendrick, A. and Fraser, S. (1992) *'Literature Review' for the Skinner Report*. Edinburgh: Scottish Office.

Millham, S., Bullock, R., Hosie, K. and Haak, M. (1986) *Lost in Care*. Aldershot: Gower.

Packman, J., Randall, J. and Jacques, N. (1986) *Who Needs Care?* Oxford: Blackwell.

Parker, R. (1966) *Decision in Child Care*. London: Allen and Unwin.

Parker, R., Ward, H., Jackson, S., Aldgate, J. and Wedge, P. (1991) *Assessing Outcomes in Child Care*. London: HMSO.

Patton, M.Q. (1990) *Qualitative Evaluation and Research*. London: Sage.

Quinton, D. and Rutter, M. (1988) *Parenting Breakdown*. Aldershot: Avebury.

Rossi, P.H. (1992) Assessing family preservation programs. *Children and Youth Services Review 14*, 77–97.

Rowe, J., Hundleby, M. and Garnett, L. (1989) *Child Care Now: A Survey of Placement Patterns*. London: BAAF.

Rutter, M., Tizard, J. and Whitmore, K. (eds) (1970) *Education, Health and Behaviour*. London: Longman.

Stein, M. and Carey, K. (1986) *Leaving Care*. Oxford: Basil Blackwell.

Thoburn, J. (1990) *Success and Failure in Permanent Family Placement*. Aldershot: Avebury/Gower.

Trasler, G. (1960) *In Place of Parents*. London: Routledge & Kegan Paul.

Triseliotis, J., Borland, M., Hill, M. and Lambert, L. (1995) *Teenagers and the Social Work Services*. London: HMSO.

The Contributors

Jane Aldgate	University of Leicester
Stewart Asquith	University of Glasgow
David Berridge	University of Luton
Moira Borland	University of Glasgow
Marie Bradley	University of Leicester
Isabelle Brodie	University of Luton
Isobel Freeman	Strathclyde Social Work Department
Robbie Gilligan	Trinity College, Dublin
Pauline Hardiker	University of Leicester
David Hawley	University of Leicester
Malcolm Hill	University Of Glasgow
Greg Kelly	Queen's University of Belfast
Lydia Lambert	University of Edinburgh
Ann Lewis	University of East Anglia
Fiona Lockhart	Strathclyde Social Work Department
Colette McAuley	Queen's University of Belfast
Janice McGhee	University of Edinburgh
Alex Morrison	Strathclyde Social Work Department
Eoin O'Sullivan	Trinity College, Dublin
John Pinkerton	Queen's University of Belfast
Murray Ryburn	University of Birmingham
Clive Sellick	University of East Anglia
David Shemmings	University of East Anglia
Ruth Sinclair	National Children's Bureau
Moira Swanson	Strathclyde Social Work Department
June Thoburn	University of East Anglia
Kay Tisdall	University of Glasgow
John Triseliotis	University of Edinburgh
Harriet Ward	Dartington Social Research Unit
Lorraine Waterhouse	University of Edinburgh

Index